D0434904

S·A·L·U·T·E!

Canada's Great Military Leaders from Brock to Dextraze

S★A★L★U★T★E!

Canada's Great Military Leaders from Brock to Dextraze

ARTHUR BISHOP

AUTHOR OF THE BESTSELLING OUR BRAVEST AND OUR BEST

McGraw-Hill Ryerson

Toronto   Montreal   New York   Auckland   Bogota   Caracas
Lisbon   London   Madrid   Mexico   Milan   New Delhi   San Juan
Singapore   Sydney   Tokyo

McGraw-Hill
Ryerson Limited

A Subsidiary of The **McGraw·Hill** Companies

300 Water Street, Whitby, Ontario L1N 9B6
http://www.mcgrawhill.ca

SALUTE!: Canada's Great Military Leaders from Brock to Dextraze

ISBN: 0-07-560010-2

1 2 3 4 5 6 7 8 9 0   TRI   6 5 4 3 2 1 0 9 8 7

Printed and bound in Canada

Care has been taken to trace ownership of copyright material contained in this text; however, the publisher will welcome any information that enables them to rectify any reference or credit for subsequent editions.

Canadian Cataloguing in Publication Data
Bishop, William Arthur, 1923-
Salute!: Canada's Great Military Leaders from Brock to Dextraze
Includes bibliographical references and index.
ISBN 0-07-560010-2
1. Canada — Armed Forces — Biography.   2. Canada — History, Military.   3. Generals — Canada — Biography.   I. Title.
U54.C2B57 1997   355.3'31'092271   C97-931097-0

Publisher: **Joan Homewood**
Editor: **Erin Moore**
Production Coordinator: **Jennifer Burnell**
Editorial Services: **Ron Edwards**
Cover Design: **Lisa Hastings**
Interior Design/Composition: **Bookman Typesetting Co.**
Printer: **Tri-Graphic Printing Limited**

To the Men and Women
of
The Canadian Forces
in the hope that
they may soon regain the respect
they so richly deserve
This Book is Dedicated

SALUTE
Canada's Great Military Leaders
from Brock to Dextraze

PREFACE

Some talk of Alexander and some of Hercules,
Of Hector and Lysander and such great men as these,
But of all the world's great heroes,
There's none that can compare...

No country for its size and brief history has ever produced so many brilliant and outstanding military leaders in every field of endeavour — in the air, on the land and at sea — as Canada. In that context, this country takes second place to no other.

Beginning with the War of 1812 against the Americans, there were: Isaac Brock, Tecumseh and Charles de Salaberry. All three were outstanding leaders — brave, exemplary — whose men would follow them into hell if need be.

- It was the British-born Brock — *The Saviour of Canada* — who said, "I will never ask men to go where I do not lead them," a devotion to duty that cost him his life at the Battle of Queenston Heights. But, by his actions in that victory and an earlier one at Detroit, he inspired an outnumbered nation, hitherto certain of defeat, with the confidence that it could win the war.
- Tecumseh, the gallant Shawnee Indian chief, who rallied his people to side with the British, was not only a brilliant tactician and strategist in battle but became renowned for his oratory which inspired his followers, and put the fear of God into the hearts of his enemies. Though born in what would later be the United States, he served as a Canadian, a fact that ranks him as one of our great military leaders.
- The French Canadian, Salaberry, saved Lower Canada from invasion with his Voltigeurs, a hardy band of only 500 highly skilled marksmen, against a superior force of 6,000 enemy troops. His leadership qualities had been evident at an early age; at 15 he was given command of a company of British grenadiers.

Their heritage was not lost on those who followed them.

- During the Great War of 1914 the outstanding military leader on either side — Allied or German — was without doubt Arthur Currie, commander of the Canadian Corps. A native of Strathroy, Ontario, his strategic and tactical genius, which has been likened to that of Napoleon and Wellington, won him the respect not only of his

British and the French allies, but his German adversaries as well. An inspiration to his men, he would be right up there in the trenches at the front line with them during the height of a battle. Ironically, for all his military leadership acumen, Currie was not a professional soldier. He was a teacher and a businessman. Before the war he dealt in real estate; after the war, he became principal of McGill University.

- Typically for the silent service, Walter Hose is a name you may not know. Well, you will. Though quiet in manner — but not in temperament — he was the one who saved the Royal Canadian Navy from extinction. Known as "Canada's Father of the Navy," as a youngster he joined the Royal Navy but after marrying a Newfoundland bride he joined the Canadian service just before World War I. In 1928 he became the first chief of the naval staff. With uncanny foresight he realized Canada would never have a proper navy without public support. He scrapped the RCN per se and concentrated on building a RCN Reserve; selling the navy to the populace while building a pool of naval trained Canadians, right across the country, who could be mobilized quickly in the event of war.

- Montgomery called Guy Simonds, a future chief of the defence staff, "the most brilliant Canadian field general" of the Second World War. But to those under him, if he wasn't the most unpopular general, he came close to it. As one of his contemporaries put it, when it came to dealing with personnel "he wasn't worth a pinch of coon shit." But men followed him because they knew he was right — and he saved lives. The job always came first. Blunt and brusque, he had no time for social graces but his genius in battle was undeniable. During the Battle of Normandy he devised "artificial moonlight" — playing searchlights against the cloud base to guide the advance. To ensure an amphibious invasion of Walcheren Island in the Schelde, he ordered the bombing of dikes to "sink the island."

- As an ace fighter pilot in the First World War, Mike McEwen developed a new method of protecting bombers en route to and from their targets. Instead of flying close escort waiting for enemy scouts to attack, he led forward sweeps ahead of the bombers to seek out the antagonists and attack them first. This worked so successfully that other Allied fighter squadrons adopted the same strategy. During the Second World War, McEwen, a native of Griswold, Manitoba, commanded 6 Bomber Group of the Royal Canadian Air Force. Under his leadership the force made the greatest number of sorties with the highest destruction and the lowest casualty rate of all the Allied bomber groups in the European Theatre.

- Rollo Mainguy began the Second World War as captain of *Ottawa* which was the first Canadian warship to sink a German U-boat. He ended the conflict as commander of HMCS *Uganda* which formed part of the Royal Navy Task Force 57 in the battle to capture Okinawa that saw the first use of *kamikazes* by the Japanese. Mainguy was scheduled to take part in the invasion of Japan when the war ended. An able administrator, following the end of the war he served in several senior capacities before becoming chief of the naval staff. In the late 1940s Mainguy was instrumental in investigating the reasons for a series of insurrections aboard RCN ships that indicated a severe unrest and dissatisfaction below decks. His subsequent appraisal, the "Mainguy Report," served as a blueprint to dramatically improve the lot of the Canadian seaman.

- Keith Hodson's talent as a World War Two fighter wing leader was matched only by his skill and ability as an administrator. In 1958, after NORAD had been formed, he became the first deputy chief of staff. As a wing leader he insisted on teamwork and discipline. He was a master strategist who would position his wing against enemy fighters then cover the vanguard squadron going into the attack. After a series of command posts he became attached to the US 9th Air Force. Hodson, who was born in the Channel Islands, was well on his way to being made chief of the air staff of the RCAF but was killed in 1960 while bailing out of a T33 jet when he became entangled in the shroud lines of the parachute and broke his neck.

- Before John Rockingham took charge of the Canadian Army Special Force in Korea in May 1951, he had already distinguished himself in battle during the Second World War. Born in Sydney, Australia, he commanded the 9th Canadian Infantry Brigade in Europe and proved to be an innovative campaigner. During the battle for the Breskens pocket in Holland in October 1944 he landed an amphibious force at the "back door" hemming the Germans in from two sides. Rockingham was a popular leader with an easy manner which sometimes belied his determined spirit. In Korea he led his force — made up entirely of volunteers — until the signing of an armistice in July 1953.

- Wilf Curtis was responsible for the phenomenal post-World War Two growth of the RCAF into one of the world's most effective and efficient air forces thanks to his initiative, drive and foresight. A First World War fighter ace, in between wars he operated his own insurance business but stayed an active reservist. When the Second World War began in 1939, he became deputy air officer commanding the RCAF overseas and in 1944 was made chief of the air staff. After the war he remained in the service and convinced the federal Cabinet that the RCAF should play a major role in NATO. As a result, under Curtis's leadership and guidance, it became the principal air defence force on the continent throughout the 1950s.

- Montrealer Jacques Dextraze had the most meteoric career in the annals of the Canadian military, rising from private to general, and chief of the defence staff (CDS). He was the only person ever to accomplish this. Joining the Fusiliers Mont-Royal in 1940, his talent for soldiering and leadership was soon recognized. By war's end he commanded the regiment. Coming out of retirement in 1950, he joined the Van Doos, the legendary Royal 22nd Regiment. In Korea he led the 2nd battalion, distinguishing himself during the Battle of Kowanh-Hi in November 1951. Before becoming CDS in 1972 he served as chief of staff of the United Nations Peacekeeping Force in the Congo (Zaïre).

In "such great men as these" the country can take justifiable pride. This compendium is my Salute!

Arthur Bishop

ACKNOWLEDGMENTS

My literary agent, Frances Hanna, was the spark plug that revved up this project and throughout she kept a very firm hand on the throttle. My heartfelt thanks.

The Regimental Historian John Grodzinski was, as usual a powerhouse of diligence in providing research in countless areas and ways.

On the naval front I am grateful to Marilyn Gurney, Director Command Historian of the Maritime Command Museum, Peter Berry who was aide to Rollo Mainguy, to Mainguy's son Dan — himself an Admiral — Desmond "Debby" Piers, a retired Rear Admiral, retired Commodore Jan Drent, Andy Irwin, president of the Naval Officers Association of Canada, the executive director, Duncan Mathieson and another of its members, Sam Huntingdon.

Datsy Seferf and Cathy Murphy of the Canadian Forces College, Toronto, were most helpful in tracking down Keith Hodson's son Michael, who in turn supplied personal details about his father.

My thanks to Françoise Dextraze, Jacques' widow, in providing me with personal information about her husband. Pierre Sénécal, curator of Le Musée du 22e Régiment was most helpful in introducing me to Lieutenant General J.J. Paradis who had been Dextraze's aide in Korea.

Special thanks also to the following: Ron Edwards for his masterful job of editing. Dave McCabe, noted editor and journalist, for his advice and guidance. Lesley Bell and Scott Malan of the Toronto Reference Library. Malcolm Morrison of Broadcast Canada. Asma Kahn the Canadian Press librarian. Keith Hodson's son Michael (Dr) and his uncle Ian. Colonel John Gibson, president of the Canadian Military Institute, and Anne Melvin the librarian, as well as my close friend Dick Malott, former Canadian War Museum curator, who was, as usual, a fund of knowledge and most helpful in various ways.

Arthur Bishop
August 1997

Isaac Brock
1769–1812

1

SAVIOUR OF CANADA
Isaac Brock

Icy, wintry winds and drizzle swept across Lake Ontario causing choppy waters and making the 30-mile night crossing by boat from York (Toronto) to Niagara Falls dangerously unpleasant. But that risk against the elements was hardly enough to deter one born and brought up on the island of Guernsey where the English Channel tides surge against the craggy granite coastline. And anyway, nothing — certainly not weather — could ever swerve Isaac Brock from his purpose. On this occasion his mission was to track down six deserters with the help of a sergeant and 12 privates from his regiment.

Desertion from the British Army, by Upper Canadians in 1802 (the year Brock arrived in Canada), was not uncommon. The soldiers were poorly paid and subjected to harsh discipline. American agents were only too quick to take advantage of these conditions by luring them across the border. It was just another step to undermine morale.

Once ashore the search party wasted no time apprehending the fugitives who were chained and returned to prison cells at Fort George on the Niagara Peninsula. Shortly afterward a far more serious crisis arose. This time it was a mutiny. When it came to his attention, Brock, typically, insisted on taking charge of the situation himself. The cause of the revolt was the severe discipline inflicted on the soldiers by the Fort George garrison commander. The mutineers' plan was to lock the officers in the cells, march to Queenston and cross the Niagara River into New York. The plot was accidentally uncovered when a servant failed to show up for work. When found, he confessed to the conspir-

3

acy and admitted that the assassination of the commander had also been contemplated.

This was a grave offence and Brock characteristically decided to act promptly and forcefully. He suspected — quite rightly as it turned out — that this was the work of the Americans in their efforts to undermine the efficiency of His Majesty King George III's forces in Canada. Once again, Brock crossed the lake by boat from York to Niagara catching the recalcitrants by surprise. The 12 conspirators were arrested, clapped in irons and thrown into jail.

The subsequent trial took place in Quebec City far from Brock's control. All 12 mutineers were found guilty. Four of them and three of the deserters were condemned to death before the firing squad. The sentence was carried out on March 2, 1804.

When Brock received the announcement of the execution he was shattered, not only by the severity of the sentence but by the acts of treason themselves and the rigid disciplinary measures that had led to them. He ordered his men paraded before him and then, after reading the execution order to them, his voice quavering, his eyes misty, he said: "Since I have had the honour to wear the British uniform, I have never felt grief like this. It pains me to the heart to think that any member of my regiment should have engaged in a conspiracy which has led to their being shot like so many dogs...."

From that day on, Brock was determined to improve the lot of the soldier in Canada. It was this very concern for his men as well as his instant decisiveness and firmness in the face of danger that, in the long run, proved to be the salvation of Canada in the War of 1812 against the United States.

Isaac Brock was to the manor born — at St. Peter Port on Guernsey October 6, 1769, the same year Wellington and Napoleon were born — the eighth son of John and Elizabeth De Lisle Brock, one of 14 children. The Brocks could trace their lineage back to the 14th century and, by Channel Islands standards, as part of the upper or governing class, were considered to be moderately wealthy.

Isaac received his earliest education at Queen Elizabeth's School in Guernsey and at age ten, by then a strong, sturdy lad, was sent to school at Southampton where he was remembered by his classmates as an excellent boxer and swimmer. But to his family, his remarkable trait was his "extreme gentleness." Later, he studied French with a Protestant clergyman at Rotterdam. Brock proved to be an adept scholar but his life as an academic was cut short. In March 1785, at age 15, he followed the example of his older brothers, and joined the British Army, buying a commission in the 8th Foot Regiment.

From the very outset he displayed an indomitable will that was to distinguish him all his life. To make up for his abbreviated education, while his fellow ensigns enjoyed the good life and high spirits in the mess and elsewhere, Brock would lock himself in his room to study. In this way, he became somewhat of a scholar with a very high literary standard.

This was a time when England was at peace after the War of Independence with America and Brock spent his early years in the army garrisoned in England. In 1789, after five years service, he purchased a lieutenancy and for a time was quartered in Guernsey, and then on the neighbouring island of Jersey. Later that year, he took advantage of the government's authorization to establish a number of new companies and bought a captaincy in the 49th Foot Regiment, which he would one day command. He joined the regiment on foreign service in Barbados in the West Indies.

Soon after reporting for duty, a professional duellist in the regiment picked an argument with him — not uncommon among officers in those days — forcing him into a duel. Brock accepted, but insisted that the exchange of shots be settled across a handkerchief instead of the usual 20 paces. The bully quickly backed down and left the regiment in disgrace.

On February 1, 1793, Napoleon declared war on Britain, and the two countries fought for the next seven years. That same year, Captain Brock contracted a form of tropical fever from which he nearly died and which was to plague him for the rest of his life. When he recovered, he was sent home on sick leave following which he was assigned recruiting duties. In 1795 he purchased a majority in the 49th and rejoined it when it returned from the West Indies the following year. In 1797 he became a lieutenant colonel, again by purchase, that same year the sailors of the Royal Navy mutinied, for better wages and working conditions, and disaffection spilled over into the army.

Since the troops of the 49th, which were quartered on the banks of the Thames near London, sympathized with the mutineers, Brock had to keep a sharp lookout for trouble. He seldom got to bed before daylight, rarely slept, always keeping loaded pistols beside him, living by his doctrine that "he who watches never sleeps."

By October the crisis had petered out and Brock, by now commanding officer of the 49th, devoted himself to honing the regiment to the highest possible standard of efficiency. This was not easy given the disgruntled mood of poorly paid soldiers at the time. But Brock showed himself to be a magnificent manager of men. While he demanded discipline in no small degree and in no uncertain terms

("Nothing should be impossible to a soldier. The word "impossible" should not be found in a soldier's dictionary."), he also empathized with his troops, displaying a deep sense of understanding, and doing his best to improve their living and working conditions. He was always ready to listen to their complaints, no matter how trivial, and was willing to go to bat for them with his superiors. In this way he instilled such a strong sense of regimental pride, honour and loyalty, that, by the end of the year, the 49th was considered to be the finest regiment in the British Army.

At this point Brock had been in the army for 12 years. At age 27, he cut a commanding figure. Tall, over six feet, broad-shouldered, dark-haired, blue-eyed and extremely handsome, he was every inch the model of a regimental military leader in appearance as well as in practice. But neither he nor his regiment had as yet seen any real active service. That was about to change.

In August 1799, the 49th sailed with an expedition under Sir Ralph Abercromby against the French in northern Holland. Brock was about to experience his first taste of battle, although initially the 49th was not involved in the assault because it was not trained. But when the Duke of York arrived later in the year with fresh troops as well as a body of Russians, the allied force took the offensive and the 49th went into battle among the sand dunes of Del Helder. Brock was knocked from his mount by a stray bullet, but refused to leave the field. To one of his brothers he wrote: "I got knocked down soon after the enemy began to retreat, but never quitted the field, and returned to my duty in less than half an hour." What had saved him was a heavy cotton handkerchief he wore over a thick black silk cravat to ward off the extreme cold. The bullet had perforated both. Throughout the expedition, Abercromby's concern for his men made a deep impression on Brock. Years later he would say: "I will never ask men to go where I do not lead them."

In early 1801, Brock's regiment was picked as the main body of a military force despatched to Denmark. However, action was limited to a small exchange of naval fire off the coast near Copenhagen. Following this, the 49th was stationed at Colchester where it remained until June 1802 when the regiment was sent to Quebec. By this time American president, Thomas Jefferson, and his secretary of state, James Madison, had begun taking a decidedly hostile attitude towards England and a friendly one to France. With the purchase of Louisiana from the French the following year, they could well afford their disaffection of England; the United States no longer needed Great Britain's assistance in securing the mouth of the Mississippi and Florida. In the spring, Brock's regiment moved to Upper Canada with headquarters at York (later Toronto) and a detachment was quartered at Fort George (later Niagara-on-the Lake).

The aura of unrest among his troops, the mutiny and the desertions so appalled Brock that he temporarily moved to Fort George and took charge himself. By implementing the humane methods of treating the ordinary soldier he had learned under Abercromby, he put an instant end to desertions. With certain restrictions, the men were allowed to visit the town. Fishing in fatigues was no longer punishable and shooting the abundant local pigeons was permitted.

Brock also began laying the groundwork for establishing a veterans' corps to occupy the border points. On October 30, 1805 he was promoted to colonel and went home on leave. While in England, his recommendations to the Duke of York for improving the military in Canada were enthusiastically accepted. By this time, the war clouds over Canada and the United States had darkened considerably. This situation had been heightened by the British Navy, which after its victory over the French fleet at Trafalgar in October, was in absolute command of the seas. It allowed the British to blockade Europe. American ships carrying food and materials to Napoleonic ports were stopped and boarded, and British deserters on them, taken prisoner. This provided the United States with the excuse it needed to take a bolder, more aggressive stand in its dealings with Canada. For this reason — "the warlike character" of the United States, he called it — Brock cut short his leave in September 1806. His sister Elizabeth wrote, "Isaac left town last evening for Milford Haven. Dear fellow; Heaven knows when we shall see him again." She could not have known how prophetic those words would be.

On his return to Canada, Brock found himself in command of all troops in the colony until the arrival of Sir James Craig as governor-general and forces' commander the following year.

Brock concentrated his energies on shoring up the country's deficient defences. He directed special attention to the Quebec fortifications, where his knowledge of French stood him in good stead. Quebec City's defences were vital because it was the key to maintaining communications with England. He had the walls facing the notorious Plains of Abraham rebuilt and designed an elevated battery of eight heavy guns that dominated the heights and controlled the south shore of the St. Lawrence River. It became known as "Brock's Battery."

Brock ran into problems with the civil government which was administered by a temporary governor, Thomas Dunn, who called himself "president". On the issues of civilian encroachment on military property, use of wasteland for military training, responsibility for the cost of the Indian Department, request for civilian labour for work on fortifications, calling out part of the militia for training and authorization to arm a volunteer corps, Brock met such stubborn resistance it was tantamount to a solid veto.

But there was one area over which Brock had complete jurisdiction and it was a vitally important one: the Provincial Marine Department. He ordered it placed under the command of his deputy quarter master. Essentially, its function in 1806 was transporting troops from one location to another. But Brock saw in it the possibility of building a strong naval force capable of action in the event of war. Under two assistant quartermasters at Kingston and Amherstburg (opposite Fort Detroit), he molded the provincial marine into a fleet that six years later would command the Great Lakes and make possible the defence of Canada.

Early in 1808 Craig appointed Brock brigadier general and placed him in command of Montreal. The former Ville Marie was a lively and hospitable place in those days and, with the bonhomie that came naturally to him, Brock thoroughly enjoyed the friendly atmosphere and social life. There was little in the way of military duties to occupy him. A few months later he returned to Quebec where he remained until July 1810. When he was then transferred to Upper Canada, he complained in his letters home of being "buried in this inactive, remote corner" while the main body of the British Army was winning laurels in Europe. He pleaded with the Duke of York and others to be allowed to join in the war against Napoleon. To one of his brothers he wrote, "You who have passed all your days in the bustle of London, can scarcely conceive the uninteresting and insipid life I am doomed to lead in this retirement."

As a diversion from ennui, Brock made several trips to the United States. On one occasion he visited Detroit and marvelled at the picturesque scenic surroundings. He did not hold the same opinion of its inhabitants, however. "As to the manners of the American people," he wrote to his brother John, "I do not admire them. I have met with some whose society was everything one could desire, and at Boston and New York such characters are, I believe, numerous, but these are the exceptions."

In another effort to avoid boredom, Brock turned to reading. Here his interests were profound, wide and varied. Among the books that graced his quarters were 12 volumes of Johnson's Works; Reed's and Bell's editions of Shakespeare; Plutarch's Lives; Hume's Essays; Arthur on Courts Martial; Rollins' Ancient History; Marshall's Travels; Wharton's Virgil; Gregory's Dictionary of Arts and Sciences;

Voltaire's *La Henriade*; Walcheren Expedition; King of Prussia's Tactics; Memoirs of Talleyrand; Wolfe's Orders; Hume's Works. To his brother he wrote:

> I read much, but good books are scarce, and I hate borrowing. I like to read a book quickly and afterward revert to such passages as have made the deepest impression and which appear to me important to remember, a practice I cannot conveniently pursue unless the book is mine. Should you find that I am likely to remain here I wish you to send me some choice authors of history, with maps and the best translation of ancient works. I till lately never discovered its exquisite beauties. I read in my youth Pope's translation of Homer. I firmly believe the same propensity was always within me, but strange to tell, I never had the advantage of a master to guide and encourage me. I rejoice that my nephews are more fortunate.

On June 4, 1811, Brock was promoted to major general and in October when Francis Gore, the lieutenant governor of Upper Canada, left for England on leave Brock became "president" and administrator of the provincial government. He was now 41 years old and still a bachelor, though women found this still very athletic-looking soldier attractive. A friend wrote him from England: "I wish I had a daughter old enough for you, as I would give her to you with pleasure. You should be married, particularly as fate seems to detain you so long in Canada, but pray, do not marry there."

That same month, the Brock family had been threatened with financial ruin. Isaac's brother, William, was a senior partner in a London banking and merchant firm that had gone to the wall. William had loaned Isaac £3,000 to purchase his commissions in the 49th Regiment without ever intending to seek repayment. However, the loans had been entered on the company's books and the receivers were asking for settlement. Isaac had no way of meeting this demand so he turned over his civil salary as administrator to another brother, Irving, to begin paying down the debt as he saw fit. This affair had come as a distinct shock to Isaac, not only because of the financial setback, but because he had always been so scrupulously careful and precise in money matters. He always required all those under him to be rigidly correct in the expenditure of public money. He once wrote to the board of accounts:

> I have to request the board to continue diligently to ascertain the sufficiency of every authority for expenditure before it sanctions the smallest charge... When expense is incurred without the most

urgent cause and more particularly when large sums are stated to have been expended in anticipation of services not yet authorized, my duty strictly compels me to withhold my approval to all such irregular proceedings.

By early 1812 he received word from England that a position might be found for him but by this time it was clear that war with the United States was imminent and could break out at any time. On February 12, Brock wrote: "I beg leave to be allowed to remain in my present command."

That same month Brock went before the Upper Canada provincial legislature to ask their cooperation in suspending habeas corpus and to pass a new militia act. Incredibly, in the face of an imminent declaration of war by the Americans, he received a frosty reception. The Legislature refused both requests. However, they passed legislation allowing the formation within each militia battalion, which were loosely determined, two "flanker," or auxiliary companies — *without pay* — which would be allowed to train up to six days a month.

In September 1811, Lieutenant General Sir George Prevost replaced Craig as governor-general and commander of the armed forces, and Brock wrote to him and outlined his war plans. The cooperation of the Indians would be absolutely vital, he pointed out, and to obtain it, the natives would have to be convinced the British were serious about waging war. Brock advocated the seizure of Michilimackinac Island, an American stronghold between lakes Huron and Superior, as soon as hostilities broke out.

Prevost was cool to the suggestion. The British government wanted to avoid a direct confrontation with the Americans as long as possible lest any hostile action might arouse and unite the divided American populace. Prevost urged appeasement. This ran contrary to Brock's experience and training. In short, Brock was a man of action who wanted to go for it and was willing to accept the risk such boldness entailed. He concluded that the only possible strategy was to take the offensive. But as a disciplined officer he would obey orders.

However, with the declaration of war by the United States on June 18, 1812 even Prevost agreed that immediate action was called for. At this time, Brock had 1,600 British regular troops at his disposal in Upper Canada. These he despatched from York to reinforce the Niagara frontier where he set up headquarters.

The attack on Michilimackinac Island took place the next day, led by Captain Charles Roberts, and it was captured intact without a shot being fired. As Brock had anticipated, this action quickly drew the Indians to the Upper Lakes region to join the British side. But then, on

July 12, American Brigadier General William Hull invaded Canada along the Detroit frontier. The result was chaos; in panic many of the Canadian militia deserted to the enemy.

Brock again went before the Upper Canada legislature on July 27, but they were lukewarm to his countermeasures, such as raising the militia quota. He couldn't believe it. Hell, this was an emergency; the future of the country was at stake. Two days later he wrote to the adjutant general at headquarters in Montreal:

> My situation is most critical, not from anything the enemy can do but from the disposition of the people — The population, believe me is essentially bad — A full belief possesses them all that the Province must inevitably succumb — This prepossession is fatal to every exertion — Legislators, Magistrates, Militia Officers, all have imbibed this idea, and are so sluggish and indifferent in their respective offices that the artful and active scoundrel is allowed to parade the Country without interruption, and commit all imaginable mischief...
>
> What a change an additional regiment would make in this part of the province. Most of the people have lost confidence — I however speak loud and look big...

It was a magnificent manifesto, a masterpiece, not so much for Brock's brilliant eloquence in denouncing the situation, as for his refusal to be deterred by it. He immediately went on the offensive. The British troops on the Detroit frontier still held Fort Amherstburg. On August 8, Brock led a striking force of 300 — mostly volunteers — from Long Point, reaching Fort Amherstburg on the 13th.

By the time the full complement — 1,300 men made up of 400 militia, 600 Indians and 300 British regulars — reached the area, Hull, with his supply lines threatened, fled back across the river to the safety of Fort Detroit. The Americans outnumbered Brock's force — 2,000 with a detachment of 500 sent out to protect an approaching supply column — but typically, on August 16, Brock, never hesitating for a minute, boldly decided to attack.

His original plan was to take a defensive stand on the American side and draw Hull's forces out into an open battle. But this would have left his own forces vulnerable from the rear. So he decided to attack the fort directly. It didn't last long. Fired at by a battery on the Canadian shore and fearing massacre by the Indians, Hull surrendered. In a letter demanding Hull's surrender, Brock had written that while he did not propose to "join in a war of extermination," that the Indians would be "beyond control the moment the contest commences." In fact, the behaviour of the Indians led by the Shawnee chief, Tecumseh, was exemplary. They merely applied the *threat* of terrorism with no intention of actually practicing it. In addition to the American troops taken prisoner, Brock's army captured 35 guns, 2,500 muskets, cattle and stores. Hull was court-martialed, found guilty of cowardice and sentenced to be shot. However, taking into account his record in the Revolution, President James Madison pardoned him.

In a private letter he wrote following the surrender, Brock gave his reasons for the boldness of the action he had taken:

> Some say that nothing could be more desperate than the measure, but I answer that the state of the Province admitted nothing by desperate remedies. I got possession [from a captured American vessel] of the letters my antagonist addressed to the Secretary at War, and also of the sentiments which hundreds of his army uttered to their friends. Confidence in their General was gone and evident despondency prevailed throughout.

Brock admitted he had crossed the river against the advice of his colonels: "...it is therefore no wonder that envy should attribute to good fortune what in justice is my own discernment, I must say, proceeded from a cool calculation of the *pours* and *contres*."

The effect of Brock's victory on Upper Canada was electric. It filled the militia with confidence, and people no longer had any doubt that Canada could be defended. It was also a blow to American morale. The sight of the defeated army hauling its wounded across the Niagara frontier in full view of their fellow US troops across the river was nerve-racking.

Brock hastened back to the Niagara front, where he knew the next blow would fall, only to learn that Prevost had negotiated an agreement with American Major General Henry Dearborn to refrain from further hostilities. He was flabbergasted. After a telling victory at Detroit, now was the time to strike — not talk! When President Madison resisted all overtures from Britain which had initiated the truce, Brock complained bitterly that the "abortive" armistice had simply allowed the Americans time to bring up more troops to the frontier.

Brock now faced the problem of defending a long line with an inadequate force always uncertain exactly where the enemy would strike. On October 12 his brigade major, Thomas Evans, crossed the Niagara River near Queenston under a flag of truce and noticed on the American side that boats were being prepared for a crossing. When he returned to Fort George, where Brock had set up headquarters, he advised him that an attack was imminent. However, Brock was unconvinced. For once in his life he had miscalculated his enemy's intentions. He felt sure the attack would take place at the mouth of the river near Fort George, but on the morning of October 13, Brock, who slept in his clothes ("He who guards never sleeps"), heard gunfire from the direction of Queenston.

The odds favoured the Americans. Brock's opposite number, General Stephen Van Rensselaer, had 6,300 troops under his command, 3,650 of them regulars. Brock had only 1,500 men and 250 Indians and these had to be scattered all along the frontier. The Americans concentrated their entire force in one spot. At Queenston, where the invasion was taking place, the only defence was a detachment of Brock's old regiment, the 49th, and some militia, 350 men in all.

Brock mounted his horse, Alfred, and rode towards Queenston in the mud and rain to assess the situation. With him were his two aides-de-camp, Lieutenant Colonel John MacDonell, attorney general of the province, and Captain Charles Clegg. Meanwhile at Brown's Point, two miles south of Queenston, Captain Duncan Cameron, commander of the flank companies of the 3rd York militia battalion, the "York Volunteers," marched his men in the direction of the gunfire. Situated on the heights above the village, the 49th Regiment, supported by a three-pound field gun and another gun at the river base below, inflicted heavy casualties on the invaders and, by the time Brock galloped into Queenston, the situation seemed to be pretty well in hand. By then, the 49th had moved down from the heights to join the battle below.

Brock, with Clegg and MacDonell, immediately rode up the slope to the single 18-pound gun redan battery halfway up the hill to survey the battle. Suddenly enemy troops led by Captain John Ellis Wool appeared on the scene. From below, Wool had seen the carnage inflicted on his compatriots by the redan and was determined to seize it and turn it on the British. He and his men had been able to achieve complete surprise by scaling the heights unseen up one of the "fisherman's" paths, a narrow, winding trail. Brock ordered the gunners to spike the gun by hammering a ramrod into the barrel and breaking it off. Then they beat a hasty retreat. They fell back so quickly that Brock and his aides had no time to remount their horses; they led them hurriedly on foot down the slope to the village. The Americans were too busy manning the redan to give chase.

But Brock knew he would have to recapture the redan. Once the Americans unspiked the gun they would control the battle. He ordered a detachment of 70 men forward to skirt the Americans who had taken cover among trees and in hollows on the right flank. From behind a stone wall he watched Wool despatch 150 of his men to circumvent them. But after a brief exchange of musket fire, the Americans began to back off. Brock seized that moment to charge with 200 troops he had rallied around him.

Sending an advance party to attack Wool's left, sword in hand, Brock leapt his horse over the wall and galloped up the slope full tilt, a magnificent figure in his scarlet tunic, but also a splendid target.

One musket shot struck his sword hand, badly bloodying it. No matter — he ignored it, waving the wounded arm to urge on his men. Then suddenly an enemy rifleman stepped out from behind a tree and from 50 yards took careful aim. Brock probably never noticed him. The bullet struck Brock in the right breast near the heart. Mortally wounded, he fell from his horse onto the ground.

Brock's body was taken to a house in Queenston. His loss was irreparable. But by his bravery and the example he had set, were a precedent for morale and discipline that in the long run saved Canada from defeat and occupation. These qualities had an immediate effect. The little British army had recaptured the heights and sent the Americans packing. The US Army never recovered from the battle of Queenston Heights. Brock's spirit continued to animate and sustain the nation for another two years, until final victory.

On October 16, Brock and MacDonell, who died only hours after his commanding general, were buried with ceremony in a bastion just outside Fort George. Across the river at Fort Niagara, American guns joined in the final salute.

On the morning of October 6, in London, Brock's brother William was asked by his wife why the guns from the Tower were firing. "For Isaac, of course," he replied good humouredly. "It's his forty-third birthday." In fact they *had* been fired in Isaac's honour. News of his victory at Detroit had just reached England.

Ironically Brock never learned that a few days later, in recognition of his Detroit victory, the Prince Regent had appointed him an extra Knight of the Order of the Bath.

In 1824, Brock and MacDonell were reburied under an imposing monument at the summit of Queenston Heights. Then in 1840, a fanatic, Benjamin Let, described as a "border ruffian," dynamited the structure, blowing it up. Feelings ran so high over the incident that on July 30, of that year, 8,000 people from all over the province gathered at Queenston to plan an even more striking memorial which ultimately took the form of the lofty column that today dominates the battlefield where Brock fell. It has been called, "the stateliest monument that has ever been raised to an individual anywhere in Canada." In Britain, Parliament voted that Brock be commemorated by a modest memorial at St. Paul's Cathedral.

But the finest testament to Brock's leadership, and perhaps the most moving, emerged from the 1840 meeting:

> Resolved — that we recall to mind, with admiration and gratitude, the perilous times in which Sir Isaac Brock led the small regular force, the loyal and gallant militia, and the brave and faithful Indian warriors, to oppose the invader — when his fortitude inspired courage, and his sagacious policy gave confidence, despite a hostile force apparently overwhelming.

Brock gave ten years of his life to Canada, in both a civil and military capacity. He entered into the defence of a country entrusted to his charge with a generous heart and a resolute determination. With limited means at his disposal he took the untrained militia of Upper Canada and mobilized it into a highly disciplined force. He rallied the Indians to his side. He set an example to the youth of the country in courage and patriotism through his infinite patience and fine judgement. Although nearly two centuries have passed, the lustre of Brock's bravery and fame lives on.

Tecumseh
1768–1813

2

THE SHOOTING STAR
Tecumseh

"I shall fight with the British!"

Following the 1811 betrayal by the Americans at Prophet's Town on the Tippecanoe river where, after assurances that there would be peace, the Indians were massacred and their village burned to the ground, the great sachem, Tecumseh, chief of the Shawnee tribe, vowed revenge. If the United States — "The Seventeen Fires" — won the war they would destroy his people. But, if the British — "The Red Coats" — emerged victorious, justice would be done, and the Confederacy, what was left of it, would be treated with fairness and respect.

At the beginning of June 1812, on the eve of the outbreak of hostilities, Tecumseh, with 30 faithful followers, set out north from the Ohio valley for Fort Amherstburg, gathering recruits in the Indian villages enroute. His journey coincided with another march north. The army of the Northwest commanded by Brigadier General William Hull, the governor of Michigan, was on its way to Fort Detroit. It was clear to Tecumseh that their intention was the invasion of Canada from that stronghold. Unbeknownst to the Americans, the Shawnee sachem's braves had been shadowing the 2,500 blue coats every foot of the way.

By the time they reached Fort Amherstburg war had already been declared and the Shawnee had been reinforced with warriors from the Fox, Kickapoo, Potawatomi, Delaware, Sauk and Wyandotte tribes. They now numbered close to 1,000. Tecumseh had intended to present himself to Colonel Thomas St. George, commander of the British garrison, and formally offer his services to King George III, the great

Father over the Sea. However, to his dismay, he found not St. George, but the bigoted, lily-livered (he was later court-martialed), Colonel Henry Proctor in charge.

Tecumseh took an instant dislike to the foppish man who was obviously a behind-the-scenes soldier. The aversion was mutual. Proctor had no time for Indians. "I don't feel these red skin savages can be of much assistance in a civilized war," he declared and dismissed the Shawnee chief out of hand. Tecumseh was furious but knew he had to play along or lose the friendship of the British. His patience paid off when Isaac Brock finally appeared to take over a few days later.

The two hit it off immediately. "Welcome Shooting Star," Brock greeted his new ally. Turning to one of his followers, Tecumseh said: "At last a *man* commands the fort!" The two sat down with their deputies to draw up war plans. Tecumseh urged an all-out attack on Fort Detroit at once. "The savage is mad!" Proctor broke in predictably. Brock silenced him. Drawing a knife, Tecumseh sketched a plan of attack in detail on a piece of elm bark. Then he concluded that, "Half the battle is already won for us because General Hull is clearly a coward." But when the plan was put to a vote, only one of Brock's officers was in favour. However, Brock, who had abstained from the vote, rose to his feet and overruled the result.

"Gentlemen," he announced forcibly, "I am very sorry to override you, but I believe you are wrong and that our Shawnee friend is right. It is, assuredly, a gamble. But all battles are gambles. The prize is exceedingly attractive." He turned to Tecumseh. "Tomorrow we shall mount an attack against Fort Detroit. Shooting Star, assemble your people at dawn, for I wish to speak personally to them of the attack."

Next morning Tecumseh's 1,000 braves sat upon a misty meadow just outside the fort as Brock stood before them. "You, the noble friends of Chief Tecumseh, are comrades of whom I am most proud. I welcome you into the army of our father, the Great King," he began slowly through an interpreter.

My message this morning is brief. Your leader has shown me the wisdom of carrying the fight across the water. We plan to attack Fort Detroit, and if you accompany my soldiers, I promise we shall all be fighting together with one aim — to drive out the Americans and regain the lands which they stole from you. As [a] symbol of my faith and respect, I ask Chief Tecumseh [to] wear this medallion, which bears the face of our leader His Majesty King George III.

Tecumseh bowed his head and Brock placed the medal, which dangled from a cord, over the Shawnee's neck. Tecumseh straightened and said quietly "My battle is yours, my brother." With those words he became a true Canadian battle leader in every sense of the word.

***

Bravery and leadership were two qualities bred into Tecumseh. One of seven children, he was born in 1768 in the village of Old Piqua, the site of the present city of Springfield, Ohio. His father, Puckeshinwa, was a sachem, or chief, of the Kiscopoke, his mother, Methoataske, a member of the Turtle band, both clans of the Shawnee tribe, a sub-faction of the mighty Algonquin nation.

The name Tecumseh had several meanings, two of them prophetic: "I Cross Someone's Path" and "A Panther Springing upon its Prey." In the vivid imagination of the native people, he was more graphically envisioned as a "Shooting Star — the Panther of the Sky."

Though small in number, the Shawnee were proud and warlike. As a young man, Tecumseh grew up wiry and strong and revelled in the stories told by the older braves of battles fought. He dreamed of one day being a warrior — and a sachem — himself.

One morning in 1774 he watched as a messenger of war, clearly identified by his war paint, loped into the village. There the braves gathered around him to learn that the "Long Knives" of Virginia had invaded Ohio, taken the Indians' land from them, got drunk and killed men, women and children. The Shawnee were urged to join the Mingo, the Delaware and the Wyandotte on the warpath.

Sometime later, in a hand-to-hand battle with the Virginians at Point Pleasant between the Kanawha and Ohio rivers, Puckeshinwa was badly wounded but returned to Old Piqua alive. The Indians lost that battle but the invaders had been temporarily stopped. However, that winter, when Puckeshinwa failed to return from a hunting foray, Methoatske took her son with her to search for him. They found him in the forest bleeding to death, from a musket shot.

"Who did this foul thing, my husband?" his wife asked. "White men," Puckeshinwa gasped in reply. Mother and son struggled to help him back to the village but the Shawnee sachem collapsed to the ground, dead. Sobbing, Tecumseh threw himself across his father's body in frustration. For Methoataske, tears gave way to rage.

"You heard who killed this good man," she shouted above the howling wind. "Long Knives! Not honourable men...but butchers. I will make you swear to kill the Long Knives when you are grown tall! You shall bring vengeance for this crime, and your name shall be known because you are the avenger. You shall think one thought — that you must kill the Long Knives who did this terrible thing. Swear now! Swear now Tecumseh! *Swear now!*"

Tecumseh raised himself from his father's corpse and stared at it both glumly and angrily. "I swear," he answered solemnly. "I swear!" Then and there, a metamorphosis had occurred that turned him from a mere youth to potentially the greatest of all the Indian chiefs.

Soon afterwards, Tecumseh experienced his baptism of fire, though at 12 years old, he was considered too young to take part in the fighting. In 1780, the Army of the West, a force of 700 Kentuckians commanded by Colonel George Rogers Clark, put Old Piqua to the torch. From the forest where the women and children were hiding, Tecumseh watched in horror as every hut, every wigwam in the village burned to the ground. His seething hatred for the Long Knives over his father's death intensified.

The Shawnee not only lost their homes but most of their possessions as well. For the moment they took refuge in one of the villages along the banks of the Ohio — "The Beautiful River." To compensate for their losses, they decided to attack some of the flat boats that plied the river from Pittsburgh carrying goods to the interior.

After much persuasion, Tecumseh's older brother, Cheeseekau, gave him permission to join the expedition. The party of 25 warriors embarked in four canoes. They chose a spot to set up an ambush on the edge of the river, and camped for the night. In his excitement Tecumseh could not sleep. Early next morning a sentinel spotted two of the 60-foot craft, lashed together as one.

The Long Knives plying their craft were caught completely off guard and the Shawnee set upon them with bloodcurdling shouts and cries. Tecumseh, lusting for blood, accounted for three of the white men in the ensuing mêlée. However, one man was spared and taken prisoner. The loot was rich, including bales of cotton and woolen cloths, barrels of sugar, flour, salt and gunpowder and chests of tea.

The white prisoner was taken to the village where he was forced to run the gauntlet as women and children pelted him with stones and struck him with sticks. He was then tied to a stake and wood was piled around his feet to be set on fire. Tecumseh was horrified. Now for the first time his fellow braves fell under the spell of his oratory, a power for which he became renowned and which would influence many future events. It also showed that Tecumseh, while brave and fearless in battle, was humane at heart and detested cruelty of any kind.

Tecumseh rushed forward and, shielding the victim, faced the throng. "Are we brave men?" he asked, "or are we like crouching animals of the kind that must crawl and hunt by night. I say if we burn this white man, even though he is our enemy, then may Skemotah drive us from his great net and leave us forever on earth to rot and die as cowards." He continued:

> To kill with honour is one thing, to butcher is another. Torturing, burning, cutting with a knife — how does it profit us? In no way! It turns us into beasts. I would be the first if I thought it signified great courage, but suddenly I do not think it takes any great courage to be cruel to a man like this, caught and helpless. No courage at all. My father died a victim of the Long Knives — murdered! But I will not let myself become the kind of animal which slew my father. I shall take vengeance on the Long Knives, but not like an animal. With courage — like a man!

In the summer of 1788 when he reached his twentieth birthday, Tecumseh's restless spirit and ambition to one day became a war chief were rewarded when his brother, Cheeseekau, formed a hunting party to explore the west. By now Tecumseh was full-grown and every inch the warrior. Standing six feet high, lean and hard, he sat tall and erect in the saddle. His hooded eyes, hollow cheeks and full mouth gave him a warm, friendly look that belied the ferociousness he could display in battle.

The hunting party set off through what is now Indiana, to the banks of the "Great Father of Waters," the magnificent Mississippi, several hundred miles north of the mouth of the Ohio river. There they camped, and hunted game while exploring the country and spoke with other tribes.

Finally they reached the prairies and enjoyed their first buffalo hunt. It was during one of these chases that Tecumseh was thrown from his horse and broke a leg. This temporarily delayed the Shawnee from pushing further south. And when they did reach Cherokee territory, they found the tribe at war with the Long Knives. They joined forces with the Cherokee and in a subsequent attack on an American fort, Cheeseekau was killed. Tecumseh now assumed leadership of the nomadic party. He refused to return home, however, until they had accomplished something worth telling about. They then headed further south.

For two years he led his party, joining with the southern Indian tribes in their wars against the Americans and the Spanish. And it was during this time that he exhibited the generalship as a battle leader that won him the respect of the other tribes. Finally, in 1790, the band, reduced to half the original number, returned to the Ohio Valley. By this time open warfare had broken out between the Americans and the Indians. At the heart of the conflict was the fact that the Indians had no protection of either person or property from the greed of the whites. Seizure of Indian lands went on unceasingly. A year after Tecumseh's return, the Indians annihilated an expedition led by General Josiah Harmar. In the fall of 1791, a second expedition led by Major General Arthur St. Clair penetrated the Indian countryside.

With a small party of scouts, Tecumseh lay in ambush near Nettle Creek, a small tributary of the Miami River, and watched as St. Clair's Army of the North-West marched north out of Fort Jefferson. He immediately sent word to the principal chiefs of the Indian Confederacy, Blue Jacket of the Shawnee and Little Turtle of the Miami. It was a slaughter. St. Clair's force was cut to ribbons. The Indians filled the mouths of the slain with earth, to symbolize their greed for land. The survivors fled in panic back to Fort Jefferson.

For the next three years the Americans made no further attempts to invade although there were the usual skirmishes with the Indians. Then in 1794 the powers in Washington commissioned General "Mad Anthony" Wayne to lead a campaign against the Indians. Wayne's force embarked at Pittsburgh on flatboats travelling the Ohio, and landing in Indian country near the mouth of the Wabash, where Wayne built Fort Recovery. Tecumseh, who had been stalking the Americans, resolved to attack the outpost. But it was not the type of assault to which the Indians were accustomed. They were used to forest fighting, not as a coordinated body, but as individuals. In a sense they were disorganized, the onus depending on each individual's discretion and impulse. This was fine among the trees but it didn't work out in the open against a heavily armed fortification defended by a series of musket volleys and artillery.

Tecumseh finally withdrew and set up camp nearby to observe the American movements. It then became a game of cat and mouse. By this time Wayne had decided to take the offensive and march right into the heart of Indian country. To deceive the Indians into believing his objective was the Indian villages along the Miami River, he proceeded in that direction. Then he swung about and stopped near the junction of the Au Glaize River and the Maumee of the Lakes. Knowing the Indians were close by and would try to surprise him, the resourceful Wayne fashioned a surprise of his own. He had his men cut logs six feet long and wrap them in blankets to resemble sleeping soldiers. His troops then withdrew behind a redoubt of fallen trees. When the Indian scouts began tomahawking the "sleeping" logs, they made easy targets for a deadly American volley.

Reconnaissance told Wayne that the Indian population was far larger than he had anticipated, so he abandoned plans for an immediate offensive and decided to consolidate. With nearly unlimited manpower he built Fort Defiance, an imposing, impressive fortification, complete with blockhouse, magazines, barracks, encircled by heavy palisades — a fence of pointed wooden upright stakes.

Indian reaction to the invasion was mixed. Little Turtle of the Miami wanted to make peace with the Americans. Blue Jacket urged war. The Confederacy council voted with the Shawnee chief. The stage was set for what became known as the Battle of the Fallen Timbers. The Indians took position at the Maumee rapids behind tree trunks felled by a tornado. Tecumseh was placed in charge of the Shawnee in the forefront of the line. He captured one of the American guns but soon had to abandon it when they were forced to retreat in the face of an American advance. Tecumseh tried his best to rally his warriors into making a stand but they were outnumbered and outfought, the main body fleeing into the woods. The battle was lost.

The army of the Confederacy had suffered a shattering defeat and the Indian villages now lay at the mercy of the Army of the North-West. They were soon ravaged and put to the torch by a cruel conqueror. The Americans now ruled the garden land of the Au Glaize, in which large tracts of Indian Territory had been ceded to them under the terms of the Treaty of Greenville (1795). But it was a pact to which Tecumseh steadfastly refused to subscribe or recognize. In fact, he turned his back on the chieftains for agreeing to such humiliating terms. In an oblique way this was to have significant, far-reaching consequences for Canada. The entire episode marked the emancipation of Tecumseh. From then on he became a man possessed.

He saw very clearly that if the Indians were to resist encroachment by the Americans, the tribes must unite as a confederation in peace as well as in war. It would have to be the responsibility of the warriors to guide their destiny, not the village chiefs who were all too willing to sell their lands to the whites for entirely inadequate considerations.

The leading spirit behind the movement was Tecumseh's younger brother, Laulewasikaw, who assumed the office of Taskswatawa — "Open Door" — to play the role of prophet and spread the word. As a first step to forming a new confederacy, Tecumseh invited the chiefs of all the tribes of the Ohio Valley to a council at Wapakonetta — the Shawnee, Wyandotte, Miami, Delaware, Ottawa, and Pottawatomi. There, after passing the peace pipe, the Prophet exhorted them to unite as one for which he promised, "The Great Spirit would give them his blessing." Though some chiefs opposed the scheme, resenting Tecumseh's popularity, the majority favoured it. After a new Indian village was established near Greenville, named Prophet's Town, on the Maumee of the Lakes, Tecumseh travelled the countryside preaching his gospel. Then, abruptly, trouble loomed directly ahead.

In 1801, General William Henry Harrison was appointed governor of the newly formed Indiana Territory. Tecumseh had no use for him. He had fought against him at the Battle of the Falling Timbers. He remained his enemy still.

Superficially Harrison appeared to be friendly towards the Indians. Tecumseh knew better. Harrison was buying large parcels of land from village chiefs who had no right to sell them. But the migration of Indians into Prophet's Town alarmed Harrison even though they gave no indication of dangerous intentions. Still he wanted pressure brought to bear to make them leave. Matters came to a head in 1810 — on the verge of war between Canada and the United States — when Tecumseh discovered that Harrison had coerced several tribal chiefs into agreeing to treaties that they had no authority to sign. Then a French-speaking spy was caught reconnoitering Prophet's Town and admitted he had been sent by Harrison for that purpose. Furious, Tecumseh demanded an audience. In August he travelled to Valenciennes with a war party for the confrontation. The meeting took place outside the handsome governor's mansion on the 12th of the month. Harrison spoke, "Your Father requests you take a chair." "My Father!" Tecumseh answered contemptuously. "The sun is my father and the earth is my mother, and only on her bosom will I repose." That said, he squatted himself on the ground, Indian fashion. Then he addressed the governor with his masterful, eloquent oratory. He spoke in English, which he had picked up from white captives:

Brother, I wish you to listen carefully, as I do not think you understand what I so often have told you. Brother, since peace was made you have killed some of the Shawnee, the Winnebago, the Delaware and the Miami, and have taken our lands. The Indians have resolved to unite to preserve their lands, but you try to prevent this by taking tribes aside and advising them not to join the Confederacy. The United States has set us an example of forming a union of their fires. Why, then, should you complain if Indians do the same thing among their tribes? You buy lands from the village chiefs who have no right to sell. If you continue to buy lands from these petty chiefs, there will be trouble, and I cannot foretell the consequences. The land belongs to all Indians, and cannot be sold without the consent of all. We intend to punish these village chiefs who have been false to us. It is true I am a Shawnee, but I speak for all the Indians — Wyandotte, Miami, Delaware, Kickapoo, Ottawa, Pottawatomi, Winnebago and Shawnee, for the Indians of the lakes and for those whose hunting grounds lie along the Mississippi, even down to the salt sea.

My forefathers were warriors. Their son is a warrior. From them I take only my existence. From my tribe I take nothing. I am the maker of my own fortune. Oh, could I but make the fortune of my red people as great as I conceive when I commune with the Great Spirit who rules the universe! The voice within me communing with the past ages tells me that once, and not so long ago, there were no white men on this continent. It then belonged to the red men, who were placed there by the Great Spirit to enjoy it, both they and their children. Now our once happy people are miserable, driven back by the white men, who are never contented but always encroaching. The way, the only way, to check this evil is for the red men to unite in claiming a common and equal right in the land as it was at first, and should be yet, for it was the gift of the Great Spirit to us all, and therefore the few cannot cede it away forever. What! Sell a country? Why not sell the air? Backward have the Americans driven us from the sea, and on towards the setting sun are we being forced *nekatacushe kalopolinto* — like a galloping horse — but now we will yield no further, but here make our stand. Brother, I wish you would take pity on the red people and do what I have requested. The Great Spirit has inspired me, and I speak nothing but the truth to you.

Taken aback, Harrison denied that the Indians were a single nation. He maintained that the Shawnee came from distant lands and had no right to speak for the other tribes. He argued that a fair price had been paid for the lands that had been sold, whereupon Tecumseh called him a liar. The meeting broke up on that note, both sides coming close to shedding blood. Harrison was left with the notion that he would soon face an Indian uprising. Tecumseh, having presented what he considered a fair proposal for peace which had been received with insults and lies, vowed to ally his Confederation with the British in the war that now seemed inevitable.

On November 15, only three months after the meeting with Harrison, Tecumseh visited His Majesty George III's 100th Regiment at Fort Amherstburg across the river from Fort Detroit. Introduced by the commanding officer, Major George Taylor, he addressed the assembled troops resplendent in their bright scarlet tunics. His oratory was brief but effective, "To my very good friends in the army of the Great King, I bring greetings from my people below the lake."

On his return to Prophet's Town, Tecumseh spread the word that he had been favourably received by the British and was certain they would accept an alliance with the Confederation once hostilities broke out. As the new year opened, a steady trickle of Indians, those too old, too young or too frail to fight, found their way to Fort Amherstburg. While the British were not entirely happy with this situation, they accepted it and even issued supplies to the immigrants.

Then, in July of 1811, a further confrontation with Governor Harrison was forced upon Tecumseh, when an emissary, Captain Walter Wilson, was sent to demand that the Shawnee surrender a pair of Potawatomi braves who had killed two white men on a homestead in Illinois. Tecumseh denied knowing their whereabouts and told the American that even if he did he would never turn them over to white men for punishment. "That is treason!" Wilson responded angrily. Then and there Tecumseh decided to meet Harrison again, face-to-face. Eighteen days later, with a party of 300 of his tribesmen, he set off for Valenciennes.

This meeting was even stormier than their first. Immediately on arrival the Americans ordered the size of the Indian delegation reduced. In the interest of keeping matters under control, Tecumseh held his temper and complied. Now Harrison told the Indian Chief that he regarded his planned trip south to enlist tribes into the Confederation as an "unfriendly act." That was too much for Tecumseh and the conference came to an abrupt halt. On his return to the village, on August 11, Tecumseh set off south with 25 of his warriors, as he had planned.

Meanwhile, although Harrison told the authorities in Washington that the Confederation must be broken and that the settlers were determined to fight the Indians, the US government refused to sanction an attack on the Indians or to send troops. Harrison, however, was determined to provoke the Indians into battle and force Washington to intervene. As soon as he learned of Tecumseh's departure, he began preparing to ravage Prophet's Town in the Shawnee chief's absence — a blow aimed at shattering the Confederacy. But to throw the Indians off guard, he spread the word that all he wanted was peace with them.

On the trek south, Tecumseh's band visited all the tribes along the Mississippi and penetrated as far as Alabama, Texas and Florida. The Indians of the south, Choctaw, Cherokee, Creek, Seminole and Osage were struck by the commanding figure of this strong, six-foot chieftain and spellbound by his eloquence. Here was a true leader in every sense of the word who inspired confidence with his oratory. "Brothers, we all belong to one family. We walk the same path. Brothers, we are friends. We must assist each other to bear our burdens. We are threatened with a great evil…we must be united, we must fight each other's battles." Tecumseh's mission to the southern states had been successful beyond his wildest dreams. But by the time the Shawnee warriors returned to the Ohio Valley they faced the spectacle of their village in utter ruins.

Tecumseh had left his brother, Tenkswatawa, in charge. He had not reckoned with Harrison's treachery. The Prophet was no warrior, he was a dreamer, a religious fanatic. Of this, the Indiana governor was only too well aware. To the American War Department, Harrison had written:

> If it were not for the vicinity of the United States, Tecumseh would perhaps be the founder of an empire that would rival in glory Mexico or Peru. No difficulties deter him. For four years he has been in constant motion. You see him today on the Wabash, and in a short time hear of him on the shores of Lake Erie or Michigan, or on the banks of the Mississippi, and wherever he goes he makes an impression favourable to his purpose. He is now upon the last round to put a finishing stroke to his work. I hope, however, before his return that that part of the work which he considers complete will be demolished, and its foundation rooted up.

With a party of 1,000 blue coats, Harrison set out along the densely wooded south-east shore of the Wabash river. The first Indians were sighted when they reached a point three miles from Prophet's Town. A mile further on, the Americans halted. Here they received a deputation of chiefs who advised them that The Prophet desired peace and requested a council with Harrison. He assured them that he, too, wanted peace and scheduled a meeting for the next day. Meanwhile, he ordered his men, who were "spoiling for a fight," to prepare to attack the village. When, next day, the Indians were confronted with the sight of the Americans bristling with bayonets, marching through the fields and long grass towards Prophet's Town, they knew they had been deceived. Soon the village was surrounded and they bravely ordered the Americans to desist. When Harrison asked where he could make camp, the Indians told him: "anywhere except in the village."

Harrison assured the Indians that they could sleep peacefully with the knowledge that his troops had no intention of attacking. That was a lie and they knew it. No one slept that night. At four o'clock in the morning the bugles sounded to begin the attack. The Indians responded with war whoops. The Battle of Tippecanoe was on! It did not last long. By first light, the Indians, their ammunition and arrows exhausted, began to retire. In the meantime, the women and children had managed to cross the river and escape. The Americans now advanced on the village killing any braves still about, setting fire to all the huts and wigwams, destroying the caches of corn, breaking everything from brass kettles to firearms. The only thing the Indians managed to salvage was a few head of cattle which they had driven away. All the hogs and fowl fell into American hands. Prophet's Town no longer existed, only the smouldering ruins remained.

The Indians had put up a stiff, if short, fight, killing 62 Americans and wounding 122 others. But Tippecanoe spelled doom for the Confederacy. Even the genius and charisma of Tecumseh could no longer rally the scattered native tribes. In fact, the battle had decided for once and for all time, that the continent would belong to the white man.

At this stage the British urged Tecumseh to come to terms with the Americans and make peace. Tecumseh wanted no part of it and, in any case, it was too late for that. On June 1, 1812, on direct orders from US President James Madison, the American Army of the Ohio, commanded by Brigadier General William Hull, began marching north from Dayton to invade Canada from Detroit. Eighteen days later the United States declared war. By that time Hull had reached Fort Wayne. From there he sent a messenger inviting Tecumseh to sit in council. At the meeting he asked Tecumseh to give his word that the tribes that owed allegiance to him "will not take part in the war." This after the humiliation the Indians had suffered at Tippecanoe!

Stunned, Tecumseh inquired, "Will the treaty lands be restored to their rightful owners?" Hull replied, "That I cannot promise." Tecumseh rose, reached forward for the peace pipe, broke it in two, threw it to the ground and stalked out of the wigwam.

Early in July, Tecumseh and his warriors crossed the Detroit River to Bois Blais (Bob Lo Island) and from there to Fort Amherstburg. On July 5, Hull arrived at Fort Detroit and a week later crossed the river with a force of 3,000 men, heavy artillery and cavalry, and occupied the town of Sandwich. From there he issued a proclamation that if any of Tecumseh's men joined the British they would be shown no mercy. In fact, Hull was in such dread of Tecumseh that he suggested to two of his officers that they disguise themselves as Indians and try to capture him. They steadfastly refused to have any part of such "foolishness."

Meanwhile Tecumseh moved to the Aux Canards River north of Amherstburg with a small force of his own warriors and a few men from the fort's militia. There, he fought the first battle of the War of 1812 — and lost. Defending a bridge spanning the marshes, he was forced to fall back when the Americans crossed the river at another point and attacked his force from behind.

But other than that minor action, Hull made no move to attack the British fortification. In the meantime, Tecumseh took several hundred of his Indians and crossed the river to the American side, shadowed by the guns of the British warship *Queen Charlotte*. On August 4, at the Raisin River, 35 miles south of Detroit, just outside of Brownstown, the warriors ambushed a supply column led by Major Thomas Van Horne. Coincidentally, they also intercepted messengers carrying dispatches south. Some of these contained complaints of Hull's cowardice and indecisiveness. This was born out when Hull, on learning of the British capture of Michilimackinac Island, and fearing an attack from the rear, moved his army from Sandwich back across the river to Fort Detroit. So much for the invasion of Canada!

Now the Americans assembled a force of 600 bent on protecting another northward bound convoy from the Raisin River. With 250 warriors and British soldiers, Tecumseh and Major Adam Muir crossed the river at Monguaga and waited in ambush for the protective force to appear. At three o'clock in the afternoon of Sunday August 9, the vanguard appeared. In the subsequent mêlée Tecumseh was wounded in the leg by a musket ball. Without his leadership Muir became confused and the British line broke. Throughout the night the badly mauled force made its way back across the river to Amherstburg where Tecumseh came face-to-face with the cowardly, hostile, distrusting and bigoted Colonel Henry Proctor who had taken over command of the fort.

***

On the afternoon of August 14, after Brock had addressed Tecumseh's warriors, they led their combined army north towards Sandwich. Cannons were hauled to the river shore and hidden behind a row of trees. There the artillerymen calculated their range so that their charges would fall inside the enemy fort. That night Tecumseh led a party of 600 braves across the river opposite Sandwich. Then in the darkness they crept stealthily forward until they formed a ring of tomahawks and rifles around Fort Detroit. Throughout the night they emitted blood-curdling war whoops and battle cries, startling the sentries on guard in the outposts and putting fear and dread into the hearts of all those inside the stockade.

Next morning Brock sent a courier across the river to demand surrender. Hull refused. At the same time the trees camouflaging the cannon were cut down and the guns opened fire, continuing all day and throughout the night. The Indians with their yelling and whooping added to the fearsome cacophony. On the following morning, with 700 of his red coats, Brock crossed the river by boat. At noon he sent a messenger forward — *too* far forward — to be deliberately captured. The man carried a fake despatch to Brock advising him that a party of 5,000 Indians from Michilimackinac Island was on its way to reinforce the attack. By this time roofs inside the fort were burning. But there was still no indication of a surrender.

In the afternoon, Tecumseh, astride his gray mustang, rode over to answer a summons from Brock who advised him that he had just learned from his scouts that an American force of 300 cavalry, sent to protect a convoy, had encamped only three miles from Detroit and was, at that very moment, riding north. "We'll be trapped between their lines and the fort unless we crush Hull's defenses in a space of 30 minutes," he told Tecumseh. The latter smiled, then nodded knowingly. A scheme had already hatched in his nimble mind. It was one based on deception and terror.

The ruse began with 1,300 British and Indian warriors alike, howling bloodcurdling war whoops at the top of their lungs. Then Tecumseh sent his 600 braves, four and five abreast, running cross a clearing near the walls of the fort. To give the impression that the Americans faced an overwhelming force of Indians, the running line of men twisted back through the forest in a circle, then just as the end of the column vanished from sight, the leaders appeared in the clearing again. All the while the air was rent with the cries and yells. Brock and Tecumseh sat breathlessly on their horses waiting as the charade continued. Suddenly Tecumseh pointed to the fort, "Look! There!" he shouted excitedly. "Hull shows his colours. Our deception worked!"

The Americans had raised the white flag of surrender. And not a shot had been fired in defence. The British and Indians now poured inside the walls of the fort, shouting and cheering, firing their rifles into the air. After the formalities of signing the surrender were completed, Tecumseh's warriors camped outside the walls while their chief was provided with a parlour on the second floor of a house on Jefferson Street that Brock had commandeered for himself.

Brock entered the room, sat down and spoke. "There is a look of pleasure on your face, my friend, " he said to Tecumseh. "I am at peace tonight. Perhaps it is because today was so very good, and the battle went well," Tecumseh replied. "Perhaps it is because I have fought beside a noble man."

"Come now, you're the one the Yankees are calling noble," was Brock's answer. "Why, whenever the citizens or the captured troops gather, one hears a single name — Tecumseh. Not one American has been attacked or molested in any way by your people. They imagined they would all be parted from their hair, I suppose. Proctor as much as said you'd bathe in the blood of the poor prisoners."

"Proctor is very foolish," Tecumseh frowned. "My people are not always easily controlled. But there will be neither peace nor honour for them until they walk as men, not animals. This lesson I have tried to teach those who fight with me."

"There's been no drinking, no violence. They behaved admirably. I wish all war could be as bloodless. And I only regret I cannot stay longer," said Brock. That last remark stunned Tecumseh. "You are leaving?" he asked. Brock explained that there was a danger of invasion on the Niagara frontier and he had to get there at once. This troubled Tecumseh, who did not relish the notion of serving with Proctor. But Brock — who presented the chief with a brilliant silken sash and a pair of the finest quality pistols, for which he received in return a finely fashioned wampum belt — assured Tecumseh that he had spoken to Proctor and there would be no problem. "I believe you actually impressed that pompous oaf," he assured him. But Tecumseh was uneasy, and with good reason. Trouble with Proctor was to erupt only 24 hours after Brock's departure.

As soon as he took command at Detroit, Proctor issued an order for all its citizens to swear allegiance to the Crown. Father Gabriel Richard, a Catholic missionary, would have none of it. The only oath he would agree to was allegiance to the American constitution. Outraged at what he considered to be an act of insubordination, Proctor had him clapped in irons. When Tecumseh learned of it, he confronted Proctor and demanded the Jesuit's release on the grounds that, as one skilled in medicine, he was needed to tend the wounded. When Proctor refused, Tecumseh threatened to abandon the British colonel and his small troop. That did it. Proctor backed down. But it was not to be the last of the differences between the two.

That winter Tecumseh went south, moving northward along the Wabash gathering a following of warriors. In April 1813 when he turned to Fort Amherstburg, he had 3,000 braves with him. It was then that he learned that his ally Brock, with whom he had formed such a close comradeship, had been killed at Queenston Heights the previous October. He was then told, to his chagrin, that Major *General* Proctor was now in command. Tecumseh's reaction was angry and terse. "Then the Confederation is in danger," he scowled, "Brock saw my people as they are — humane, courageous, capable of governing themselves wisely. Proctor thinks of us as savages."

But in the interests of defeating the Americans, the two adversaries formed an uneasy alliance. Together with a combined force of 2,500 men they marched south to the rapids of the Maumee River in Ohio where Harrison had built Fort Meigs opposite the site of the Battle of Falling Timbers. To reinforce Harrison's garrison, General Green Clay, with 1,500 Kentuckians, was moving from the north.

An argument over strategy quickly developed between the two leaders. Tecumseh offered a plan to draw the Americans — a mixture of blue coats and settlers wearing coonskin caps — out of the fort. Proctor cut him short. "I am quite capable of planning the strategy of this campaign. Please remember that I am in command, and that I have had the benefit of professional military training."

Tecumseh was furious but swallowed his pride. Next day Proctor took his soldiers up the Maumee river in small boats to set up artillery north of the fort, while Tecumseh led his warriors overland to the south. By the time his men were in position, General Clay's army appeared within striking distance. The Indians attacked, killing 450 Americans while the rest escaped across the river to Fort Meigs.

That was the only success achieved during the siege of the fort and in May 1813 the campaign had to be abandoned when reinforcements failed to arrive. The force returned to Fort Amherstburg, where summer had set in. Though Tecumseh did his best to prevent it, he was faced with wholesale desertions as his warriors, disillusioned by the way they had been treated by Proctor — for example, when the British troops received beef rations, Proctor ordered horsemeat for the Indians — drifted south back to their villages and their families.

The hostility between Proctor and Tecumseh, which had been increasing daily, reached a climax on September 11, 1813, the day after the British lost control of the Great Lakes during the Battle of Put-in-Bay. That defeat meant the supply line to Fort Amherstburg had been severed. At dawn that day, Tecumseh called a meeting of his warriors on a bluff overlooking the Detroit River to tell them of the naval defeat and that an American army was marching from the north ready to strike. "But as they march," he announced, "the leader of the Great King's soldiers already gathers his goods and prepares to flee, afraid for his life. If he is a coward, and if his men are cowards, then I ask that they leave us their weapons so that we may fight the Long Knives when they cross the river." His words were met with an angry growl from the assembled braves. Proctor, who had been watching and listening from his carriage nearby, beat a hasty retreat to the safety of his quarters. Then he sent for Tecumseh.

Tecumseh accused Proctor of cowardice. "I came to the house of the Great King to fight, not to run," he spat out contemptuously. Proctor replied that it seemed more strategic to withdraw, then make a stand later. "I will fight. You will fight with me," Tecumseh answered angrily. Proctor offered a compromise. Fall back to the Thames River and make a defence at Chatham or Moraviantown. Tecumseh turned and marched from the room in disgust.

On September 19, General William Henry Harrison's army was ready to cross the river. Proctor's troops put Amherstburg to the torch and retreated hurriedly north to Sandwich followed by Tecumseh and his braves. The following day another American army of 5,000, set sail across Lake Erie. At the same time 1,500 cavalry also got under way.

On the night of September 27, at the sight of the Americans crossing the river, the British broke in panic and fled from Sandwich east towards the Thames. Tecumseh's force of 1,000, all that was left, trailed behind them in the darkness. By noon next day, Proctor was already in flight up the road towards Moraviantown. But Tecumseh decided to make a stand at Chatham where he found some tag ends of the British army who agreed to fight with him. Tecumseh was determined to hold the two bridges crossing the Thames into the town. However, Harrison's force, spearheaded by the Kentuckian forest fighters, was simply too overwhelming in numbers and too overpowering in artillery support. Tecumseh was wounded in the arm but continued to fight. Finally, the defenders had no choice but to retreat east toward Moraviantown.

On October 4, Tecumseh learned that Harrison had captured most of Proctor's ammunition supply. The signs were not bright and by nightfall, an exhausted Tecumseh had a premonition that the end was near. "I am weary," he said, "and I feel we shall never leave this ground."

Next morning, on the curved road near the Thames river, Tecumseh finally caught up with Proctor and urged him to make a stand against Harrison's troops. But the British commander had totally lost his nerve. "No, no!" he groaned. "We cannot withstand the onslaught of the American army. It is impossible!" Tecumseh aimed his pistol at Proctor's stomach. "Are you going to refuse me again?" he snarled. "I do not believe you will this time!"

Proctor broke down completely, dropped to his knees then crawled to his cot and, whimpering, buried his head in the blankets. Sickened at the sight of Proctor's sobbing, Tecumseh said to one of his aides, "Since there is no choice left for victory, the only course remaining is honourable defeat. We fight!" When an aide pointed out that Proctor was in no condition to lead, Tecumseh replied, "I will organize the armies myself."

Tecumseh now deployed his warriors and the British troops in a wide line running north-west from the river. Beneath the British forces nearest the Thames and another wooded area farther north lay a dense, low, swampy area. By placing his Indians beyond the swamp, Tecumseh hoped to split the Americans into two prongs. By noon the battle lines were drawn.

At four o'clock in the afternoon, the bugles of the Kentucky horsemen sounded and the first ragged lines of whooping buckskin-clad riders charged into the woods where the British and Indians had entrenched themselves. This was where the Kentuckians were at home — in the forests. The British line soon broke and the troops began surrendering in droves.

Tecumseh kept darting in and out through the woods, his smoking pistol in one hand, his knife in the other, exposing himself fearlessly, shouting words of encouragement. Suddenly he was seen to stagger and fall. A single bullet had killed the great leader. Word passed down the line: "Tecumseh is dead." Indian morale broke down immediately. Without the leadership of the Shawnee chieftain, the braves turned and fled. His body was never found. A legend was lost — swallowed up in the muck and mire of a swampy battlefield. But his legacy never died.

Tecumseh never realized his dream of uniting all his people under a single Confederation. Nor did he survive to see the Canadian victory over the American invader which his bravery, leadership and brilliance had done so much to bring about. Tecumseh was not only a great leader in battle, a tactical and strategic genius, but with his bravery and oratory, he was also an inspiration to his people. He was a patriot with a fierce sense of loyalty, a man who abhorred cruelty and torture. Though he was born in America it was Canada that he served in time of war. By that very fact, he ranks as one of our great military leaders.

No prayers were said for Tecumseh but one eulogy marks him as the most farsighted statesman of his race:

Sleep well, Tecumseh, in thy unknown grave,
Thou mighty savage, resolute and brave,
Thou, Master and strong spirit of the woods,
Unsheltered traveller in sad solitudes,
Yearner o'er Wyandot and Cherokee,
Could'st tell us now what hath been and shall be!"
From Norman S. Gurd's *The Story of Tecumseh*

The Tecumseh Stone, his monument, can be found in Amherstburg.

Charles de Salaberry
1778–1829

3

DEDICATION TO HONOUR
Charles de Salaberry

During the capture of Quebec, the 60th Regiment of Foot (Royal American), which had been raised in New York and Philadelphia in 1775, had played such a prominent part that General James Wolfe awarded it the regimental motto: *Celer et Audax* — Swift and Bold. In 1797 it was employed against the French in Jamaica. Its officers were drawn from many nations including, England, Prussia, Switzerland, and Hanover. Among them were two French Canadians, Jacques des Rivieres and 21-year-old Charles de Salaberry who was brigade major and aide-de-camp to the commander of the 4th Battalion.

With such a cross-section of nationalities, keeping peace in the mess wasn't always easy, particularly with the Germans, known for their swordsmanship, and their belligerency. One of them had drawn Rivieres into an unequal duel and killed him. Next morning at breakfast he boasted, "I have just despatched a French Canadian to meet his Maker." Outraged, Salaberry sprang to his feet. "After breakfast you'll have the pleasure of seeing if you can despatch another," he challenged.

It was almost foolhardy, for Salaberry was a mere novice with the sword. The only thing he had going for him, and it was a moot point, was his youth. It was clear from the very start that he was no match in skill and experience against his older opponent, who toyed with him, setting him up for the kill. Parrying a weak lunge by Salaberry, the German drew blood, slashing him across the left temple. Salaberry's supporters dragged him from the fight, but he would have none of it.

Dabbing his wound with a handkerchief, he returned to the duel with renewed vigour, determined to win.

Thrusting and slashing, his strength and energy seemed to grow by the minute. Now he had the upper hand, as the Prussian swordsman began to tire. Salaberry was quick to take advantage. Feigning an attack to the right shoulder, he took a tremendous swipe to the left waist. One last lunge and it was all over. The German crumpled to the ground, cut to ribbons.

Salaberry had won the respect and admiration of his fellow officers and no one ever challenged him again. Subsequent to the incident, one of his commanders wrote to the Duke of Kent of his protégé: "He is a young man of distinguished bravery and he will make an excellent officer because he has a dedication to honour in his soul."

Distinguished bravery and dedication to honour, were two attributes built into the very backbone of the tradition of the Salaberry family, stretching back to the 16th century. In 1587 when, at the Battle of Coutras one of the Salaberrys, a Bourbon officer, killed a leading Guise warrior but spared a less adept comrade who was wounded, Henry of Navarre proclaimed "*Force a Superbe, Mercy a Faible.*" Roughly translated it means: "Strength against the Mighty, Mercy to the Weak." It became the family motto and part of their coat of arms.

From then on the Salaberrys continued to distinguish themselves in war, against the Moors, English, Infidels and Christians. They also served their country in public life. In the early 18th century, Charles Simon de Salaberry was named military governor of the Ardennes. His oldest son was in charge of the Treasury Department, while a nephew held the position of state councillor.

The first Salaberry to come to Canada, or New France as it was then called, was Michel, grandfather to Charles. He arrived in 1775 as captain on a merchant vessel. In 1748 he married Madeleine Louise (his second marriage), the daughter of a colonial seigneur from whose mother he bought Beauport at Quebec, one of the oldest seigneuries in the New World. In 1752 Madeleine gave birth to a son Louis who joined the British Army and fought in the American Revolution distinguishing himself at Saratoga where he was wounded.

In 1778 Louis married Francoise Catherine Hertel de Pierreville. In the first Lower Canada election in June 1792, Louis won a seat in the new elected assembly. Then two years later he was commissioned, along with two others with the rank of major, to form a new regiment, the Royal Canadian Volunteers, to ensure security against the United States. In 1791 when Prince Edward, the Duke of Kent was stationed in Canada, he and Louis became close friends. This alliance was to play a significant part in the military career of Louis's eldest son, Charles, who had been born on November 19, 1778, in the manor house at Beauport, the eldest of four male offspring.

As an infant, Charles-Michel d'Irumberry de Salaberry gave little indication of the strength and determination that he would later display as a soldier. He was so sickly with colic that his parents feared he would not live. But he did survive and grew up so hale and hardy that by the time he was 14, under the sponsorship of the Duke of Kent, he was accepted as a cadet in the 44th Regiment of Foot. After a year of basic training, he obtained a commission as an ensign in the 60th Regiment of Foot — the Royal Americans — with which he was sent to St. Vincent, where he officially began his military career on July 28, 1794.

As producers of sugar, the islands in the West Indies were of vital economic importance to both England and France, who were then at war. At the time Salaberry arrived, the main theatre of operations was the Island of Guadeloupe, which a year earlier had been taken by the British. But the French had returned in strength and had regained control of Grande-Terre, the eastern half of the island. To retake it, General Sir Charles Grey sent for reinforcements, among them the 60th Regiment.

Many of the troops came down with malaria. But Salaberry, the sickly child, seemed immune to the disease. His good health singled him out for special duties and earned him a promotion to the rank of lieutenant as well as command of a grenadier company — at age 15!

In late September the French landed by sea on the western side of Guadeloupe and, 2,000 men strong, laid siege to the city of Basse-Terre where the 60th Foot was left to hold out. Salaberry's grenadiers withstood attack after attack. On one occasion they absorbed 500 musket shots and 50 artillery shells within the space of five hours. Casualties were fearful and mounted steadily so that by December 10, when the order came to evacuate, Salaberry and two others were the only ones in the entire company who had not been wounded. This was the 16-year-old commander's baptism of fire and it is to his credit that, at so tender an age, he was able to maintain such a high standard of discipline under the severest of battle conditions. His amazing stamina had served the strapping youth well as it would on more than one occasion.

In another action that winter, the capture of Martinique, Salaberry again distinguished himself. By this time the Royal Americans had been reduced to a force of only 200, but Martinique was gained without a single loss. Salaberry was now transferred to Halifax where he was engaged in recruiting duties at which he proved most successful. Then in July 1799, he returned to the West Indies and was promoted to the rank of captain. There he remained until December 1804, when, after six months leave at home in Canada, he was posted to Great Britain.

In London he joined the 5th Battalion of his old regiment now under the command of Lieutenant Colonel Francis Baron de Rottenburg. The Baron introduced revolutionary changes in drill techniques which Salaberry would later employ when he commanded his own regiment. Among them were: free style marching, which was faster and less tiring than the standard staccato style; quick, silent drill; shorter commands; carrying rifles at the trail instead of shouldered at the slope; and, most innovative of all, "maneuvers by bugle call."

Salaberry's recruiting experience in Halifax now paid off handsomely. Travelling about England to enlist men for the Duke of Kent as well as for Rottenburg, he would re-enlist men from other regiments that had been disbanded. Competition among recruiting officers for these eligible, well-trained soldiers was keen. That Salaberry was so successful among his peers was greatly appreciated by Kent and Rottenberg, but General Sir George Prevost resented the fact that, in his zeal, Salaberry was hiring some of his best men away from him. This was unfortunate. Prevost, an unforgiving individual with a malicious nature, was to become governor-in-chief of Canada, and Salaberry would have to serve under him. Prevost had been commander of St. Vincent in 1794 when Salaberry served there, but there was no contact between the ensign and the commander.

In 1807, Salaberry's battalion was posted to Cork in Ireland where he was promoted to the rank of major and made aide-de-camp to Rottenburg, then a major general. Two years later, in an effort to reduce the Napoleonic threat, a campaign was planned to capture Walcheren Island at the mouth of the Scheldt River in Holland, occupied by the French. The objective was to create a diversion for the allied land forces. On July 30, Salaberry led his men ashore in the first wave. At first the assault proved successful, one objective after another falling to the British. Rottenburg was impressed with Salaberry as a fighting officer. But heavy losses and the outbreak of a frightful fever — one that would plague Salaberry for the rest of his life — soon dashed British hopes for a victory. The expedition was called off in September. The Earl of Chatham, who had headed it up, was forced to resign. Soon afterward, Rottenburg was posted to Canada and he brought Salaberry with him as his aide-de-camp. They arrived in Quebec on April 19, 1810.

At the time, Lower Canada was politically in a state of turmoil. The problem was taxation. The merchants and businessmen, who were primarily English-speaking, and who dominated the government Executive Council, wanted taxes to be based on land. The landowners who, for the most part were French-speaking, and held the majority in the Legislative Assembly, wanted taxation based on imports.

It was an abrasive issue that called for delicate political handling. But the prejudiced governor, Sir James Craig, on the advice of English extremists, totally misread the situation as racial rather than economic and on May 15, 1809 dissolved the assembly. Then when the new body adhered to the same view as its predecessor, Craig lost his head altogether. In late February 1810 he dissolved the new assembly and fired a number of French Canadians from government and militia posts, among them Charles de Salaberry's father, Louis, who lost his pension as well. When the newspaper, *Le Canadien,* took umbrage, Craig had the editors and the printer thrown in jail.

With relations between Britain and the United States fast deteriorating, this intolerable state of affairs became daily more precarious. The British government wasted no time. It dumped Craig and replaced him with General Sir George Prevost to clean up the mess.

A look at the defences told Prevost how desperate the situation had become. Upper Canada had 1,500 Regulars defending a 1,500 mile border. In Lower Canada there were five British battalions — approximately 4,500 men. But it was the French Canadian position that worried him. After Craig's inane performance, their attitude towards British rule was hostile to say the least. Prevost needed their loyalty in the worst way. With the arrival of Charles-Michel d'Irumberry de Salaberry in Canada, he saw the answer to the thorny problem facing him.

Despite their earlier differences over recruiting, Prevost was willing to forgive — temporarily — because he saw in Salaberry a heroic French Canadian figure who his countrymen would not only be proud of but would also respect. Salaberry had also been trained in modern battle tactics and drill by the brilliant Baron Rottenburg. On April 1, 1812, not a moment too soon, Prevost gave Salaberry the militia rank of lieutenant colonel and two weeks later signed an order for the formation of a corps of light infantry called the Canadian Voltigeurs (rovers or rangers) of which Salaberry became commandant and superintendent. It was an impressive position for the 34-old French Canadian to hold in the British Army. But Prevost's prejudices against the French Canadian were far from forgotten.

The Voltigeurs numbered just over 500, each armed with a light infantry musket and a knife. Their uniform was grey trousers, red sash, crossbelts, short boots and light bearskin caps. Their drill, à la Rottenburg, was simple infantry manoeuvres with the emphasis on sharp shooting. To become a Voltigeur, a man had to be between 17 and 35 years old and stand no less than five foot three inches tall.

It was at this time, during the formative stages of the Voltigeurs, that Salaberry got married. His bride was Marie-Anne-Julie de Rouville, daughter of a wealthy seigneur whose estates included seigneuries at Rouville, Chambly, Saint Olivier and elsewhere. The couple made their home at the Chambly seigneurie.

Salaberry proved to be a harsh disciplinarian — though a fair one. His men made up a song about him:

> There's our Colonel
> With Satan in his soul
> Who'll be the death of us all.
> There is no beast of prey
> That would dare stand in his way;
> And no matter how far you seek,
> You'll find our Colonel is unique.

Salaberry took whatever measures he saw fit, even physical confrontation, to maintain order in the ranks. One afternoon he was told that things were getting out of hand in the drill hall. A troublemaker, Roger Rouleau, was stripped to the waist, taking on all comers and creating chaos. Salaberry marched into the hall and ordered the man to get dressed. Rouleau yelled back, "I'd like to see you make me!" Suddenly Salaberry lunged forward, seized Rouleau's shoulder in a vice-like grip, and threw him to the floor so forcibly it was a wonder it didn't crack the boards. There was no more trouble from Rouleau. Meekly, he pulled himself off the floor and got dressed.

While the Voltigeurs were training, the War of 1812 was beginning to have its effect on Lower Canada. The key was the St. Lawrence River which formed the lifeline for supplies and reinforcements to Upper Canada and had to be kept open. Montreal, which controlled access to the upper St. Lawrence, was dangerously close to the American border. Prevost was forced to adopt a defensive strategy to protect it.

As soon as Prevost learned that US President James Madison had declared war — on June 18, 1812 — he established a line of troops extending from Saint-Jean to Laprairie to guard Montreal. Salaberry was assigned the most advanced posts along the 45th parallel (the Canadian-US border) from Saint-Regis to Yamaska. His headquarters were at Saint-Philippe de Laprairie. The most direct invasion route was along the Richelieu River, but it was also the most heavily defended and therefore the least likely one for the Americans to take.

By now Salaberry had, in addition to his four companies of Voltigeurs, also part of the regular troops under his command: all of the Sedentary Militia, some battalions of the Embodied Militia and all of the Indians, numbering usually between 90 and 250.

The American strategy against Lower Canada which, of course, was aimed at capturing Montreal, was led by the American commander-in-chief, Major General Henry Dearborn, who took command of troops assembled at various points on Lake Champlain.

Acting on intelligence that Dearborn was preparing to march, Salaberry had bridges destroyed and roads blocked with felled trees. By November 17, Dearborn was marching on Odelltown, Lower Canada, with 6,000 men supported by artillery. To meet the threat, Salaberry positioned his men on the north shore of the Lacolle River. Close to 1,000 of Dearborn's troops, commanded by Colonel Zebulon Pike, crossed the border on the night of November 19 but were spotted by the British officer of the day allowing a forward detachment to escape. Unknown to Pike, another American party had also crossed the border. In the darkness and confusion the two groups opened fire on each other. After a short, heated exchange among themselves they finally withdrew. That ended Dearborn's campaign for the moment and for the rest of the winter the Lower Canada frontier remained reasonably undisturbed.

The following spring and summer Salaberry spent most of his time at his headquarters in Saint Philippe. His wife, Marie-Anne, who was with him, gave birth to a son in May. During the summer the British fleet on Lake Champlain set fire to the American barracks at Swanton, Vermont and Plattsburg, New York, and destroyed blockhouses at Champlain. The Voltigeurs covered the ships' return to base down the Richelieu River.

Meanwhile, on July 23, General John Armstrong, the US secretary of war, submitted plans for the capture of Montreal, which he estimated as being the "weaker place," with two armies totalling 10,000 men, the largest force the Americans fielded during the entire war.

The first army, made up of 7,000 troops commanded by Major General John Wilkinson, would advance through the St. Lawrence Valley. The second, led by Major General Wade Hampton, assembled at Burlington, Vermont, was to move up the Champlain Valley and join up with Wilkinson's army just south of Montreal. Because the British had no force comparable to that of the Americans, the capture of Montreal would be a pushover. Or so they thought. To disguise how small his force really was, Salaberry, in his usual innovative way, constantly moved his troops from one location to another to give the impression that he had far greater numbers at his disposal than was actually the case.

Hampton's first move was to transfer his army across Lake Champlain to Plattsburg which he did by September 18. This caught Prevost off guard. He had anticipated an attack on Kingston, an assault the Americans had actually planned originally, but had discarded due to the garrison's strong defences. So Prevost had left Major General Sir Roger Sheaffe in charge of Montreal and hurried upriver to Kingston.

In the meantime, on the 19th, Hampton moved his force north, Salaberry's Voltigeurs began blocking all the roads leading to Odelltown and tore down the bridge across the Lacolle River. By nightfall Hampton's troops had reached Chazy and early next morning he had them on the march again to Champlain at the top of the lake. From there they surrounded Odelltown and captured it.

Salaberry had too few troops to mount a counter-attack. All he could do was contain the Americans until reinforcements arrived. This he achieved by having his Indians ambush American patrols. Their fear of the Indians also kept them from probing too far and discovering how few troops Salaberry had. He then had his Voltigeurs block the roads with felled trees and throw up wooden defences, while his Indians constantly harassed the Americans. Hampton quickly realized that he might run into much stiffer resistance than he had anticipated. Unable to determine Salaberry's real strength — or weakness — he decided to withdraw back across the US border, improve his supply lines and mount an advance towards Montreal from a different direction — the Chateauguay Valley.

By late September most of the streams had run dry and the Lacolle River was low. This state of affairs caused concern for both sides. Hampton worried about a lack of water for his troops. Salaberry feared that the reduced effectiveness of the rivers and streams as natural defence barriers would make it easy for the Americans to advance when and where they chose.

On September 23, Hampton's forces had fallen back to Chazy and began advancing towards Four Corners, at the head of the Chateauguay Valley. After a three-day trek they established camp and began building and improving a roadway back to their supply base at Plattsburg.

All these movements had been carefully reconnoitered by Salaberry's scouts. He now positioned the bulk of his forces in the valley to cut Hampton off and made his own headquarters in a stone tavern on the banks of the Chateauguay River south of Sainte Martine.

The Americans may have had numerical superiority but they also had their share of problems. Their supplies were inadequate. Rainy weather meant delays in bringing up food. Their worn-out summer uniforms were too light for the cold autumn weather. And at night they lived in fear of harassment from Salaberry's sniping patrols, many of them made up of the dreaded Indians. All this began to create serious morale problems. Then, on October 1, on orders from Prevost, Salaberry penetrated the American defences in a surprise raid with 200 of his Voltigeurs and some Indians.

This quixotic attack, against vastly superior numbers and a well-armed camp seems to have been a deliberate attempt on Prevost's part, going back to his recruiting grudge against him, to discredit — even sacrifice — Salaberry. Prevost's private correspondence to his wife revealed his strategy.

It turned out to be somewhat of a fiasco. To begin with, the element of surprise was lost when an Indian prematurely opened fire on a sentry. Then, by the time they had penetrated the outer defences, the Americans rallied and tried to outflank them. This was not the kind of fighting the Indians cared for and they withdrew, taking most of the Voltigeurs with them. That left Salaberry and three others to fend for themselves. Somehow they managed to fight off their assailants until dusk when they slipped through the American lines to their own. Next morning, Salaberry tried to rally a renewed assault, but the Indians refused to participate. Without them, he knew any new attempt would be hopeless and the raiders withdrew.

Knowing that an attack by Hampton was imminent, Salaberry directed his energies to shoring up his defences. In this, he showed a genius for planning and phenomenal appreciation of battle tactics. He blocked all the roads and destroyed all the bridges. Between La Fourche, where the English river flows into the Chateauguay, and Spear's, where the Outarde River joins it, he set up advance posts. Between them half a dozen gullies or ravines crossed the area which Salaberry had chosen as his battlefield, the best possible option along the entire length of the Chateauguay River. Salaberry fortified each of the ravines with log defences running from the river bank, across the cleared fields on either side of the road into the woods and a swamp on the right flank. About a mile in advance of the line of defence, were two fortifications in a position to slow down the American advance and alert the main force that the enemy was on his way. The woods on the right flank in advance of Salaberry's own lines provided cover for some of the Indians and a few buglers.

Behind the main defence on Bryson's Ravine was Grant's Ford which, on face value, would provide Hampton's troops with access to the left flank. However, this weakness Salaberry covered with fortifications on both banks of the river and another post was built further up the river on the swampy and wooded south bank.

Once again, Salaberry employed the ruse of deceiving the enemy about his actual strength by marching units close to the American positions, then when they were out of sight of the Americans, changed uniforms to give the impression of a number of different units being concentrated in the area. The ruse worked. Hampton reported to Armstrong, "the enemy is hourly adding to his strength." In fact reinforcements *had* arrived. A militia unit, 1,400 strong, commanded by Colonel "Red" George Macdonnel took up a reserve position at Morrison's field.

On October 16, Hampton received orders from American Secretary of State General John Armstrong, to advance to the mouth of the Chateauguay River. About 1,500 militia would not leave New York State. It was their prerogative to refuse to fight on foreign soil. Hampton assigned them to guard the road to Plattsburg and the supplies at Four Corners. It was five days before his lead units crossed the American border into Canada. By this time, Hampton had a fair idea of where Salaberry had placed his forces from American-born settlers in the area who acted as guides. Hampton planned a two-pronged attack; an advance party would push through the brush and swamp on the south side of the river, led by Colonel Robert Purdy, while the main body concentrated on a frontal charge. Purdy began his attack on the night of October 25. The main assault took place next morning.

In the dark, Purdy's three infantry regiments soon got bogged down in the tangled maze of the swamp. By dawn they had made little progress but, although wet and disillusioned, they nevertheless continued to work their way forward upriver. At this point on Tuesday, October 26, Hampton ordered his remaining force, under Brigadier General George Izard, to begin the frontal attack as soon as they heard gunfire. That would be the signal that Purdy had made contact with the Canadians.

They heard shots all right, but they weren't American. The gunfire had come from the Voltigeurs the moment that Purdy's infantry came into view. Now Salaberry ordered four of his companies to move forward and asked Macdonnel to send in a company of 40 Chateauguay Chasseurs to support the Voltigeurs defending the forward positions against Purdy's Americans.

By two o'clock in the afternoon, however, the only signal Hampton had received from Purdy was that he had reached an impasse. He decided to go ahead with the main assault anyway, even if it left his left flank exposed. The battle lines were clearly drawn. Salaberry with 500 Voltigeurs, 150 Indians and Red Macdonnel's 1,200 militia reserves faced Izard's force of 5,000 and Purdy's 1,500 to 2,000 troops. This would be the only battle of the War of 1812 fought entirely by Canadians and Indians without the backing of British regulars, and an uneven one it was, to say the least. But Salaberry was certain he would win. He not only depended on his nerve but on the meticulous way he had planned his defenses and his flexibility in battle.

By this time, Purdy had been forced to retire. Climbing a tree to survey the situation, Salaberry saw that the enemy was divided. Then and there he decided to force the Americans' left flank and to sound bugles from all quarters of the field to give the impression that Hampton faced a much larger force than really existed. Purdy had sent one of his men forward to demand a Canadian surrender, whereupon Salaberry, standing on a tree stump from which he conducted the battle, shot him dead. That was generally credited with being the start of the battle.

Izard's forces now made their attack. It was a brave attempt but they soon became totally demoralized by the blare of bugles which seemed to be coming from everywhere, and the chilling war whooping of the Indians who sniped at them from behind the fortifications and trees in the woods. A message from Purdy that he was being besieged by superior numbers convinced Hampton that he was not only overwhelmed but that his troops would soon be ripped to shreds. He decided to hold his ground overnight but in the morning ordered a withdrawal.

The Americans left their dead — at least 50 — and many of their wounded on the battlefield. The Canadians gathered up the enemy wounded and sent them back to their field dressing station. Salaberry's casualties had been incredibly light: five killed, 16 wounded and three missing.

The retreat was made in disarray, the Americans discarding their equipment and belongings — knapsacks, muskets, ammunition, provisions, shovels and personal effects — en route to Piper's Road where, on October 29, they made camp. But harassed all night by the Canadians and Indians, early next morning they fled across the border, back to the United States.

Half the American forces marshalled to capture Montreal had been stopped. But the other army, under Major General Wilkinson, was still moving down the St. Lawrence. On November 11 they were forced to fight a rearguard action against a force of 800 Canadians, including three companies of Voltigeurs commanded by Colonel John Morrison, at John Crysler's farm near Morrisburg, but it failed to halt the advance. Next morning Wilkinson received a report of Hampton's defeat. Totally unnerved, he decided to call off the campaign and retire across the American border. The threat to Montreal had come to an abrupt, inglorious end.

The Battle of Chateauguay, fought at the incredible odds of 12 to one, had been an enormous success. Its importance was that it prevented the two American armies from joining forces which would inevitably have resulted in the capture of Montreal and the eventual fall of all Canada to the United States. It had also been an exemplary display of field generalship and extraordinary courage by Salaberry. His father chided him, "You are, I believe the first general to win a battle mounted on a stump. Believe me, change your mount!" In a more serious vein, the Honourable Juchereau Duschesnay, whose father and uncle took part in the battle wrote, "It is difficult to know which to admire the more — his personal courage as an individual or his skill and talents as a commander."

General George Prevost, however, was far from generous over Salaberry's leadership or the part played by his Voltigeurs. In his general order, issued on the day after the battle, he stated that the Voltiguers were merely an advanced guard sent out to protect the work parties. He recommended awarding colours to some of the reserve regiments who hadn't even seen action and made no reference to Salaberry's role in the battle, stating that he had himself taken charge once the fighting began when, in fact, he was many miles away, safe behind the firing line.

Salaberry, who never took credit for his accomplishments, saw red. Determined that Prevost should not earn kudos for a victory towards which he had contributed nothing, he fired off a fiery dispatch to the attorney general setting the record straight by outlining the true story. He need not have worried. There were too many prominent Canadian families represented on the battlefield who knew the truth for Prevost, as Salaberry himself put it, "to tarnish the little glory that I have gained."

The general public got the real story which was published in the *Gazette*. After studying Prevost's report, Duschesnay wrote to Salaberry, "My wishes will not be completely satisfied until your virtues, your talent and your services will have been recompensed in a most fitting way and until we can unanimously claim that we have given justice to the Hero of Chateauguay."

From England, the Duke of Kent wrote to Charles's father, Louis: "I saw with dismay that the report did not render him [Charles] sufficient justice… Over here everyone attributes to him all the honour and looks to him as the hero who saved the province of Lower Canada…I have also spoken about this with the Duke of York who appears perfectly convinced that it is to your son that we owe it all."

The reply to Prevost from Colonial Secretary Lord Bathurst indicated that nobody had been taken in. It concluded with this statement which must have been a bitter pill for Prevost to swallow:

> To Colonel Salaberry, and to all officers under his command in general, you will not fail to express His Royal Highness' most gracious approbation of their meritorious and most distinguished services.

Later the Legislative Assembly of Lower Canada passed a resolution that read in part:

> …this Assembly deeply appreciates the valour and discipline shown by the non-commissioned officers, soldiers and militiamen of the little band under the immediate command of Lieutenant Colonel Charles de Salaberry, in the memorable defeat of the American army…at…Chateauguay and that these [thanks] be communicated to them by the officers commanding these units, who are asked to thank them for their courage and exemplary conduct.

But Salaberry had not heard the last of General Prevost, not by a long sight. After a fall campaign of forced marches, and several skirmishes, his troops were exhausted, their uniforms tattered and torn from slogging through the swamps and forests. On November 23, Prevost ordered 300 men to attack Four Corners, a hopeless task against a force of 900 Americans. The Canadian troops would be exposed to heavy rains and severe frosts in uninhabitable conditions. Predictably it failed. The weather and life in the swamps left Salaberry so crippled with fever and rheumatism that in January 1814, he was granted a short furlough which he and his wife, Marie-Anne, spent in Montreal. He considered retiring from the army but, on the last day of the month, he was summoned from his sickbed to march to Coteau-du-Lac where it was feared the Americans would attack from French Mills on the Salmon River.

Salaberry quickly assembled a force totalling 600 men from his Voltigeurs and four companies of the 49th Regiment and began a forced march up the St. Lawrence. But the American assault never materialized and, after losing 30 of his men from frostbite, Salaberry marched his force back to Montreal where he arrived on February 4, sicker than ever.

Later that month, after being appointed an inspector field officer, he resigned as commander of the Voltigeurs. Then, in March, Major General Wilkinson, with an army of 2,000, once again invaded Lower Canada down the Richelieu River, captured Odelltown and placed Lacolle under siege. This threat brought Salaberry back in the forefront of the fighting. A company of Voltigeurs was quickly sent to relieve the siege. With a force of 800 troops Salaberry drove Wilkinson's force back to Plattsburg.

By July, Major General George Izard had replaced Wilkinson and, with 6,000 men, encamped at Champlain just inside the American border. The British responded to this new menace by sending Salaberry and 2,200 troops, with some artillery, to take up a position at Odelltown to prevent another invasion.

This coincided with the arrival of 16,000 British troops in Lower Canada following Wellington's defeat of Napoleon's army on the Iberian Peninsula. Prevost put together an army of 11,000 with the objective of destroying the American naval base at Plattsburg. The campaign quickly fizzled out with the defeat of the British fleet, and Prevost ordered his troops withdrawn. By September there was little activity on the frontier and on November 18, Salaberry applied for retirement at half pay and became seigneur of Chambly.

In July of the following year — the Treaty of Ghent was signed on Christmas Eve of 1814 ending the war — Salaberry received a special gold medal commemorating the Battle of Chateauguay and much later was created a Companion of the Order of the Bath.

Salaberry settled into civilian life comfortably and with relish. He completed the building of his manor house, a handsome stone structure on the Richelieu River near Fort Chambly. In December 1815 he drafted a plan for building a canal around the raids on the Richelieu between Chambly and St-Jean to open a water route between the St. Lawrence and Lake Champlain that would connect with the traffic travelling down the Hudson River. This led to his appointment as commissioner of interior communication for Kent County and the establishment of a company, Proprietors of Chambly Canal. The waterway was completed in 1843 and became a significant economic resource during the First World War.

In 1818, when his father-in-law died, Salaberry took his seat in the Legislative Council alongside his father. Both father and son played significant roles in rousing public opinion to delay passage of the controversial Union Bill introduced by the British in 1822 to unite the two Canada's which would reduce the French Canadian majority in the Lower Canada Assembly.

That was Charles's final involvement with public life. Thereafter, he spent his time with his family and friends and busied himself running his estate. On the evening of February 26, 1829, at a neighbourhood party while in conversation with his host, Salaberry suddenly became pale, excused himself and collapsed with apoplexy. His wife carried him home and a doctor was called. Next morning he had recovered all his faculties except his speech. Surrounded by his family he died peacefully that morning at the age of 51.

Salaberry was laid to rest in the churchyard at Chambly where a large tombstone marks his grave. He was one of our greatest military leaders whose fame and feats at the Battle of Chateauguay has been likened, even in his own lifetime, to that of the legendary Leonidas, the King of Sparta, who held the bridge at Thermopylae with a handful of his soldiers against the Persian invader. Salaberry had inherited a proud legend and more than lived up to it.

Ironically, although a number of streets throughout the Montreal and the Richelieu Valley, some parks, a building and a regiment have been named after him, his name is little known. Outside his native Quebec, he is probably not known at all. Yet, two statues were built to commemorate him. The first of these was conceived shortly after his death in 1870 by a fervent patriot, Jacques Dion. But it took a decade of campaigning — letters, speeches, door-to-door canvassing — to see it realized. Finally, on June 7, 1881 it was unveiled at Chambly by the governor-general of Canada, the Marquess of Lorne.

The other monument which was built in 1882 and depicts Salaberry with sword drawn, stands alongside statues of Montcalm, Wolfe and Frontenac in the façade of the National Assembly buildings in Quebec City.

The site of the Battle of Chateauguay itself is commemorated by a granite obelisk, built in 1895. More recently, in 1970, Parks Canada opened an interpretation centre and site museum nearby which includes memorabilia, relics and other materials relating to the battle.

Arthur William Currie
1875–1933

4

THE VERY MODEL OF A
MODERN MAJOR GENERAL
Arthur Currie

Blasphemy! On June 13, 1927 foreshadowing the McKenna brothers' TV series, *The Valour and the Horror* and Paul Cowan's so-called documentary, *The Kid Who Couldn't Miss*, The Port Hope, Ontario *Evening Guide* took solid aim at the man whom the noted Canadian military historian, Donald Dancocks, rightly described as "the finest general this country has ever produced." A front-page article, simply headed Mons, read:

> Cable despatches this morning give details of the unveiling of a bronze plaque at the Hotel de Ville (the City Hall) at Mons, commemorative of the capture of the city by Canadians on November 11, 1918. This is an event which might properly be allowed to pass into oblivion, very much regretted rather than glorified.
>
> There was much waste of human life during the war, enormous loss of lives which should not have taken place. But it is doubtful whether in any case there was a more deliberate and useless waste of human life than in the so-called capture of Mons.
>
> It was the last day; and the last hour, and almost the last minute, when to glorify the Canadian Head Quarters [*sic*] staff the Commander-in-Chief conceived the mad idea that it would be a fine thing to say that the Canadians had fired the last shot in the Great War, and had captured the last German entrenchment before the

bugles sounded eleven o'clock, when the armistice which had been signed by both sides would begin officially.

Canadian Headquarters sounded the advance upon the retreating Germans, unsuspecting that any mad proposal for further and unnecessary fighting was even contemplated. The men were sent on in front to charge the enemy. Headquarters, with conspicuous bravery, brought up the rear. The fighting may have been more severe than was expected. Certain it is the Germans did not take the attack lying down.

Of course, the town was taken at the last minute before the official moment of the armistice arrived. But the penalty that was paid in useless waste of human life was appalling. There are hearts in Port Hope stricken with sorrow and mourning through this worse than drunken spree by Canadian Headquarters. Veterans who had passed through the whole four years are buried in Belgian cemeteries as the result of the "glories of Mons"...

It does not seem to be remembered that even Ottawa, neither by government nor Parliament, gave Sir Arthur Currie any official vote of thanks, or any special grant as an evidence of the esteem for his services. And this is the only case of this kind in connection with any of the commanding officers of the war. He was allowed to return to Canada unnoticed by officials of the government or of Parliament and permitted to sink into comparative obscurity in a civilian position as President [*sic*] of McGill University. The official desire to glorify Mons, therefore, deserves more than passing or silent notice. Canadian valour won Mons, but it was such a shocking, useless waste of human life that it is an eternal disgrace to the Headquarters that directed operations.

The author of this slanderous critique was a sometime newspaperman, a paid Liberal Party hack, William Thomas Rochester Preston, known as "Hug the Machine" Preston for the political patronage he enjoyed. But he was also called a lot of other things as well, none of them very flattering — "an unprincipled rogue," "a professional liar," and a "rotten swine." Among his credits were: fighting conscription in 1917, and involvement with the notorious West Elgin ballot-stuffing case at St. Thomas in 1902.

Currie was stunned, shocked — and angry! Mons had been anything but an "eternal disgrace." British General Sir Henry Horne, commander of the British Army, called its capture "just about the best thing that could have happened." Currie said, "I appreciated the national pride our country would have if we finished the war with the old battlefield in our possession, and though we were anxious to take it, *we did not care to suffer many casualties in doing so.*"

Contrary to what Preston wrote, Prime Minister Robert Borden cabled Currie, expressing thanks "for the heroic conduct and glorious achievements which have brought so much honour and credit to Canada."

It would have been uncharacteristic for Currie to take such libel lying down. All his life he had stood up to challenges. This one was to be no exception. Although he had been warned that it would be impossible to get a favourable verdict from a jury, he was determined to fight back. In July, 1927, legal papers were served on Preston as well as, Frederick Wilson, the owner of the *Evening Guide.* Thus began on April 16, 1928, one of the most dramatic court cases in Canadian history, one that became known in the press as "the fifty thousand dollar libel suit."

*** *

Canada was a scant eight years old when Arthur William Currie came into the world on Sunday, December 5, 1875, the third of seven offspring of Jane, and her husband, William Currie, (the family name was changed from Curry in 1887) who was described as a "successful and prosperous, farmer." He also "held numerous public offices" locally — locally being the small western Ontario town of Strathroy, 30 miles west of London. Arthur's grandparents had emigrated to Canada earlier in the century from Scotland and Ireland to avoid religious persecution, bringing their considerable old-world agricultural skills to the fertile London farming area.

As he grew up on the family's 300-acre farm, there was nothing remarkable at first about Arthur's personality or behaviour that gave an indication of his future emergence as Canada's "finest general." He attended a one-room school at nearby Napperton. He worked hard and when he finished school he qualified for entrance into Strathroy Collegiate Institute. As an "excellent student" there, he began to develop a fierce determination and a coolness under pressure. This was particularly evident in his debating classes, where he refused to be either hurried or harried in making his point. He also had a very strong memory.

As a teenager Currie was popular with his school pals who knew him as Art, and had an engaging sense of humour — "the life of the party." He grew up a big fellow, six-foot-four-inches tall, already weighing 200 pounds and could easily hold his own in a scrap. Raised a strict Methodist (though he switched to Anglicanism), he had his own cryptic religious code. "I believe in God, in Jesus and in the power of prayer," he stated flatly, a tenet he lived by all his life.

With his vigorous debating skills, Currie planned on taking up law. However, the death of his father when he was 15 years old, prevented it. The family could no longer afford to send him to college. He turned to teaching, instead. In 1893, he graduated from the Strathroy Model School with a third-class teaching certificate, but there were no teaching jobs available. Lured by the call to the Canadian West, Currie bought a $25 train ticket to Vancouver, arrived after a six-day journey, and hopped the ferry to Victoria where a maternal grand-aunt, Mrs. Orlando Warner, took him in as a boarder. It was at that same Alston Street establishment that he met another roomer, Lucy Sophia Chaworth-Musters, daughter of a retired English army officer who later abandoned her. Lily, as the Warners nicknamed her, was destined to become Arthur's wife.

Currie's only qualification for employment was teaching but his third-class Ontario certificate was not acceptable in British Columbia. He went back to school to upgrade it and it finally, in the fall of 1895 he found a job in a "one-room school, with outhouse" in Sidney, north of Victoria. At 19 he had charge of 30 students ranging in age from six to 18, earning himself all of $60 a month. A year later he was back in Victoria, teaching at Victoria High School. The following year he made the most momentous decision of his life. On January 5, 1897 he enlisted as a gunner with the 5th Regiment ("the Dandy Fifth") Canadian Garrison Artillery.

His first duty as a militiaman hardly augured a bright military career. Assigned as an orderly to the colonel of the regiment just before its annual inspection, he fell in at the rear instead of the front of the column, and received his first reprimand. Then, when it came time to present the long-time medal to the commanding officer, Currie dropped it — for which he received a fierce glare.

But after a few such near misses, Currie took to soldiering like a duck to water, whether it was drill, parades, rifle practice, social events or sports (he was an atrociously poor athlete but an excellent organizer). He rose through the ranks quickly and on December 19, 1900 was gazetted a second lieutenant.

He also suffered a bitter disappointment. When the Boer War broke out in 1899, the 5th Regiment sent a small contingent but Currie was not among them. He was in hospital with a stomach ailment that would periodically plague him. While recuperating, he decided to quit teaching — it simply didn't pay enough to cover his expenses as an officer (he had to pay for his own uniform, for one thing), and that of a future husband. He and Lily Chaworth-Musters had decided to get married.

Currie found a job with Matson and Coles, an insurance firm, where he became so successful, that when the owner left to go into publishing, he inherited the position of partner. In 1906 he was made provincial manager of National Life Assurance of Canada. In the meantime, he and Lily were married on August 14, 1901 and their first child, one of three, a daughter Marjorie, was born on December 9, 1902. Married life so agreed with Currie that, a big man anyway, he began to put on weight. By this time, he had been promoted to the rank of major and was made second-in-command of the regiment.

But the insurance business and the militia were not his only interests. He was an active Freemason, a card-carrying Liberal and a member of the BC Rifle Association of which he was made president, all the while developing his amazing administrative skills. While he was serene and good-natured most of the time, he could swear with the best of them, particularly when he lost his temper.

In 1908, during the land and building boom, he made another giant step in his life. He became a partner in a newly established real-estate firm, Currie and Power, and made a lot of money. On September 1 of the following year, Currie took command of the 5th Regiment. At 33 he was a burly young man with a calm appearance and a mien of authority and self-confidence. His first action as CO was to quell the bitter strike by the BC coal miners. As it was to mark his career so often, Currie's assessment of the situation, his timing and decision to act, won out and considerably enhanced his military career. When the 50th Regiment (Gordon Highlanders) was formed, Currie was given command on January 12, 1914. Shortly afterwards the bottom fell out of the real estate market and Currie, along with many others, found himself holding property worth a fraction of the price for which he'd bought it and found himself facing bankruptcy. Then, on August 4, the late-afternoon edition of the Victoria *Daily Colonist* carried the banner headline: BRITAIN AND GERMANY AT WAR — and recruiting for overseas service became Currie's top priority.

It had come as no surprise. On Sunday, June 28, the Archduke Francis Ferdinand of Austria-Hungary was assassinated in Sarajevo, triggering the events that led to the Great War. On August 3, Germany invaded Belgium and Britain issued an ultimatum demanding respect for Belgian neutrality which Germany and Britain had agreed to by a pact in 1831. Competition for recruits among the three Victoria militia units was strong, but Currie outmanoeuvred the others by opening a recruiting office where the crowd gathered daily to scan the bulletins in the windows of the *Colonist*.

There now came a turning point in Currie's career as a soldier. Sam Hughes, the irascible minister of militia and defense, whose son, Garnet, was a major in Currie's regiment, offered him command of one of four infantry brigades being formed at Valcartier, Quebec, one of the most prestigious, important military postings in Canada. His regiment would form part of his new brigade. Before he left, he had a few loose ends to clear up. His firm, which he entrusted to his partner, Roger Power, owed him $10,000. He also found himself entangled in a problem. To avert bankruptcy, he had borrowed mess funds from the regiment and was accused of misuse. It was probably with a sigh of relief that he left for Quebec on August 27.

Currie's new command, the Second (Provisional) Infantry Brigade was composed of the 5th, 6th, 7th and 8th Battalions each 1,000 strong made up of hardy men, volunteers all, 28 to 35 years old, from the north-west, interior BC and the coastal cities. It was one of three brigades that would form the First Canadian Division. At Valcartier most of the time was spent on the firing range. No one knew what to expect in the way of battle conditions in France but certainly a prime requisite would be to have men who could shoot straight.

Currie devoted himself to learning the best way to command 4,000 men and inspire their trust. He never once left camp, keeping long hours from 5:30 in the morning to 11:30 at night — all the while getting to know his non-commissioned officers (NCOs), as well as officers, who would have to lead. He was genuinely popular and amazed everyone with his enormous energy.

The Canadians arrived at Plymouth on October 14. Here Currie met Lieutenant General Sir Edward Alderson who would command the Canadian Division. A close friendship developed between the pair. Later, when asked to assess the Canadian brigadiers, Alderson replied, "Currie is out and out the best." The winter spent at Salisbury turned out to be the worst in 60 years. It rained 89 of the 123 days.

This served to illustrate just how poorly, thanks to Sam Hughes' inefficiency, the Canadians were equipped. Their boots got so soggy they disintegrated. Hughes blamed everyone in sight but in actual fact the fault was entirely his own for insisting that, given the country's limited industrial capacity, everything had to be Canadian-made.

For example, the contingent's 133 motor vehicles were of five different makes, and eight manufacturers supplied the 853 wagons. Uniforms tended to fall apart. Then there was the MacAdam shovel named after, and patented by, Hughes' female secretary. In combat it proved so use-less it had to be discarded but not before 25,000 had been purchased at $1.35 each. But the worst travesty of all was the unreliable, constantly modified Ross rifle, a throwback to the Boer War. It proved so danger-ously ineffective the troops threw it away in disgust. As Currie pointed out: "after firing a few rounds the shells seem to stick in the bore and are not easily extracted... This seems to me to be a point where the most careful investigation is necessary, as a serious interference with rapid fir-ing may prove fatal on occasion." Events were to prove him right but such out and out criticism did not endear him to Sam Hughes.

By the time the training on Salisbury Plain had come to an end, Cur-rie had achieved what he had set out to do: size up his officers and their capabilities down to the most junior lieutenant. He now had a well-coordinated brigade working together as a team. Then, towards the end of 1914 he was informed that his 6th Battalion was to be converted to cavalry and replaced with the 10th. Reports reached Currie that its officers were of a poor calibre and he feared that the unit might upset the closely knit organization he had trained to perfection. He asked for the 11th instead because it was, he argued, "the most efficient and best officered battalion." Commander Alderson curtly rejected the request.

On February 14, 1915 the Second Brigade arrived at the port of St. Nazaire and proceeded by train to Hazebrouck in northern France, close to the Belgian border. There, it was assigned to the British Fourth Divi-sion on a line north-east of Armentières along the River Lys where the Canadians were first introduced to trench warfare. Nothing in their field training had prepared them for this. In fact, no one had expected the war to degenerate into one of such stagnation. The Germans had counted on a quick victory. When the advance was halted at the Marne, both sides, the Germans, and the French and English, raced to occupy the Channel ports. This resulted in each side digging in to form an unbroken line of trenches from the Swiss border to the English Channel coast.

Currie's highly disciplined Second Brigade quickly adapted to the trench warfare routine established by the British. Before dawn the troops stood on readiness for a possible enemy attack. Once that danger passed, they breakfasted, shaved and carried out chores. At dusk they were given a hot meal and the daily ration of rum. At night reinforcements would arrive and repairs and improvements to the trenches be made. In no man's land, engineers strung barbed wire while patrols took place.

Men learned to keep their heads down (helmets had not yet been issued), and the snipers were busy. A far worse danger was artillery. In reserve, behind the lines, the Canadians were out of range of the field guns and life was fairly normal. Off duty the troops enjoyed the cafés in the towns and the hospitality of the villagers.

Currie used the "instructive week" in the trenches to observe what had been learned about this new type of warfare and how it could best be employed. He was absolutely tireless in his search for knowledge. A British lieutenant colonel, Edmund Ironside, later the Chief of the Imperial General Staff (CIGS) said, "He wished to be treated as a student and was absolutely devoid of 'rank.' I remember saying to myself, 'Here is a cheery, shrewd individual who will lead.'"

One thing that struck Currie about the generals and senior officers he met was that none of them shared the dangers with their men. This was the first war in which they did not lead their troops in battle. They headquartered in safety 50 miles or so behind the lines living in comfortable billets while their men struggled in the muck, mire and pestilence of the trenches. Currie was of a different calibre. He believed in setting an example.

On February 24 his brigade suffered its first casualties — the first Canadian combat losses of the war — four dead and 20 wounded. Then, on March 1, the unit boarded buses which took them to a new sector farther south where the brigade was reunited with the rest of the Canadian Division. This was a comparatively quiet part of the line and after two weeks they were relieved and sent to the rear where they underwent further training. In April the division received orders to move to Ypres to relieve a French division.

The 17-square mile Ypres Salient was the one break in the solid line of trenches and had seen the bitterest fighting of the war. In October and November of 1914, British, French and German casualties reached a shocking 250,000. On April 14, 1915 the Canadian Second Brigade was the first of the reinforcements to arrive and they were disgusted by what the French had left behind. The trenches were short, shallow and uncovered — typical of the French emphasis on offense at the expense of proper defences. There was little barbed wire, and unburied corpses and human excreta was everywhere creating a terrible, nauseating stench.

It became quickly apparent to Currie, now a brigadier general, that this was a highly vulnerable position. The Germans could, and did, fire from three directions, making movement by daylight untenable. Even more menacing was an entry in Currie's diary on April 15: "Attack expected at night to be preceded by the sending of poisonous gas and sending up 3 red lights (reported by prisoner who came into French lines)." This turned out to be a false alarm — but only temporarily.

The Second Brigade was responsible for the right half of the Canadian Division's front. The Third, commanded by Boer War hero,

Brigadier General Richard Turner VC, was on the left, while the First was held in reserve north of the town. Currie immediately put his men to work reinforcing the trench defences, a task that had to be carried out at night in darkness.

True to his policy of sharing the danger with his men, Currie set up his headquarters in a badly shot about cottage in the village of Wieltz which regularly came under enemy fire, though he preferred to spend most of his time up at the front.

On Thursday, April 2, at five o'clock in the afternoon, the Germans unleashed 149,000 kilograms of chlorine gas that drifted towards the French Poilus and colonial Zouaves and Tiraileurs holding the line on the left of the Canadians. The French fled in disarray, choking, crying, falling, dying, leaving a gap in the line four miles wide. The Germans swarmed through it, driving all the way to the Canal de L'Yser. That left Ypres virtually defenceless, and the Canadian Division wide open to attack. But with the help of the British, the next day, the Canadians managed to mount a counter-attack to try to close the hole between their left flank and the canal.

While fighting raged all around Currie's brigade it was not assaulted directly, although it came under heavy shelling. With his trenches secure, Currie despatched his 10th Battalion to support the Third Brigade on his left. It proved to be a disaster — the battalion was decimated. But Currie did not learn about it until the following day and, meanwhile, that night, he rushed three of the 7th Battalion's companies in response to a call for help, to plug a gap in the Third Brigade's line. But that was it, he'd spent the last of his reserves. He signalled Turner that "the 2nd Brigade could give no more help."

Next morning, Saturday, April 24, at 4:00 a.m., the Germans launched a second gas attack, this time against the Canadians. But the poisonous fumes came as no surprise this time around, and the defenders took certain measures — one of them being to urinate into a handkerchief and hold it over the nose and mouth — to neutralize the deadly effects. Currie's brigade bore the brunt of the subsequent assault by the German troops, but made a determined stand. All morning long the Germans threw in wave after wave and by noon the sheer force of numbers began to tell. The Third Brigade was in trouble but Currie was powerless to help; all his reserves had been used up.

He appealed to Alderson to send reinforcements from the British division. But communications became confused. Turner's brigade had been ordered to withdraw leaving the Second Brigade completely exposed. Currie set off by himself to track down the British Division HQ but when he reached it the commander refused to supply reinforcements. When Currie got back to his own HQ he learned that his 8th Battalion was holding on valiantly. Fortunately the German commands had also become confused and by nightfall they called off all further attacks. In the darkness Currie set off for the front to survey the Second Brigade's line. By morning two British companies had arrived but would only take orders from their own HQ, so that they were no help in stabilizing the situation.

All day long the battle continued with the Canadians hanging on by the skin of their teeth. Currie appealed to Alderson for artillery support and reinforcements but received neither. Meanwhile, the two British companies evacuated their trenches for no apparent reason. By five o'clock in the afternoon, with no help in sight, Currie decided he had to do something to save his brigade. He issued the order to "retire at dusk." The withdrawal back to Gravenstafel Ridge where they dug in was orderly. Some hours later they were finally relieved by a British brigade. Typically, Currie was the last to cross the canal.

He was roundly and widely applauded for his conduct. It was largely due to his efforts that the Second Battle of Ypres blunted the psychological impact of poison gas. From then on it was just one more of war's horrors. Alderson told Currie his brigade had "done the best." He was called the "outstanding figure" of the battle and King George V appointed him a Companion of the Order of the Bath (CB), while the French made him a commander of the Legion of Honour.

Ypres had cost the Canadian Division 6,036 casualties, a third of its strength. Four thousand replacements were sent out from England but the new Sir Arthur received only 700. His Second Brigade was still in weak shape for the division's next action which took place two weeks later. This was a badly conceived joint Anglo-French operation begun in May near Festubert, 20 miles south of Ypres. The Canadians went into the line on May 17.

The Second Brigade's objective was a German strong point. The lack of preparation and the imprecise maps provided appalled Currie. He was sure the attack would fail and asked for a postponement until the front could be reconnoitered and a proper plan drawn up. Alderson rejected the proposal and it went ahead as planned. It failed, as Currie had predicted. The preliminary bombardment had not been able to cut the barbed wire defences and his 10th Battalion had been cut to ribbons. He was promptly ordered to make a second attack. But now he was given time to plan for the assault properly. After making sure that the artillery cut the barbed wire, he drew up a 12-point programme that underscored his care in preparation and meticulous attention to detail. It provided for bridging parties to help the infantry across drainage ditches, work parties to consolidate the infantry's gains, supply parties to bring up additional ammunition, supplies and water, and observation officers to ensure coordination between the infantry and the artillery. He was also keenly conscious of the need to instil morale in his troops. As they assembled for the operation, Currie mingled among them, patting them on the shoulder and offering words of encouragement. "Now boys, don't forget, I'm depending on you!"

The planning paid off so well that, although the attack was five minutes late getting under way, within half an hour the objective was in Canadian hands. This, of course, pleased Currie but as always, he was distressed over the casualties, in this case 53 officers and 1,200 men. It concerned, and also horrified and sickened him that the British had such a disregard for waste of human life. They were still playing war by Boer War rules.

They seemed to ignore the need for painstaking care and preparation for any offensive no matter how large or small. Even the best trained troops were no match for machine-guns, artillery fire and barbed wire entanglements. Currie was the first, and at the time, the only one to recognize the need. There was one consolation for the Canadians. At Ypres the Ross rifles had proved to be a disaster. Alderson now had them replaced with the British Lee-Enfield rifles.

It came as no surprise that on September 14, Currie was promoted to major general. At 39, he was one of the youngest to attain that rank in the Great War. Earlier he had been told that a second division was to be sent to France and that a Canadian Corps would be formed under the command of Edwin Alderson who had picked Currie as his successor to take over the First Division. "Currie is the one who I have no hesitation in saying would, with a good staff, command a Divn [*sic*] well," he had told General Headquarters. Turner was given command of the Second Division, his appointment officially preceding Currie's, making him the senior Canadian in France.

Currie now had under his command 18,000 men, 76 field guns and howitzers, as well as 5,600 horses, and he wasted no time seeking the confidence of those under him. He had a special talent for achieving just that. He won over his staff officers by soliciting their opinions, weighing their views and bringing clear-cut, common sense solutions to their problems. In this way his subordinates felt at ease with him. He rarely applied the heavy hand of command except when absolutely necessary, and because of it, he was popular among his troops.

But hand in hand with the elixir of division command — "the most effective level of battle control" — came the bitter taste of political meddling. Reorganization to form a Canadian Corps (a Third Division was already in the making) created vacancies, as well as promotions, within the First Division at the brigade command level.

The case in point was the appointment of Sam Hughes' son, Garnet, as commander of the First Brigade. Though both father and son had been influential in getting Currie his first field command, he was compelled to cast personal feelings and obligations aside. Simply put: Garnet Hughes was not a competent officer. In Currie's own words he had "practically no experience in military matters." Currie fought the appointment but it was a battle he was bound to lose. With pressure from the defence minister as well as his corps commander, Garnet Hughes got the appointment in the end. But that was not the last that Currie was to hear from Sam Hughes.

Shortly after assuming his new command, Currie learned that his wife and daughter, Marjorie, were coming to England. The other news from home was not so good. His business interests in Victoria were sagging and he was being pressed for payments by his creditors.

In France the Canadian Corps was relatively inactive during the winter of 1915-1916 which it spent in the Ploegstreet (Plug Street) Wood adjacent to the Ypres Salient and thus was spared the slaughter suffered by the Allied armies being hurled across no man's land, trapped by barbed wire and cut down by machine-gun fire. At horrendous cost, the French failed to take Vimy Ridge, while at Loos, the British army, under the inept leadership of General Sir John French, was, to all intents destroyed. It cost French his job. In December 1915 he was replaced by General Sir Douglas Haig, who earlier in the war, had said, "The machine-gun is a much overrated weapon…"

During this period, Currie's First Division became expert at raiding enemy trenches. To Currie, no man's land did not exist. He regarded it as "merely an outpost of our entrenched positions." The raids not only boosted Canadian Division morale but produced prisoners and documents and demoralized the Germans. A letter taken from one dead victim read, "I hope that the Canadians are not in the trenches opposite your front, for they suddenly on the darkest night jump into our trenches, causing great consternation and before cries for help have been answered disappear again into the darkness."

Currie soon found himself in the company of the notables of the day. Several times he met King George who invested him with his CB. Also, Marshal Joseph Joffre, the French commander-in-chief, presented him with the medal of the Legion of Honour. On his leaves to London to be with his family, he became acquainted with Lord Kitchener and Winston Churchill. He was also on friendly terms with the new British commander-in-chief, Sir Douglas Haig. That was quite remarkable, given Haig's deep mistrust and contempt for amateur soldiers — and colonial ones in particular.

Life in the trenches that winter was particularly miserable and uncomfortable. It was cold, rainy and muddy. Currie, as always, was sympathetic to the plight of his troops and made regular visits to the trenches to ensure they were taking proper care of themselves, especially the condition of their feet, and that they were properly clothed and fed. On several occasions he narrowly escaped injury from enemy bombardment. What concerned him even more was getting lost in the trench systems which were virtual interlocking mazes. To overcome that problem, he took along an aide, Henry Willis-O'Connor who, he said, proved to be "an infallible duck-board guide."

While Currie went to pains to ensure the welfare of his officers and men, he demanded a strong sense of discipline in return. Not the pukka, spit and polish subservient British type, but one of a more rational nature. Currie had his own code: "discipline is simply self-control which makes you do the right thing at all times." As long as his men behaved themselves, he was satisfied. But if they stepped out of line, they would be dealt with harshly.

In early April 1916, the Canadians were back in the Ypres Salient. By this time Haig had replaced Sir Edward Alderson with General Sir Julian Byng as commander of the Canadian Corps. By the end of May an attack was expected because the Germans could be heard digging tunnels to plant mines near or under the Canadian trenches. Currie proposed an assault on the earthworks by his most experienced troops. Byng rejected it on the grounds that it would encroach on the territory of Brigadier Malcolm Mercer's Third Brigade and nothing more was done about it. Then, on Friday, June 2, a bright sunny morning in the Salient, all hell broke loose.

Currie had been inspecting his reserve brigade, the Third, when heavy German artillery fire signalled an attack to the north, where the Third Division was protecting Currie's left flank. Mercer was in the front line and fell, fatally wounded. The 4th Canadian Mounted Rifles, the battalion which bore the brunt of the attack, was cut to ribbons suffering 89 per cent casualties. Leaderless, the Third Division was incapable of stopping the German advance as the enemy swarmed across no man's land and occupied the key positions of Observatory Ridge, Hill 61, Tor Top, and Mount Sorel. With the Germans enjoying a commanding view from these heights, the Salient stood in jeopardy.

In panic, Byng ordered a counter-attack. Currie protested that it was premature, that the enemy's position and plan of action was too obscure for the Canadians to regain lost ground. He favoured a cautious reconnaissance to locate the Germans and determine the best site from which to launch an assault. But Byng rejected Currie's advice and told him to proceed as directed. It was the same old story. Not enough time to plan and prepare properly, and, as Currie had predicted, the attempt failed. It cost the corps 1,700 casualties and Byng finally conceded that Currie had been right and gave him responsibility for a new operation to recapture the lost positions while allowing him plenty of time — five days — to mobilize his strategy by scheduling the attack. The date was June 7. However, the weather interfered and the heavy rain forced Currie to pull his division to the rear and give his men time to rest up for the coming campaign.

The attack started at 1:30 a.m., June 13. It was the first one planned and executed by the Canadian Corps. It was not only an enormous success, but it became a model for the method and meticulous planning that Currie would employ, with varying modifications and improvements, in every single offensive he launched during the entire war.

On this occasion, he reorganized his division into three composite brigades so that the four battalions of the First Brigade, so badly hurt in the earlier attacks, could be rested and held in reserve. Then he rehearsed his troops so methodically that each man knew where he was to go, what he was supposed to do, and what he was liable to encounter. And, another stamp of Currie's style was the overwhelming artillery support, larger than had ever been employed on a battlefield before — every gun in the Canadian Corps, and a number of British weapons, was brought to bear. To unnerve the Germans and wear them down, between June 9 and 13, they were subjected to four massive bombardments, each lasting half an hour. Then the attack itself was preceded by a ten-hour shelling.

Though it was a dark, rainy, gusty night, the exhaustive planning and practice and the inordinately heavy artillery back-up, paid off quickly. Within an hour, at a cost of 1,214 casualties, the Canadians had overrun Mount Sorrel, driven off the Germans, and restored the original defences. "Almost too easy," Currie remarked later.

This unqualified success established Currie as one of the rising stars of the British Army. *The Times* of London wrote that, "he gave further proof of his gifts as a military leader. Nothing was left to chance. Everything was made ready." It drew congratulations from Haig. It also won the respect of Byng who, henceforth, would rely on Currie's judgement, with the result that they became lifelong friends.

In August 1916, the Canadian Corps was transferred to the Somme in northern Picardy as part of the British Reserve Army — later the Fifth Army — under General Sir Hubert Gough. The British offensive in that part of France, aptly known as Santerre, from the French *sang terre* — land of blood — was designed to take the pressure off the French, who were being decimated at Verdun, and the Russians, mounting a last gasp offensive in the east. It would become what the Germans called *Das Blutbad* — The Blood Bath — with horrendous losses to both sides. For the British, it began disastrously. On the very first day, July 1, they lost 60,000 men. By the end of August, this casualty list had risen to over 200,000, a figure matched by the enemy.

It was in the midst of these killing fields that Currie's First Division took up station near Pozieres Ridge on September 3, relieving an Australian Division. The battered, barren, shell-shocked countryside made the Ypres Salient look like a desert. Not a tree was left standing and the roads were so continually blasted that they changed shape from one day to the next. Bombarded day and night from the moment of their arrival, the Canadians suffered severe casualties. "Hell, pure hell," Currie wrote in his diary after beating off the nightly three or four enemy attacks.

Currie knew that morale would suffer if his men were forced to simply sit still and get, in his words, "blown to bits." They needed to fight back. It was with some relief, therefore, that on September 6, he received orders from Corps HQ to take out a small salient on Pozieres Ridge which the Australians had been unable to capture after a series of attacks. With his usual penchant for planning, Currie worked with Garnet Hughes for two days to prepare the assault which took place before dawn on September 9, preceded by the usual artillery barrage. It took only 23 minutes for the First Brigade to attain its objective. Admittedly it was a minor success, but a success nevertheless, after a string of failures.

Two nights later the Second and Third Divisions relieved Currie's badly depleted battalions. In the six days they had been in the trenches they had lost 2,390 men killed and wounded. On September 15, the two relieving divisions captured Courcelette assisted by several tanks, one of the first use made of these armoured vehicles. Two days later the First Division returned to action to consolidate the village.

For a week it rained continuously and the troops had to struggle through mud so thick and gooey they could advance only a few yards without rest. It reminded them of Western Canadian gumbo. "It was like walking in caramel," someone remarked. By the time Courcelette had been secured on September 24, the division had incurred a further 1,000 casualties. The survivors were exhausted though somewhat cheered by a message from Haig that read, "the result of the fighting of the 15th and following days was a gain more considerable than any which attended our arms in the course of a single operation since the commencement of the offensive." But there was no respite; Haig ordered the attacks continued.

The next objective was Thiepval Ridge, guarded by three powerful positions in front of it: Zollern Graben, Hessian Trench, and Regina Trench. Currie's First Division, flanked by Turner's Second on the right and the British 11th on the left, was to storm the fortifications shortly after noon on September 26, following a three-day artillery barrage. It was an utter fizzle. The British division veered off to the left which put it out of touch. After a steady advance the Second Division had to give up all the ground it gained. To Currie it was a dismal set-back. Then on September 28, his division was pulled out of the front line, but only for a short time. On October 3, his troops were ordered back to the front where they were assigned the capture of Regina Trench, the only position on Thiepval Ridge still in German hands.

Currie left nothing to chance. He personally reconnoitered the ridge to get the lay of the land. He exhorted the artillery to give him the strongest possible support. He coaxed and, as usual, rehearsed his men down to a fare thee well. Although he kept it to himself, Currie was suffering from a stomach disorder at the time, but this did not deter him from his usual precise planning and preparation. But despite it, the operation, which got underway at 4:50 a.m. on October 8, turned into a fiasco.

The artillery failed to cut the barbed wire. That held up the attackers. Only a handful of Brigadier George Tuxford's Third Brigade got through to reach the redoubt. Two battalions of the First made it to the adjacent fortification, the Quadrilateral. But, cut off from supplies, particularly hand grenades, they were unable to sustain fierce German counter-attacks that afternoon. After a powwow with Byng, Currie bitterly called off any further operations. Incensed over Garnet Hughes' bungling and failure, as far as Currie was concerned, the brigadier's days in the First Division were rapidly drawing to a close.

When it came time for the First Division to leave the Somme on October 7, Currie had no regrets. In fact he looked back on the abysmal experience with some rancor, not the least of which was his disgust at

Sir Hubert Gough's incompetence as a commander. He vowed, ruefully, that he would never again serve under him.

Ten days later, the Canadian Corps, under the command of Lieutenant General Sir Julian Byng, took up positions in the muddy, waterlogged trenches 30 miles to the north paralleling Vimy Ridge, the 450 foot high, four mile long, promontory dominating the Artois Plain that the Germans considered impregnable. And with good reason. Since its capture in 1914, the British and French had failed to dislodge its occupants at a fearful loss of 190,000 men killed. Nevertheless, as part of the planned joint Allied spring offensive, the Canadians were ordered to take the vital redoubt, whatever the cost.

That they succeeded with a minimum of acceptable casualties was a direct result of the lessons Currie learned from the outcome of the Battle of Verdun which he thoroughly absorbed, improvised and implemented. On February 21, 1916 the Germans had attacked the sacred French fortress but the Poilus hung on tenaciously, albeit at a frightful loss of 500,000 men, though they inflicted casualties of 400,000 on the enemy. Then in October the French Army mounted a series of brilliant counter-attacks that Currie considered "one of the the greatest victories in the history of the wars of the world."

On his return to his own HQ, he prepared a report on his observations and recommendations simply entitled "Notes on French Attacks, North-East of Verdun in October and December, 1916," which he delivered as a lecture at Canadian Headquarters on Saturday afternoon, January 20, 1917. It was, and remains, one of the most important, significant and far-reaching military documents ever laid down, one that underscored the fact that Currie had discovered the key to tactical success on the Western Front.

Ignoring, and oblivious to, the modern concepts of the sophisticated rifle, the machine-gun, motor traction, wireless communications, and the airplane, the majority of Great War field generals — "near-sighted men caught in a revolving door," was the way the Canadian writer Ralph Allen described them — still measured war by Napoleonic standards: armies of enormous, unprecedented size bent on crushing each other through sheer weight of numbers. Infantry blindly charged into battle with banners flying, backed by cavalry and artillery.

After two-and-a-half years of this aimless, senseless slaughter for virtually no ground gain, only the French commander-in-chief, the "Hero of Verdun," Robert-Georges Nivelle, whom Currie had intently interviewed, had arrived at a viable alternative. His answer was concentrated and skillful use of firepower. While this fell short of actually breaking the stalemate strategically, it could at least gain a tactical field advantage. Currie had questioned the generalissimo studiously at length and had been left with the indelible conviction that the Great War could only be won by effective use of artillery — not attrition! His prescience was not unjustified. An estimated 60 per cent of the casualties sustained during the Great War were artillery-inflicted although Currie's objective was to "exploit gun power to the limit for the purpose of saving infantrymen's lives."

On this premise he tabled the following dicta. Without coordinated artillery support, the infantry could not be expected to succeed. Its first task was to neutralize the enemy guns. This included the blinding of observation posts with smoke shells. At Verdun, use of poison gas shells had also proved effective; burdened with respirator helmets the efficiency of the heavy gunners dropped by 60 per cent. Artillery would no longer be limited to pounding enemy trenches and fortifications but could be effectively used to harass enemy activity of virtually every description: transportation routes, supply depots, camps, headquarters and command posts as well.

Prolonged bombardment formed an essential, integral part of the pre-assault build-up. To confuse the enemy as to the exact date and time of the attack, barrages similar in weight and intensity were laid down at intervals on several days preceding the actual assault. This also forced the enemy to retaliate and reveal his own gun positions.

But in addition to wearing down enemy resistance prior to the battle, Currie had also quickly grasped another of the basic requirements for the modern assault — the need for firepower combined with movement. During the attack itself, a creeping barrage covered the infantry. This called for precise coordination and timing. A wall of fire preceded the troops at the rate of 100 yards every four minutes. However, the success of the advance ultimately rested with the foot soldier. Currie believed that, "it is the personal conflict of the infantry which determines the fate of a battle, and which actually gains ground...cruel and violent as it may be." Therefore the platoon had to be a self-reliant, self-sufficient unit with maximum flexibility. This called for intensive training "carried out on ground as similar to the area over which they had to attack as it was possible to find," as Currie noted.

Currie also strongly advocated improved, broader, intelligence gathering and more productive use of it. Before launching an offensive, he believed it was essential to obtain a precise, accurate profile of the enemy from every possible standpoint: his strength and weaknesses, his exact position, his morale. This was secured by regular surprise night trench-raids in which documents, armaments and instruments were seized and prisoners taken and interrogated.

At Verdun, French aerial photographs proved to be far superior to those of the British. Currie insisted that the Royal Flying Corps raise its standards accordingly because such reconnaissance was vital to success. During the battle, 190,000 maps to scale were produced from the photographs and every single commander, down to the smallest unit, was provided with one. Currie took this measure a step further and set a new precedent. He insisted on supplying maps not only to unit commanders, but non-commissioned officers as well. This was an unheard of and unprecedented delegation of authority and responsibility within the British Army.

Currie combined all these elements with his commensurate insistence on intense training and preparation at every level. As the war progressed, he made innovative use of such technological advances and developments such as the tank — which he employed en masse — and the percussion fuse shell for severing barbed-wire defences. His blueprint for tactical success was not only adopted by the Canadian Corps but eventually by several British commands as well. The Canadian historian, John Swettenham, provided this significant endorsement when he wrote that, "no later Corps attack when planned by Currie was ever unsuccessful." But Currie might never have had a chance to demonstrate his planning prowess if it weren't for a disagreement with Sir George Perley, the newly appointed first minister of overseas military forces in Canada.

Currie had been Perley's logical choice as the senior officer to help him sort out the problem of inadequate numbers of qualified replacements being trained for the front at Shorncliffe. This situation had become critical due to the mismanagement of Sam Hughes who, as a result of Currie's constant complaining, lost his job as minister of militia.

But although Currie was by far the most capable and experienced person to tackle the recruitment and training problem, his wariness about possible political meddling disturbed Perley. He perceived potential friction between government and military when what was needed was accord. Perley gave the more amenable, less dogmatic, Richard Turner the nod. It turned out to be a sound choice. More importantly, it made Currie the senior Canadian officer in the field, leaving him in the fortunate position for the Allies, of being able to see his theories implemented. This contributed greatly to the final victory.

By the time the attack on Vimy Ridge got under way on Easter Monday, April 9, 1917, it had been preceded by a week-long artillery bombardment. Currie's doctrines had filtered into the ranks of the other three divisions that now made up the Canadian Corps of 100,000 men, the Second, Third and Fourth. As a consequence, despite drenching rain, the assault went off like clockwork. While it was not exactly a pushover — Currie's First Division suffered 3,202 casualties — incredibly, by early afternoon, the battle was all over. Currie later described it as, "the greatest day the Corps has ever had." The American historian, William Manchester, wrote that, "the Canadians won the reputation of being the finest soldiers on the Western Front." And, while Vimy Ridge was supposed to have been an impregnable fortress capable of resisting assault, the London *Morning Times* noted that "the Canadians took it on a time table."

Over the next month Currie's First Division distinguished itself with the capture of two key enemy positions east of the ridge, the villages of Arleux and Fresnoy, during the British attempt to pierce the Oppy-Mericourt defences in preparation for a major assault against the vaunted German Drocourt-Queant Line. Despite being badly let down by poorly disciplined and disorganized British troops on either flank, in both instances the Canadians succeeded, marking themselves as the outstanding battle formation of the Western Front. One general applauded them as, "the pride and wonder of the British Army." Currie summed up his philosophy when he wrote: "The great lessons to be learned from these operations is this: if the lessons of the War have been thoroughly mastered; if the preparation and support is good; if our intelligence is properly appreciated; there is no position that cannot be wrested from the enemy by well-disciplined, well-trained and well-led troops attacking on a sound plan." By this time Currie had become something of a legend, and official recognition was soon forthcoming.

On Monday, June 4, Currie learned that he had been appointed Knight Commander of St. Michael and St. George. With the honour went a promotion to commander of the Canadian Corps. But it was a miracle that he lived to see the day. On the previous morning he had just left his headquarters to deliver a telegram to a signal station when a German airplane dropped a bomb on the encampment killing two of the occupants and wounding 16 others. For one who so blithely ignored danger, this was Currie's closest brush with death during the entire war.

Currie's appointment had the full blessing and sanction of the British commander-in-chief, Sir Douglas Haig. The two got along together like day and night. Haig chided Currie, "Give me fat counselors," he said referring to Currie's 250-pound girth. But Currie was far from being intimidated. On one occasion when Haig revealed plans for an assault and asked Currie his opinion, he replied gruffly, "Sir, I don't think it's worth a damn."

Currie assumed his new duties on June 8 at the Corps Headquarters in the chateau at Camblain l'Abbe. It wasn't all that cut-and-dried, but as Currie had been warned, and had already guessed as much himself. As senior Canadian officer overseas, Richard Turner challenged the appointment. He wanted it himself. But Haig would never agree to that. While he respected Turner as a warrior, as a field commander he considered him incompetent. Sir George Perley, ever the diplomat, smoothed things over neatly by getting the prime minister's permission to allow Turner authority over administrative matters at the front and by elevating both Turner and Currie to the rank of lieutenant general. But that was only smoke.

A furious flame burned brightly in the breast of Sir Sam Hughes who, though in disgrace, still had powerful connections, including the Canadian-born Lord Beaverbrook. Hughes wasted no time enlisting his friends in an effort to see that his son, Garnet, succeed Currie as commander of the First Division. With Byng's approval, Currie had already decided on Archie Macdonnell, a feisty twice-wounded veteran of Canada's pre-war army, as his successor. The thought of Garnet taking command was anathema to Currie, quite out of the question. Hell, he'd already fired him once for his bungling and ineptitude. No! He'd fight the proposal tooth and nail even if it meant tendering his own resignation.

Though browbeaten, cajoled, pressured and threatened from all sides for obvious political reasons ("his father wants him to get the position and God help the man who [falls] out with his father"), Currie stood his ground. He adamantly refused to accept command of the Corps if there were any strings attached. With that ultimatum, Perley, his deputy, Walter Gow, and Turner, among others, finally caved in.

But Garnet Hughes wasn't through by any means. He refused to accept the dictum lying down and demanded an audience with Currie to restate his case and convince — or force — Currie to change his mind. On the evening of June 14, the pair met in the latter's suite in the Carleton Hotel in London. Currie, who described the encounter as a "three hour wrestling match," remained steadfast. The appointment was Macdonnell's and that was that — period! Case closed! Whereupon Garnet Hughes barged out of the suite raging, "I'm not finished with you! I'll get you for this yet!"

Menacing words, not to be taken lightly. Garnet Hughes meant every one of them. Currie had made his point and won his day. But, at the same time, he had incurred the uncompromising malice and wrath of the impetuous, ill-tempered and vengeful Sir Sam Hughes. He was a dangerous enemy who, to his dying day (and, in effect, beyond the grave), wielded his substantial influence to dangle a sword of Damocles over Currie's destiny for a decade to come. As Currie later admitted, "From the time of my refusal he never ceased to blackguard me and to minimize my influence and authority with my own men."

One of the first steps that Currie, a fierce, confirmed nationalist, took as the new commandeer of the Corps, was to firmly establish with both those looking in, as well as those looking out, that this was going to be a Canadian show, run all the way by a Canadian — and don't you forget it.

To illustrate his point, he picked Dominion Day, July 1, 1917 as a symbol. During the two years the Canadian Army had been in France the date had been passed as just another day, ignored and unrecognized as a milestone of Canadian unity. Not this time around. For the 50th anniversary of Confederation, with the former Canadian governor general, the Duke of Connaught, as his guest, Currie staged a spectacular celebration. It included a concert of 188 massed bagpipes and a "grandstand" fireworks display with every gun of the Canadian Artillery at the front firing off three giant salvos every two minutes. It was a splendourous, memorable occasion indeed, but next day it was business as usual.

As part of a fresh offensive scheduled to begin at the end of July 1917, in order to prevent the Germans from bolstering their left wing forces in Flanders, and to create a diversion, Currie elected to attack Hill 70, a designated enemy position near Lens, a coal-mining centre north of Vimy Ridge. Over the strong objections of several senior British First Army officers, Currie insisted on extra field gun support to initiate "an artillery killing ground" preparatory to the actual assault itself. Haig overruled the dissenters unequivocably. After the Vimy experience, he had absolute faith in Currie's artillery-oriented method of assault, as did his men who had nicknamed him "Barrage." Rain delayed the attack for several weeks. In the meantime, Currie transferred his headquarters from the sprawling chateau at Camblain l'Abbe to a less ostentatious set-up in a country house at Coupigny. It was characteristic of Currie to want to stay in the closest possible touch with the front line.

The Canadian strike went off as planned at 4:35 on the morning of August 11 after the enemy had been duly pulverized by one of Currie's furious, incessant, unrelenting bombardments, which was becoming Sir Arthur Currie's trademark. In less than half an hour Hill 70 had been overrun. Now came the crucial test — consolidating the gain. For the next eight days the Canadians beat off 35 different German counter-attacks at the overwhelming odds of 28 battalions to 69. "Our gunners, machine-gunners and infantry never had such targets," Currie gloated afterwards. Enemy losses numbered between 25,000 and 30,000 compared to less than 8,000 for the Canadian Corps. As a result, just as Currie had anticipated and hoped, the Germans were forced to divert two divisions from the critical main battle line at Ypres to reinforce their position at Hill 70. The official German history conceded that, "The fighting at Lens cost us, once again, the expenditure of considerable numbers of troops who had to be replaced...The whole previously worked out plan for relieving the fought-out troops in Flanders had been wrecked." Currie had good reason to rejoice over his first victory as Corps Commander which he described as "great and wonderful."

Following the battle for Hill 70, Currie enjoyed two weeks respite on leave with his family in England. On his return to France he was plagued with diarrhoea which lasted for three weeks. The Germans added to his discomfort; they had found the range of his headquarters which they shelled repeatedly. Typically, Currie stubbornly refused to be dislodged.

By the fall of 1917, the Allied offensive in Flanders had completely bogged down. Rain and mud made forward progress impossible, but Haig obstinately insisted that the battle, "continue well into November." He was convinced, that by that time victory would lie within grasp. He bullheadedly believed, against the misgivings, and objections, of almost everyone else, including British Prime Minister David Lloyd George, as well as Haig's own closest aides and advisors, that the key lay in the capture of Passchendaele Ridge north-east of Ypres. Once this final bastion was secured, cavalry would be free to romp across the flat Belgian countryside and bring hostilities to a swift conclusion. This pipe dream represented one of the gravest, most misguided calculations of the entire 1914-18 conflict and very nearly lost the Allies the war. It was also the costliest battle the Canadian Corps ever fought.

By the end of October Haig was desperate. Since the start of the offensive on July 30, the British had suffered 200,000 casualties in a futile attempt to capture the ruined Belgian village. As late as October 9, an attempt by the Australians ended in a slaughter. Now Haig's reputation, indeed his future, was on the line. By this time he knew that his only hope was to enlist the Canadian Corps.

Currie had strong reservations and didn't mind saying so. His first reaction was: "Passchendaele! A name for a lot of mud and grief, for a lot of crack-brained fools in London to play with! What do they care? Do they get killed? What's the good of it? Let the Germans have it — keep it — rot in it! Rot in the mud...It isn't worth a drop of blood." After a careful analysis, study and survey of the situation he concluded that the Corps would sustain at least 16,000 casualties. Would it, he asked, be worth it? His answer was a bureaucratic shrug that orders are orders. "I carried my protest to the extreme limit," he said, "which I believe would have resulted in my being sent home had I been other than the Canadian Corps commander."

Battle conditions in the sector far exceeded Currie's worst fears. There had been no salvage of any kind, most of the dead were still left unburied. The only cover still in existence was to be found in water-logged shell holes and ditches. Not a tree or hedge could be seen anywhere. The depth of water and slime precluded the possibility of digging trenches. Buildings had been reduced to rubble. And the area behind the lines wasn't a whole lot better. Regardless of the handicaps and problems facing him, Haig knew that Currie would give it his best shot.

But on one major point — to Currie at least — Haig refused to acquiesce or be mollified and firmly put his foot down. Under no circumstances would he agree to serve with General Sir Hubert Gough's Fifth Army. He had experienced enough of Gough's bumbling, fumbling and indecision on the Somme to last him a lifetime and he wanted no further part of him. A reconnoitre of Gough's section of the Passchendaele front reinforced his convictions. It revealed an atrocious, slovenly lack of proper preparation — in fact the general attitude was one of defeatism. Rather indiscreetly, though at least tacitly, Haig bulletined General Sir Henry Horne, commander of the First Army with whom the Canadians had been serving that, "the Canadian Corps should be sent to General Plumer [Sir Hubert — Second Army] and not to Gough because the Canadians do not work well with the latter."

In tackling preparations for his "losing" battle, Currie set new standards in proficiency and attention to detail, even for him. Every evening at 9:00 he led a conference with his planning staff to review the daily progress in every phase of the operation — artillery, communications, roads, light railways, tramways and maps — and a comprehensive report was made to Second Army HQ promptly each morning. There were snags, and not just the bloody mud. There was the bloody British red tape too, which was just as aggravating, and binding. A case in point was the 140 missing field guns from the assigned 360 artillery battery for the corps. When Currie complained of this shortage, Second Army Artillery HQ promptly presented him with 140 requisition forms representing the missing weapons as if that cleared everything! Currie went into a rage. "Godammit. I can't fight the battle with requisitions!" he stormed. Next day he got his guns.

It was tough slugging, but Canadian inventiveness, ingenuity and backwoods experience overcame the problem of roads which Currie regarded as "essential to victory." In the manner of the old Ontario country corduroy byways, plank roads were put up over the quagmire. Engineers constructed a light railway which the negative-minded British had pooh-poohed as an impossibility. And solid artillery platforms were built to prevent the guns from sinking into what reminded the western Canadians of bottomless gumbo.

That same mud presented a serious problem for evacuating the wounded. The medical officers reckoned that because there were no landmarks on the shell-torn battleground, the stretcher-bearers would get lost at night. Therefore evacuations would have to be made during daylight, thereby increasing the danger from enemy fire. And in the absence of roads, the deep, soft muck and the shell holes would require six men to carry a single stretcher. It would also take at least six hours of this exhausting drudgery to carry a man from a first-aid post to a point where transportation was available. The conquest of Passchendaele would be no ordinary undertaking.

As had become his custom, Currie favoured a headquarters post as close to the lines as was practical without inviting undue risk. Declining the comfort of a chateau far to the rear, he chose a small somewhat dilapidated hut, that had seen better days, in the tiny hamlet of Ten Elms, from which to conduct his operations. The crowded structure became the venue of regular conferences in which Haig, Plumer and the Corps commander put their heads together. Not infrequently Currie would ask the C in C: "Is this battle really necessary?" The standard response was "some day I will tell you why, but Passchendaele must be taken."

At a briefing held October 23, Currie outlined his plans for the capture of Passchendaele Ridge. As usual, he had left nothing to chance. The operation would be carried out in four stages. On October 26 and on the 30th, the Third and Fourth Divisions, under Major Generals Louis Lipsett and David Watson respectively, would initiate the attack to establish a foothold from which to complete the assault. With a hiatus to regroup and restage, between November 6 and 10, the First Division under Archie Macdonnell, and the Second led by Harry Burstall, would complete the final stages by occupying the ridge.

But first, there was, as the British say, a spot of bother — temporary and picayune maybe — but bother all the same. For no explicable reason, except perhaps to stir up the dung, Gough wanted the start date advanced to October 22. But Currie wasn't buying. Any such change, he argued forcefully would upset the timetable, be premature and render it impossible to reach the objectives. Plumer backed him to the hilt, to Gough's intense consternation and rage. It would not be the last Currie would hear from him.

Though they had total faith in his judgement and meticulous penchant for pre-planning, Currie's troops were under no illusions as to the formidable difficulties they faced. To the Germans the appearance of the Canadians in the sector only a week earlier spelled trouble. They were ready and waiting behind a ring of virtually impregnable, entrenched concrete pillboxes almost invisible in the mud. And conditions ruled out any chance of taking the enemy by surprise on the part of the assailants.

The battle began right on time, at 5:45 a.m., October 26, after a heavy overnight rainfall. It was a mess. Men struggled in waist-deep mud, falling into water-filled shell holes from which there was no rescue. But the Canadians ploughed steadily ahead, both divisions reaching their objectives before the end of the day. It didn't escape Currie's notice that Lipsett's Fourth received no support whatsoever from Gough's Fifth Army on his left flank.

But this petty vendetta was only just getting warmed up. On the eve of the scheduled second assault of the first phase to get under way October 30, Gough asked for a postponement; he needed time to reorganize, he claimed. "Refused to do so," Currie noted angrily in his diary. He wasn't about to be goaded into something so innocuous. But he was also acutely aware that by denying Gough his request he had ensured a lack of protection for his own left flank.

On October 30, after suffering 2,321 casualties, the Third and Fourth Divisions established a strong attacking position from which the final assault on the ridge could be launched. Relieved by the First and Second Divisions, the next week was spent shoring up the position, moving guns into place, laying down duck-walk planking to make roads and walkways and narrow-gauge tracks for light railway lines. The work was not without losses in men killed and wounded, but the sacrifice and rugged effort paid off.

At dawn November 6, the Germans were caught completely by surprise despite a preceding 48-hour artillery bombardment. Within three hours the ridge had been overrun. With the announcement in the London press the next day that Passchendaele was now in British hands, Haig's reputation, for the time being at least, was secure, thanks to his faith in Currie's military genius and the bravery of the Canadian Corps.

But the battle wasn't quite over. On November 10, the Corps carried out the final phase of the operation, quickly and efficiently. Despite heavy rain, or perhaps because of it, the Canadians again achieved total surprise and took all their objectives in nothing flat. Almost predictably, it was a different story on the left. A thoroughly disgusted and disgruntled Currie noted in his diary that Gough's Fifth Army, "retired in very bad and pronounced disorder, amounting to a panic." This left the Canadian First Division in a tenuous predicament — cut off and forced to defend itself against a series of determined German counterattacks. However, Archie Macdonnell's troops hung on tenaciously until the Germans were finally forced to concede defeat and withdraw. Four days later the Battle of Passchendaele was all over.

The victory earned unanimous praise from every quarter. The British papers crowed: "a very fine and gallant operation...the Canadians had never shown greater doggedness or determination," said *The Times* of London; "fine and thrilling act of courage," wrote the *Daily Chronicle*. The French awarded Currie the croix de guerre, and paid him the unique honour and distinction of being the only general invited to Paris to receive it. The Belgians made him a grand officier de L'Ordre de la Couronne and pinned the croix de guerre to his chest. Even the Germans conceded: "The enemy charged like a wild bull...there was no means by which positions could be held." And, finally, Currie himself was triumphant: "I am proud to say, the Corps delivered the goods. The fellows never worked so hard or fought with such grim determination...No finer feat of arms has ever been performed in this or any other war...the Canadians were the only troops that could have taken the position at that time and under the conditions under which the attacks were made."

But Passchendaele stuck in Currie's craw. The battle had cost the Corps 15,654 casualties, only marginally fewer than Currie had predicted. And for what gain? Bitterly, he told Canadian Prime Minister Sir Robert Borden that, "the venture was by no means worth the cost...it was won to save the face of the British High Command who had undertaken all through the autumn months unsuccessful and highly disastrous attempts."

As he had promised preparatory to the battle, following the war Haig offered Currie his reason why Passchendaele had to be taken. "It was [at this time] that I learned," he explained in 1919, "for the first time the true proportions of the mutiny in the French Army in 1917 and the strength of the Peace Party in France and also in England that year." It thus became vital to prevent the Germans from launching an attack against the French. To boost the morale of the French and British armies and, the French and British governments, Haig decided the Ridge must be captured. The price was paid in Canadian blood, and the ramifications were to cause Currie consternation beyond the battlefield.

Canadian casualties at Passchendaele, and Currie's role in particular, quickly became a political football in Canada where a federal election had been called for December 17 over the issue of conscription. Its introduction had become necessary due to insufficient volunteers to replace the growing number of casualties. One of the most bitter elections Canada ever experienced quickly developed. The country was split in two. The Laurier Liberals and Quebec were on one side, against conscription, and the rest of the country, the Conservatives and the Union Party were on the other. The opponents of conscription lashed out in every direction with wanton disregard for the facts, as Currie was soon to learn to his dismay.

George Waldron, a nobody Liberal candidate who'd never seen a shot fired, claimed "that the Canadian casualties [at Passchendaele] were excessive" and demanded "that the conduct of the Army should be inquired into." That same day, in a speech to the House of Commons, Sir Wilfred Laurier, the Liberal leader, announced that Currie had resigned as Corps commander. Currie was flabbergasted, perplexed that " a man like [Laurier] could descend to such false and dishonourable conduct, and could willfully lie in the hope of getting some advantage for his party." Although he strongly favoured conscription — for more than anyone else he knew how critical the replacement situation had become — Currie had stood aloof from politics all along. His credo was simply, " a soldier in the field has no time to indulge in matters political." He was relieved when Borden and the Union Party won the election handily with 153 seats, to the Liberals 82.

Shortly after Currie had to deal with a brush fire on his own doorstep that threatened to undermine the *esprit de corps* of the Canadian Corps and totally disrupt it. It arose out of plans to reorganize the British Army. Due to a manpower crisis, the number of battalions in each division was to be reduced with the surplus troops assigned to bring all units up to strength. The English proposed that the Canadians follow suit, creating two additional divisions which could provide for an extra corps. That sounded fine, except for one thing: they needed competent personnel to administer it. With a Canadian Army under his domain, Sir Edward Kemp, Perley's replacement as overseas minister, jumped at the opportunity to increase his prestige and stature among his peers. Naturally, Richard Turner, too, embraced the idea; it virtually assured him a corps command. And it would also produce a number of staff openings for the accumulated "desk" officers idling their time away in England, a direct manifestation of Sam Hughes' inept system of recruiting.

Currie saw such expansion of his command from a corps into an army as an erosion of efficiency, not because of what the expansion required in terms of size and responsibility, but because of the present lack of experienced staff officers — "the hardest of all to train" — to implement and administer such an enlarged organization. Not only would the identity of the corps be affected by such readjustment, with a resulting loss of morale but, most importantly, its fighting ability and capacity would suffer as a result.

Though it lost him his chance of promotion to the rank of full general (a promise from Haig) which would have made him one of the most eminent and prominent officers in the entire British Empire (and a colonial one at that!), Currie presented a counter-proposal for preserving his precious Canadian Corps and at the same time increasing its strength — made possible with conscription coming into being — within the existing composition on the Corps. The Canadian government, all the way up to Borden, heartily concurred. And it was also a decision enthusiastically received by those within the Corps itself who recognized the personal sacrifice Currie had made on their behalf. But the full benefit, the real impact, the true significance of it all was still to be felt. And that day was not far off. However, at that very moment things did not look all that bright.

After Passchendaele, the British and French armies, which had been bled white, were stalemated; they couldn't move forward another inch. The Italians were hanging on by the skin of their teeth. Bolshevik Russia had dropped out of the conflict entirely, leaving 177 German divisions free to strengthen the Western Front. Obviously, logically, the time was ripe for a German strike to win the war before the full force of the Americans, who had entered the war in April of 1917, could be felt. Almost predictably, it began like a thunderclap on March 21, 1918 at 4:40 in the morning on a 50 mile-wide front between Arras and St. Quentin.

On the right wing, near the Somme, Sir Hubert Gough's Fifth Army collapsed completely before the German juggernaut, surrendering 400 guns and thousands of prisoners — a major breakthrough. It was no surprise to Currie who noted, "the 5th Army did, as was expected, damned poorly." For his nemesis, Gough, who was replaced a week later, Currie had the final word, "When a man shows unmistakable signs of weakness, get rid of him at once re-Gough."

Before the advance was halted exactly a month later, the Germans had recouped 230 square miles of lost territory, and had reached the River Marne, a mere 40 miles from Paris. The French commander-in-chief, Henri Petain, losing his nerve, had withdrawn his army to the French capital. At another point, the Germans had come within 12 miles of Amiens. But General Erich Ludendorff failed to press his advantage. Because only one of his armies had broken through, he ordered it to stand pat while the other two caught up. It was a tactical error but, in any event, it made no difference in the long run. Major political and strategic events were rapidly overtaking the situation in the field. The Americans now had more than 180,000 men in France, with more arriving daily. The British were receiving reinforcements, troops originally slated for the Italian Front which Lloyd George, having lost faith in Haig, had previously denied him. But most significantly, all Allied forces had been placed under a single unified command headed by the ebullient, aggressive Marshal Ferdinand Foch in April 1918.

As the German onslaught ran out of steam, having sustained a total of 348,300 losses, the war once more wallowed into a stalemate. But Foch was determined on one final offensive that would end the war. As it turned out the Canadians were destined for the vanguard. The Corps was certainly a logical choice. During the German assault it had been fairly inactive — a well earned rest after the battles of 1917 — occupying part of the Lens-Arras Front. But for Currie it had been a time of annoyance, frustration and irritation. Two days after the attack began, two of his divisions were removed from his command. Three days later, both of the others, along with his Corps headquarters, were placed in reserve. Currie fiercely resented the move — and said so, in no uncertain terms. In appealing to Haig's General Headquarters to have his command restored he wrote. "My staff and myself cannot do as well with a British division in this battle as we can do with the Canadian Divisions, nor can any Corps Staff do as well with the Canadian Divisions, as my own. I know that necessity knows no law and that the Chief will do what he thinks best, yet for the sake of the victory we must win, get us together as soon as you can."

Not content to leave it there, Currie also signaled Sir Edward Kemp, whom he found entirely sympathetic. Kemp immediately contacted Lord

Derby on the grounds that, "the Canadian Corps has become…most efficient under its present leadership, and it is believed that the high morale which exists in the Corps is undoubtedly due to the fact that it has been kept together as a unit under Lieut.-General Sir Arthur Currie, in whom the troops have unbounded confidence." Orders from the British secretary of war despatched to Haig's GHQ, to reunite the Canadians, soon reinstated the status quo, not, however, without some degree of umbrage on Haig's part. "I could not help feeling," he grumbled, "that some people in Canada regard themselves rather as allies than as fellow citizens of the Empire."

At this time Currie composed a message to the Canadians under his command which, while lauded by the English and French media as well as senior field officers, and suitably memorable, failed to inspire or draw rave notices from those serving under him. But, at any rate, it deserves mention here. In part, it read:

> Canadians, in this fateful hour, I command you and I trust you to fight as you have never fought, with all your strength, with all the determination, with all your tranquil courage. On many a hard fought battle you have overcome this enemy. With God's help you shall achieve victory once more.

Contemporaries described it as, "an order which should rank among the great documents of Canadian History." It probably has. *The Times* of London said it, "struck a note that drew a response from the whole Empire." Well, not quite. Alexander Ross, one of Currie's most faithful brigadiers, scoffed that, "it was not the stuff to feed the troops. Appeals to higher ideals made them ill." Arthur Saunders, a battalion commander, said the men simply "didn't understand what Currie was talking about." It might be generous to concede, however, that given the circumstances, Currie could well have been trying to console himself.

The Canadians were assigned defence positions at Vimy Ridge which amounted to nothing more than hit-and-run trench raids. But, even in this relatively timid atmosphere, Currie was, once more, and certainly not for the last time, perturbed over the poor performance of the British soldiers on the Corps' flanks. Although, conceding that their courage was beyond reproach, "compared to Canadians," he noted,

> these troops seemed prone to govern their actions rather by rule than by principle; this gave wonderful results as long as experienced officers were in command, but without these a soldier lacking in initiative, be he ever so ready to conscientiously carry out

every order to the letter, is not likely to show presence of mind in untried emergencies...[or] to quickly grasp a situation and act with vigor and determination when unforeseen circumstances arise.

But Currie's disdain for the way the British Army was run went a lot deeper than his disappointment with poor Tommy Atkin's fate in the field. In June, he had the opportunity of trumpeting his views to the prime minister himself, Sir Robert Borden, who had journeyed to London to meet with the British War Cabinet. Currie pulled no punches, he laid it on the line and backed it up with facts and figures. There was general incompetence, disorganization and confusion, and a conspicuous failure to remove incompetent officers. Too many British divisions were improperly trained and organized, or were led by incompetent officers. Take Passchendaele, for example. It was "not worth the Candle!" Statistics? Try this on for size. During the autumn and spring of 1917-18, the Canadian Corps put out 375,000 yards of barbed wire to thoroughly protect every trench and supporting entrenchment. By contrast a Portuguese Corps had put out no barbed wire, while two British Corps put out 30,000 and 36,000 yards of barbed wire; respectively. One British commander told Currie he didn't even have any barbed wire; that his men had been employed laying down lawn-tennis courts instead!

Lloyd George was delighted with Borden's report. Currie's views confirmed his own suspicions and feelings about Haig. In fact, he felt so strongly on the matter and was so impressed with Currie's "great ability, his strength of purpose, and his lack of the fetishes common to the British officers," that he confided to his war minister, Lord Milner, that, if the war lasted into 1919 he would give Currie command of the British Army. Nor were his credentials and qualifications lost on the Canadian prime minister who wired his Cabinet in Ottawa:

> The Canadian Army is admittedly the most formidable striking force in the Allied Armies. Probably it is the best organized and most effective unit in the world today. It has come on wonderfully since last year and this is due, not only to the courage, resourcefulness and intelligence of the men, but to the splendid and unremitting work of the officers, and to Currie's ability. I believe he is the ablest Corps Commander in the British Forces; more than that, I believe he is at least as capable as Any Army Commander among them.

By the summer of 1918, Currie had brought the Canadian Corps to the very peak of efficiency. This required major organizational and structural changes. The number of machine-guns had been tripled. The intelligence gathering, analyzing and distribution methods had been streamlined. But the most important innovation was the use made of the engineers. By fusing the three engineering companies and the single pioneer battalion originally assigned to each division into one battalion, and by adding reinforcements, an engineering unit of 1,000 men was now available to each division sufficient to cope with any task without the collateral support of the infantry. Significantly, it meant more rest for the troops who had been taking turns at fighting one day then working as engineers the next.

As a result of these improvements, the Corps now boasted twice as many engineers, and three times the number of machine-guns as any other corps. It also had a great deal more mechanical transport and artillery. When Marshal Foch heard about it, he decided to see for himself. The Corps impressed him as, "an Army second to none, deriving its immense strength from the solid organization of each of its component parts, welded together in battle conditions."

The kick-off to what became become heralded as "Canada's 100 Days," the final Allied offensive of the Great War, the one that would end it all, began at 4:20 a.m., August 8, 1918. The initial objective was to clear the Amiens railhead east of the city. The operation was based on the element of surprise — there would be no pre-assault bombardment — and would be led by tanks which had been employed en masse for the first time, briefly though successfully, at Cambrai in November 1917, ushering in a new era in battle. As part of General Henry Rawlinson's Fourth Army, the Canadian Corps would spearhead the attack. Because the Canadians had developed the reputation of being shock troops — an omen that an immediate assault was in the offing — to preserve secrecy, the Corps waited until the very last minute to move south to the Amiens sector under cover of darkness. And, just to throw the enemy right off track, a talkative signals section freely dispensed disinformation that the Corps was headed towards Ypres to the north. This marked a technological advance in warfare, the first use of wireless deception.

During the battle build-up, Currie was his usual tireless self, a commanding figure, pleasant, calmly reassuring, puffing on his ever-present pipe, working round-the-clock, at least 18 hours a day. Catching a nap whenever time permitted, he seemed to be everywhere. At dusk on August 7, the eve of the attack, mounted on his gelding charger, Brock, Currie rode out to survey the final concentration points. Pleased with the preparations, beaming with confidence, he stood in his stirrups, turned to his staff officers and, with a jaunty wave of his riding crop, announced defiantly, "God help the Boche tomorrow!"

The attack exceeded all expectations. It was the Allies' most successful day of the war. The Canadians advanced an astonishing eight miles, and the Australians on their left, a total of seven. At a loss of 3,868 casualties, the Corps took 8,000 German prisoners. All told the enemy lost 27,000 men, along with 400 guns and countless mortars and machine-guns. Small wonder Ludendorff called August 8, "the blackest day of the German Army in the history of this war." The ruse, the secrecy, the surprise had all combined to work to perfection. One German captive complained that his headquarters had miscalculated the Canadians' position by 70 miles.

However, the Fourth Army had outdistanced itself, which left it in a quandary as to what to do next. Currie's alert reaction was cryptic. "The going seems good: let's go on!" Next day the Canadians pushed ahead a further four miles into the Somme defense area. But then resistance began to stiffen. The Germans moved in seven divisions and by August 10 the initial attack ground to a halt. Currie rested his troops temporarily for a fresh assault reinforced by the British 32 Division. But, as Currie had expected, its leadership proved to be inept. Ignoring his advice, its commander attacked before his division was properly prepared and lost 2,000 men without gaining a foot of ground. To Currie who knew exactly the right moment to attack as well as when not to attack, this failure underlined the pronounced difference between British ineptitude and Canadian efficiency. That night he replaced the British with Louis Lipsett's Third Division and the advance continued, but only figuratively.

The Amiens battle had succeeded. The Corps had penetrated 22,000 yards (12.5 miles) into enemy territory. Four of 16 German divisions had been routed, and 10,000 prisoners taken. Two hundred guns had been captured and 25 French communities liberated. The offensive had served its purpose. By inflicting 75,000 casualties and taking 22,000 prisoners in four days the British Fourth Army had created panic in the German High Command. "The war must be ended," Ludendorff declared. Next day, the Kaiser instructed his foreign secretary to put out peace feelers. But, on the Amiens front, occupying the trenches abandoned by the British in 1916, the Germans were preparing to make a firm stand. Haig decided that a renewed offensive could only result in disaster. On August 14, he ordered the Canadian Corps transferred to the Arras Front as part of General Sir Henry Horne's Fifth Army.

On August 23, at his new headquarters at Noyelle Vion, Currie began plotting the part the Canadian Corps, as the assault force, would play in the campaign to bring an end to the war. For the initial stage of this offensive the Canadians had been handed a formidable assignment. The objective was to strike east along the Arras-Cambrai road and smash the vaunted Drocourt-Queant Line in which, according to Currie, "the Germans had placed their trust...If we can break it, victory might yet come in 1918."

Once that formidable fortification had been secured, the Corps would then outflank the vaunted Hindenberg Line, of which that defence was a part. Before that objective could be reached, however, an array of tough, well-entrenched defence systems, studded with strong machine-gun nests, faced the Canadians. The first of these were the former British trenches on Orange Hill, which had been captured by the Germans in the spring, and the heights of Monchy-le-Preux. Directly behind them lay the heavily fortified Fresnes Rouvroy Line, then finally the dreaded Drocourt-Queant obstacle, the Corps' main objective. But that was far from the end of it. To the rear of that fortification lay a natural waterway defence, the Canal du Nord, as well as a series of subsidiary posts protecting the textile town of Cambrai. Altogether, in Currie's estimation, they represented the strongest defensive positions on the Western Front.

As usual, Currie's preparations and reconnaissance were accurate down to the last detail. This was critical, because temporarily he had to make do with only two divisions, the Second and Third, both of the others were still en route from Amiens. Knowing the Germans would expect a dawn attack, over the objections of First Army General Headquarters, Currie decided to strike at night, something he normally took pains to avoid. At 3:00 in the morning of August 26, the Germans were caught completely unawares. The Canadians arrived in Monchy-le-Preux for breakfast. By suppertime they had overrun the outer defences, advanced three miles and taken 2,000 prisoners. Their own casualties numbered less than 1,500.

Storming the Fresnes-Rouvroy Line was another matter. It seemed impregnable at first. It took three days of bitter fighting before the Canadians finally captured the northern section of the entrenchment. By that time they had gained only five miles of ground at a cost of 5,801 casualties and both the Second and Third Divisions were totally exhausted. Currie replaced them with Watson's Fourth and Macdonnell's First which wasted no time in overcoming the remaining segment of the line on August 31.

Next came the famed and much feared Drocourt-Queant Line, the hinge to the German defences. Currie expected a hard fight. "We have decided to put up all our strength against it," he noted in his diary, "[but] not to attack until we are ready, and then go all out."

Beginning at dawn, September 2, incredibly, almost unbelievably, in "one of the finest feats in our history," in Currie's opinion, by employing their three assault divisions against nine defending German divisions, the Canadians smashed through one of the strongest defences they had ever run up against, in a matter of hours, and crushed the Buissy Switch main support system beyond it. That was enough for the enemy, who retreated across the Canal du Nord. (When Kaiser Wilhelm learned of the defeat he moaned, "We have lost the war. Poor Fatherland!") But, Currie cautioned against pursuing the fleeing Germans across the waterway. It was heavily defended on all sides and, besides, the Corps needed to catch its breath and take time out for repairs. The encounter had been a bitter one as Currie had expected and had cost the Canadians 5,622 casualties, bringing the total since the beginning of the Arras-Cambrai offensive to 11,423. It was some consolation that these losses were proportionately far lower than in previous battles, an appreciable decrease from one man killed or wounded in every two, to one in five.

But the respite was short-lived. On September 15, Currie received orders to cross the Canal du Nord in preparation for an attack on Cambrai. His superiors at GHQ, even Haig, favoured a frontal attack, but Currie considered the canal virtually impassable and a head-on assault potentially costly, almost suicidal. His plan was to cross the waterway to the south, at the time occupied by British troops, where the canal was unfinished, shallow and dry. It was there that he reckoned on breaking right through. The British tried to dissuade him. Sir Julien Byng warned him that it would be the most, "difficult operation of the war." But Currie refused to be discouraged or deterred and at 5:20 a.m. on September 27 as hundreds of Canadian guns broke the dawn silence, infantry from the First and Fourth Divisions swarmed over the canal quickly overrunning two trench systems. It was another overwhelming Currie success and victory for the Canadian Corps during which a further 3,000 German prisoners were taken. Both Haig and Horne, who had voiced such strong misgivings, now proffered their personal congratulations. Sir Henry Rawlingson went so far as to call it "a marvelous feat." But the Canadians had little time to bask in all that glory.

For the next four days they had to ward off a series of determined enemy counter-attacks, made possible by the resistance being encountered to the south by Byng's Third Army against the Hindenburg Line. This lack of progress had allowed the Germans to rush in reinforcements against the four Canadian divisions whom they mistakenly believed, from the tenacious resistance they put up, to number at least 12. On October 1, Currie decided to seize the initiative by boldly committing his entire force in an effort to clear the enemy from the high ground north of Cambrai.

But the initiative would not be his for long. The Germans resisted so stubbornly — "We have never seen the Boche fight harder," Currie wrote. "He is like a cornered rat and I believe will fight most desperately until beaten absolutely and totally." — that the Corps commander decided to call off the action, but not before his men had captured 7,000 prisoners, netted hundreds of machine-guns and inflicted heavy losses on the Boche.

The next step for the Canadians was to take Cambrai. That operation was but a single — though important — part of the general Allied offensive now in progress with the Americans on the right engaging the enemy in the heavily wooded Meuse-Argonne region of north-central France; the French in the middle, in the Champagne country; and the British on the left tackling the Hindenburg Line. It represented the first fully concentrated, coordinated Allied military effort on the widest front of the war aimed at daily increasing pressure on the German government, and its High Command and it marked the beginning and the end for the Fatherland.

It was another stellar performance in the catalogue of Canadian Corps victories, although, in the early morning before the attack on Cambrai, Currie had become nervously apprehensive. He had orders to hold off until the Third Army had occupied Awoignt, a village to the south-east. As usual, the British had not kept pace with the Canadian advance and Currie feared that delaying his own progress would benefit the enemy; the element of surprise could be lost and the Germans could use the time to stiffen their defences. By 1:30 a.m. on October 8, Currie decided to wait no longer. Disregarding headquarter instructions he gave the signal for the assault to proceed.

He need not have concerned himself. The Canadians caught the Germans flat-footed in the process of evacuating the city which they had started to put to the torch. By 8:30 that morning the Corps had completely secured what was left of it. The operation had been a complete walkover and a fitting climax to the six week Arras-Cambrai campaign. During that period, the Canadians had advanced 23 miles, taking 19,000 Germans prisoner, and capturing 370 artillery weapons as well as 2,000 machine-guns. They had suffered 30,000 casualties, which was not disproportionate when considered in the context that the Corps of 100,000 men had been constantly engaged against a quarter of the entire German Army leaving all the 5,000,000 Americans, British and French troops fighting on the Western Front, to cope with the rest of it.

After the fall of Cambrai, the Germans knew they were beaten. On the Western Front they were falling back everywhere against the relentless joint American, French and British onslaught. In Palestine the British had ripped the Turkish Army to shreds. In Salonika the Bulgarians had been beaten so soundly they pulled right out of the war. At home, an angry, starving Bulgarian populace heaped abuse on the men in uniform. The country was close to anarchy. Desperately, Field Marshal Paul von Hindenburg, chief commander of the Central Powers, told the Cabinet, "the only right course is to get out of the fight." The only reason they were still in it was the British and French refusal to agree to US President Woodrow Wilson's Fourteen Points Peace Proposal and insist on an unconditional surrender instead.

On the day that Cambrai fell, Ludendorff ordered an orderly withdrawal east to Germany's final bastion, the Hermann Line, which ran from the River Scarpe in the north, through Valenciennes to the River Oise in the south. Civilians were evacuated and demolition teams went to work in the towns, villages, bridges, roads and railways. At the same time all supplies were either destroyed or removed. The Germans were determined that their scorched earth preparations would make an advance as difficult and time-consuming as possible.

On October 17, the Canadians were given some inkling of what lay in store when, to their surprise, the Germans failed to respond to the pre-assault artillery bombardment. In fact, they were drawing back from the Canal de la Sensee under cover of fog and mist. There was another curious thing. The Canadians could see a number of fires and hear a series of explosions.

Once across the canal, what greeted the Canadians was just what the enemy had intended, a devastated wasteland in which all avenues and routes of transport, as well as buildings, had been destroyed, taxing the Corps' engineers' abilities and energies to the utmost. In addition, because the countryside had been stripped of all farm produce, the civilians had to be fed. After three days, most repairs had been made, and the 40,000 liberated inhabitants provided with food, partly through the willingness of many units to forfeit 15 per cent of their daily rations.

Rain and fog impeded progress as the Canadians struggled forward, around and over obstacles the German demolition teams had left in their wake. But at least they enjoyed the strange, new sensation of not being shot at — for the time being anyway.

As they neared Valenciennes, where the Germans intended to make a stand, they began to run into roadblocks fortified with machine-guns and they also came under some long-distance shelling. Much of the area had been flooded by blasting the dykes along the Canal de l'Escaut opposite the city so that the only course now open to it was from the south. And that was blocked by the heavily defended Mount Houy.

To overcome this handicap, Sir Henry Horne envisioned a two-pronged assault. A corps from his First Army would concentrate on capturing the hill, while the Canadian Corps would cross the canal and secure the city. But the scheme misfired. On October 28, the British 51st (Highland) Division stormed the stronghold but was unable to hang on in the face of three fierce enemy counter-attacks. Subsequently, Horne commissioned the Canadian Corps to undertake the entire operation by themselves.

Currie assigned a single brigade to the task, a notion the British senior officers scoffed at. If an entire division couldn't succeed, how in hell could a mere brigade secure such a bastion? Currie would show them how — Canadian style. As he had so ably demonstrated in the build-up to all his battles, Currie once again placed a premium on paying the price in shells instead of lives. As he had done so many times before, he again drew on his corps artillery commander, Brigadier General Andy McNaughton, to support his attack — "the last great barrage of the war." It was a "good one" as McNaughton had promised him. His gunners expended a total of 2,140 tons of shells, the equivalent to the amount exploded by both sides during the entire Boer War. It was so good a one, in fact, that when the Tenth Brigade assaulted Mount Houy at 5:15 on the morning of November 1, 1918, it met only token resistance. By 8:00 a.m. the hill was in Canadian hands. Twenty-six hundred Germans had been killed and 1,800 taken prisoner. The attackers had lost only 400.

The way was now left open for the Canadians to paddle across the Canal de l'Escaut and enter Valenciennes. During the afternoon, the Germans fought back vainly and by nightfall had not only abandoned the city but the entire Hermann Line as well. The Canadian Corps had fought and won its last battle of the Great War.

But that victory also served to illustrate the contempt, disdain and superior attitude that most British field commanders felt and displayed toward "colonials." The happy citizens of Valenciennes had laid on an elaborate celebration to thank the Canadians for freeing them. When Horne heard about it, he insisted that the 51st Highlanders, who had done little to distinguish themselves in the battle, and he, as army commander, should be the subject of the official address of thanks as well as receive the flag. Currie was livid. But he was to suffer still further indignity. Horne ordered that the British lead the march past with the Canadians bringing up the rear! Currie did not disguise his disgust at what he considered to be a glaring example of Imperial snobbishness and bad manners. "The act of the Army is unaccountable," he raged, "and is resented by the Corps."

Meanwhile the chase went on. On November 6, the Canadians crossed into Belgium and three days later were within a mile of Mons. By this time Currie knew an armistice was imminent. He was anxious to arrive in the town where the war had begun for the British but with the end of hostilities almost in sight he was unwilling to take chances to occupy it. He need not have worried. Around midnight on November 10/11 Canadian patrols began filtering into the town. At first there was sporadic resistance from machine-gunfire but this quickly petered out and by 2:00 in the morning it was clear that the Germans had quietly evacuated the town. Then at 7:30 came the word — the Armistice would go into effect at eleven o'clock.

The war was over, but for Currie the "battle" of Mons would be fought all over again, not around the rolling, pastoral countryside of Belgium this time, but in a drab courthouse in the pretty, peaceful little town of Cobourg on the shore of Lake Ontario, ten years later. He would win this battle too, but not without experiencing some of the fiercest rancour, bitterness and enmity he had ever known.

Under Currie's command the Canadians had built a remarkable reputation. No less authority than the eminent British historian, Sir Basil Liddell Hart, wrote, "It is a simple statement of fact that the Canadian Corps was the outstanding formation on the Western Front on either side; no nation could match it." Hugh Guthrie, a future Canadian defence minister, praised Currie as "undoubtedly the greatest soldier this country has ever produced and probably one of the greatest soldiers the world has ever seen."

Immediately after the war the Canadian Corps was assigned to the occupation forces in Germany. In January 1919, Currie arrived in London to take part in the army demobilization programme which got under way in February. That month, at the request of the Canadian prime minister, he attended the peace conference in Paris. (Currie held to the view that the fault with the Treaty of Versailles lay not in the terms but in the Allies' lack of "will and guts to see it through." In other words: the soldiers won the war, the politicians lost the peace.) In August Currie and his family set sail for Canada where he was soon to learn that the rascally, vindictive Sam Hughes, now a senile 66, but still active politically, had gone to great lengths to undermine him.

Hughes' vendetta of vengeance over Currie's refusal to appoint his son, Garnet, a division commander, began with a letter to the prime min-

ister. Dated October 1, 1918, it condemned the former Corps commander for his "useless massacre of Canadian boys…[when] the only effect
was to glorify the General in command." Borden ignored it, but on
March 4, 1919, Hughes went public with his accusations, protected from
liability by the sanctity of his seat in Parliament. With a wilful disregard
for facts, he pinpointed the capture of Mons as his main argument:

> Were I in authority, the officer who, four hours before the Armistice
> was signed, although he had been notified that the Armistice was
> to begin at eleven o'clock, ordered the attack on Mons needlessly
> sacrificing the lives of Canadian soldiers, would be tried summar-
> ily by court martial and punished as the law would allow.

Hughes got the publicity he'd been looking for — in spades! His com-
ments caused an uproar, though perhaps not quite in the way Hughes
had envisioned or wanted. In the House, members of Parliament
rushed to Currie's defence. Cy Peck, a Victoria Cross holder, praised
Currie as "one of the great Canadians, and one of the great commanders we have had in this war." Richard Cooper called him "our greatest Canadian soldier," and upbraided Hughes, and others like, him who
"stand back 3,500 miles away," from the battlefield and level false
accusations. The press took up the cudgel. The Toronto *Globe* wrote,
"The terrors of the war have been great and manifold for our gallant
men in France, but Sir Sam Hughes is a greater [terror] than any of
them." In May, Sir Edward Kemp, in his official report on overseas
operations, stated that, "General Currie has made a high place for himself in history; he measures up to a proud standard compared with
other great generals of the war; he was ever considerate of the men
under him, and always exercised patience and foresight in dealing with
the problems which came before him."

But this didn't deter the irascible Hughes, who continued his
attacks, contending that "many Canadians would be above the sod
today," had it not been for Currie's self-seeking glory. Currie was not
a man to take such recriminations lying down. Angrily he replied in
writing labelling Hughes "a liar," and "a cur of the worst type," and
challenged him to "repeat his charges outside the walls of Parliament…[where] I shall see what protection the law of Canada will give
me against his malicious slander." No fool, Hughes backed off, but the
damage had been done. Currie would say "some mud always sticks
when thrown," and in his own case that was to prove only too prophetic
some years later.

All this ruckus failed to diminish Currie's homecoming. He was welcomed as a national hero. He was immediately elevated in rank to full general and appointed inspector general of Canada's Armed Forces which, in reality, made him chief of the general staff, with headquarters in Ottawa.

Shortly after, Currie went on a coast-to-coast speaking tour captivating audiences with his articulate, gifted oratory. He proved to be a real spellbinder but the tour exacted a heavy toll. The pressures of war and the excitement of the aftermath finally caught up with him. By the time he reached Victoria he was completely exhausted and, under doctor's orders, confined to his hotel room. However, this did give him the chance to wind-up his business affairs, but what he found, shocked him; he was bereft. He had been completely wiped out because of the mismanagement by his partner who had disappeared.

On his return to Ottawa in November 1919, his main task was to reorganize the country's armed forces. He soon found out that this was a completely different ball game from wartime command. He had to cope with budget cuts, restrictions, changes and political interference. Even the militia, Canada's military mainstay, got short shrift. Frankly, the appointment was not what Currie had expected, not his cup of tea at all, and he felt decidedly uncomfortable with it. He had also become disenchanted with the Borden government.

Unlike the British Parliament which rewarded its wartime field generals with monetary grants, in June 1919, the Canadian Cabinet "did not in the least favour the proposal" of "a money grant for General Currie." As he would state later, "I am in the unique position of being the only commander of a British Force who had not received from his Government even a vote of thanks."

Then in 1920, Currie's fortunes abruptly changed. In April, he was appointed principal of McGill University. This earned him a salary of $17,500 a year, $5,500 more than he had been paid as inspector general. In addition, he was made a director of the Bank of Montreal which added $4,000 to his income. Then unexpectedly, in July, the government belatedly expressed its appreciation for Currie's past services when the Commons at last passed a resolution expressing Canada's thanks "to the General Officer Commanding, to the Officers, non-commissioned officers and men of the Canadian Corps."

As the new principal of McGill, Currie's first step was to raise funds for the institution which had become rundown both physically and administratively. A sum of $5 million was needed to repair buildings, erect new ones and hire new staff. With characteristic enthusiasm and energy, Currie showed himself more than equal to the task. During a three-week whirlwind cross-country tour, he raised $6,400,000. It made possible a much-needed metamorphosis of what had become a beleaguered institution.

Currie, now 44, went about the restoration and reorganization with a zeal that must have given some of the faculty — who doubtless had considered him little more than a figurehead when they appointed him principal — to have pause for second thought. Currie was a tireless workaholic, a real dynamo, who put his heart and soul into the job, whether it was administration or student relations — and he loved every minute of it. A revitalized McGill University thrived under his leadership.

But in addition to his duties as university president, Currie also found time for other activities. He served a term as president of the Canadian Legion, as well as nine years as president of the Last Post Fund, an association established to aid veterans and their widows, and also engaged in charity work with the Montreal Anti-Tuberculosis and General Health League and the Canadian National Committee for Mental Hygiene. In addition, he acted as president of the Conference of Canadian Universities from 1925 to 1927.

Currie also had considerable influence with the government. He was directly responsible for persuading Prime Minister Arthur Meighen to appoint his old mentor, Sir Julian Byng, as governor-general. Following William Lyon Mackenzie King's election in December 1921 he proposed an amalgamation of the departments of militia, the Canadian Navy and Air Force, into a single department — the Department of Defence. King took his advice and in January 1923 the Department of National Defence was inaugurated.

In general the 1920s were kind to the Curries. They enjoyed living in Montreal, the job, the extra-curricular activities and the social life. Then in the middle of 1927, just when they had been planning a vacation in Hawaii with their two children, the Port Hope *Evening Guide* printed the Mons article. Currie immediately cancelled his travel plans and unhesitatingly decided to take legal action against both the owner of the paper, Frederick Wilson, and the perpetrator of the article, William Preston — much against the advice of his friends. The *Evening Guide* had a circulation of under 1,000, they pointed out. Besides, this was Sam Hughes country and, although he had died in 1921, many people still revered him and believed his ridiculous accusations against Currie. A jury from that area would hardly be impartial.

But Currie was determined to see justice served and would not be dissuaded. Represented by William Norman Tilley, the noted counsellor for the Canadian Pacific Railway, Currie went for the jugular, claiming $50,000 in damages. From the start, he was in for a tough battle.

Preston, who represented himself, and Wilson, who was represented by a Toronto lawyer, Frank Regan, had done their homework. They had delved into Currie's unfortunate business past and had been fueled with plenty of ammunition, most of it jaded, by Garnet Hughes, still bearing a grudge. They looked for anything to smear Currie's character. On April 16, "the fifty thousand dollar libel suit" opened in the drab, musty, sweltering Cobourg courthouse with no less than 19 reporters covering the proceedings, tapping out a record 72,000 words a day.

The key witness for the defence at the start of the trial was Colonel Reginald Orde, judge advocate general for the Department of National Defence. Regan badgered him constantly on the matter of accuracy and availability of departmental documents, operational orders and unit war diaries. His intent was to prove that there had been a substantial number of Canadian soldiers killed on November 11, 1918, after Currie had been informed that the armistice would go into effect at 11:00 that morning.

When it became obvious that this point could not be made precisely, Regan alluded to the fact that the records might have been tampered with, to conceal the facts. "I want to establish that the records are inaccurate," he told the court. This drew a sharp rebuke from the presiding judge, Mr. Justice Hugh Rose, who was, Tilley had told Currie, "the best judge you can have for this trial." To steer the case back on track, Justice Rose ordered Regan, "to prove that the statements in the [*Evening Guide*] article are true."

But Regan persisted by maintaining that, "these records which deal with the publication of the casualties to the world were deliberately falsified for the purpose of keeping from the world the knowledge of the loss of life..." and held Orde responsible for suppressing this information. This brought a sharp response from Tilley who charged, "Now, what my friend is trying to do is to add insult to injury by this method of presenting the case." Justice Rose agreed, adding that since none of the allegations had been made in the *Evening Guide*'s article, that Regan's argument was "irrelevant."

Tilley then cross-examined Orde himself. Had his department given Currie "a list of the dead and those that died from wounds prior to the attack?" he asked. Orde confirmed that it had. "Did that list show any deaths on the 11th?" Tilley queried. It did not, Orde replied. This was a blow to the defence. Regan now took another tack. He brought into question Currie's reputation among his men. When asked his opinion, Albert Mason, a sergeant major with the 20th Battalion, who had earlier testified that he had counted three dead Canadians in Mons on November 11, answered, "He was not as popular as...other generals."

"My Lord," Tilley objected. "I did not suppose we were having evidence as to popularity, or a beauty contest, or anything of that kind."

Regan interjected that "I am dealing with his humanity, how he felt towards the private soldier, and how he acted towards him." This did not satisfy Justice Rose. "I think I will cut this short by disallowing the question."

Regan tried rephrasing it. "Was Sir Arthur Currie considerate of the comfort of the soldiers?"

"I won't allow that either," the judge snapped.

Regan refused to give in. He asked Mason, "to give us an instance where he failed to consider the comfort..."

Justice Rose again cut him off, "That is disallowed."

"I had not finished the question," Regan argued.

"Well, it's disallowed anyway."

Regan simply would not be stopped. He next tried to show that Currie was "vainglorious and consumed with the idea of his own importance" by introducing into evidence the fact that, while Sir Henry Horne, an army commander, had only one aide-de-camp Currie, as a mere corps commander, had three.

Justice Rose threw it out. "Nonsense!" he asserted.

Regan now tried to enter operational orders going back to August 1918, with the argument that, "I want the jury to get the real facts of how the Canadian Corps was driven for the last one hundred days of the war, so that they..."

"That," interrupted Justice Rose, "has nothing to do with the case."

"...so that they can decide..."

"It has nothing to do with this case."

"I had not finished my Lord," begged Regan.

"Well I am quite sure," the judge answered angrily, "that it has nothing to do with the case, whatever point you are making of it."

On another point it seemed that Justice Rose's patience had become exhausted. "Mr. Regan," he admonished, "you put a witness in the box, and you cross-examine, you lead, and you coax, and you do all the things that the book says you must not do."

"I think it is my duty," Regan pleaded in defence, "to make this observation: I think you should know that we have had great difficulty in getting witnesses."

The judge could contain his composure no longer. "What in the world has that got to do with the manner in which you are going to examine the witness when you call him," he barked unsympathetically.

At times the inanity of Regan's questions, and his answers to the judge, drew loud guffaws from the gallery. This rankled Regan who was already showing the strains the case was having on him. "I don't like this unseemly laughter," he complained. "I am getting sensitive to it."

On Saturday, April 21, the last day of the first week of the trial, Fred Wilson, owner of the *Evening Guide,* took the stand. The article in question, he said, had its genesis from a story published in the Toronto *Globe* on June 13, 1927 about the unveiling of a monument in Mons. He suggested that Preston, who seemed knowledgeable about the subject, "write an article" which he would publish.

Regan tried, unsuccessfully, to cite Wilson's sources and establish credibility. When he questioned him about the "rumours" and "common talk among soldiers" he must have sensed his argument was weak. When Tilley objected by arguing that "a newspaper cannot say there is a common rumour about that is disparaging of some person, and then put it in the press, and justify by proving the rumour. He must prove the fact." The judge sided with him. Clutching at straws, Regan asked Wilson if there was "any malice on his part towards Sir Arthur." "None whatsoever," was the response. No ground gain there. But when Currie and his entourage retired for the weekend to the Dunham Hotel he knew the fight was far from over and realized that Regan, for all his buffoonery, had scored some salient points. The question still hung over the dank courtroom: "Did Currie know, or should he have known, that the fighting would cease within a matter of hours?"

With the resumption of the trial on Monday, William Preston pleaded his own case. He began by complaining of the coverage the case was receiving in the press which was openly sympathetic towards the plaintiff. Justice Rose ruled that any favouritism, if it indeed existed, would be treated as contempt of court.

Tilley now sought to put to rest the earlier testimony of Frederick Lingard, a Port Hope resident and former member of the Fourth Artillery Brigade, who stated that while on duty at brigade headquarters between 10:00 and 11:00 p.m. on the evening of November 10, 1918, he had received word of the impending armistice. So far no one had disputed this so-called "evidence." Now came the turn of the plaintiff's side. Tilley called Colonel Alan Magee to the witness box. Magee, who had served at Corps Headquarters swore that the first word of the armistice did not arrive until 6:30 a.m. November 11. He ruled out any earlier reference to it as clearly "impossible." Another witness, John Clark, formerly commander of the Seventh Brigade, short of calling Lingard a liar, testified under oath that "Lingard's message I would characterize as ridiculous. I don't believe that it ever occurred." As to an attack on Mons, Fred Loomis, who commanded the Third Division, stated that on the morning of November 10, Currie "visited me to impress on me the necessity…not to take any serious offensive in the way of a heavy attack or a set piece with artillery; in other words to avoid casualties and losses." The wind was beginning to blow in the right direction.

Tilley now paraded four witnesses before the court, all of whom testified that there had been no fighting, no opposition in Mons on the morning of November 11. In fact Eric Finley, a captain with C Company of the 42nd Battalion maintained that, "There was nobody to fight." Regan tried to discredit this testimony by alleging that the four veterans, all of whom had been staying with the Currie party at the Dunham Hotel, had conspired to "make it up." He soon realized he had overstepped the line. An irate Justice Rose warned: "if you will persist in making these irregular unauthorized speeches, I shall have to, instead of scolding — I am very tired of scolding — I think I shall have to ask you to let one of the other counsel on your side conduct the case."

The climax to the trial came when Currie took the stand on Friday, April 27. Under Tilley's succinct querying, he stressed that the tactics employed at Mons were deliberately designed to minimize casualties. "…the troops entered, and in a few hours afterwards had gone through the city out the other side." He also pointed out that he did not select Mons as a Canadian objective. That was determined by First Army headquarters. Although he was aware that armistice talks were under way, he had been told by Sir Henry Horne that, "the wish of Marshal Foch was there should be no relaxation of the pressure" on the retreating Germans. It was feared that the enemy, if given time, might make a stand on the River Meuse.

Now it came Regan's turn to cross-examine. One observer called it a "grotesque" exhibition of trying to discredit a national hero. But Currie was more than a match for his antagonist. When asked his opinion of Sir Sam Hughes' allegations in Parliament, he called them "foolish." Now Regan pondered whether they were any different from the charges made by the defendants in the Port Hope *Evening Guide*. Currie was ready for him. "Oh, that is not foolish," he replied. "That was deliberate."

This rankled Regan and he lost his temper, telling Currie to keep his insinuations to himself. Then in an attempt to embarrass him he forced Currie to admit that he had been having a bath when he learned of the impending armistice. Currie replied that a bath was "a good thing to have in the morning." Back came a tart retort from Regan ringing with sarcasm "if the mere fact that the war was going to end didn't interfere with your ablutions?" Currie demonstrated that he too could dish out the medicine. "That is not all right Mr. Regan and, as you remarked to me, you are asking me to be careful about my insinuations; I suggest that you obey your own behest."

Regan took a shot at him from another direction. Noting that the Canadian Corps had defeated 47 German divisions in the last 100 days of the war, he asked, "Don't you think...that in the dying hours of the war, you might have spared your men a trifle more than you did?"

CURRIE: "No. You are the man that is suggesting that those men who did that should lie down and quit within two days of the final victory."

REGAN: "I didn't say that."

CURRIE: "Oh, yes, you spare them, you say quit."

REGAN: "I don't mean to lie down and quit."

CURRIE: "Well, that is what you are suggesting."

REGAN: "No it isn't."

CURRIE: "Yes it is. You would have them disobey orders; you would have them mutiny, practically; you would have them guilty of treason, and act in an unsoldierly way, right at the very last. Those were not the men who did that sort of thing."

Regan was losing ground and he knew it. But still fishing, he decided to drag things out. He quoted from books, reports and other material and took issue with Currie over their meaning. Tilley let him run on, giving him all the rope he wanted. After Currie had been in the witness box for an exhausting seven hours, Justice Rose finally adjourned the court for the weekend.

The high point of the drama took place on Monday, April 30, when the court reconvened to hear the final arguments. Regan led off. He was his usual relentless self. Everything in the *Evening Guide* article was true, he maintained. He reminded the jury of Lingard's "message" ignoring the mountain of testimony charged against it. He concluded by telling the jury that, "Currie is asking you for $50,000 and I am asking you not to give him a cent...Give him nothing. Our only desire was to give justice to those dead soldiers at Mons."

Preston followed suit. His delivery was impassioned. "I believed what I wrote in this article," he contended. The attack on Mons, he alleged "was madness. Cursed — I will not say anything else, and it was greater madness to decide that the fighting must go on until 11 o'clock...I therefore impeach Arthur Currie before this bar on behalf of the widows, the sons, who lost their fathers, and the fathers, who lost their support with needless, reckless, needless war-waste of life in his attack on Mons."

Tilley had the final word and he made the most of it. "This is a libel suit," he began, "not an enquiry into the war." He then went over the points of contention in the article one by one. "There is not one of these sentences referring to Sir Arthur Currie that has been justified," he stated. "How easy it would be for unscrupulous persons if, in a libel suit, it were permitted with impunity, to sow the seeds of suspicion and spread the idea that there were some things that have not been brought out. That has been done at this trial. You can consider this the meanest of libels. Here is a charge that a general, at a time when such action was useless, gave an order that meant loss of life, so that he might get glorification. That is a charge by a man who dips pen in ink and writes and prints it all inside of four hours." He charged that the conduct of Preston and Wilson had been reprehensible and concluded: "Gentleman of the jury, you are entitled in considering your verdict to consider that the fact that someone says something gives nobody the right to repeat it."

Justice Rose's charge to the jury next morning was a classic, with the central points of the suit spelled out in black and white. "I cannot stress too strongly upon you," he said, "[that] a comment cannot be justified as a fair comment upon a matter of public importance unless the facts upon which the comment is made are stated and stated truly."

"You are not concerned here," he told the jury, "with what these defendants meant [in their article]; you are concerned here with the idea that they conveyed to the ordinary reader." He then reviewed the trial and commented that: "The newspapers are very fond of calling it the fifty thousand dollar libel action." This was of no concern to jurors, he said. "What the jury do is consider what will more or less compensate the plaintiff and what will mark the extent of their disapproval of the conduct of the defendants...I do not think the jury are concerned with any question as to whether the defendants can pay easily or not."

The jury got the message, loud and clear. After retiring to deliberate at 11:47 a.m., the 12 jurors filed back into the courtroom three hours and 39 minutes later. The foreman addressed the judge: "On behalf of the jury, I beg to submit that the defendants are guilty of libel, and that the award of 500 dollars be given to the plaintiff." When the jury was polled it was found that 11 to one favoured the guilty verdict. Ironically, the lone dissenter turned out to be a returned soldier.

It had been another great victory for Sir Arthur Currie, one applauded and welcomed far and wide. Prime Minister Mackenzie

King gave the verdict his own endorsement, a simple message that, "It could not have been otherwise." From the mayor of Mons came this fitting tribute: *"Ville de Mons félicite son glorieux libérateur pour nouvelle victoire remportée sur détractuers."* (The city of Mons congratulates its glorious liberator for his new victory over his detractors.) A father from Aurora, Ontario, whose son had been killed at Passchendaele, cabled, "Not for a moment did we think the verdict could be other than it proved to be."

When Currie arrived home at Windsor Station in Montreal, he was greeted by an excited throng of well-wishers from all walks of life, accompanied by a military band. A procession lined the sidewalks as his car drove him to his house on McTavish Street on the edge of the McGill campus.

Three weeks later the defendants sought to have the Cobourg court decision overruled. Predictably, and justifiably, the appeal was denied. With court costs, Currie was awarded a total of $5,737, though he only collected a part of it, $5,229.09. It was too large a debt for a small-town newspaper and it pushed the Port Hope *Evening Guide* and its owner, Fred Wilson, to bankruptcy. The charlatan, William Preston, his reputation ruined, paid nothing and was never heard from again.

But the real loser was the obnoxious Frank Regan. His handling of the case, his shocking treatment of Currie, aroused public indignation and rage, some of it in the form of physical threats. One writer labelled him a "slacker," another, said she would have "scratched his eyes out" had she been present at the trial. His reputation in tatters, his career as a lawyer was finished, but there was no end to his incredible gall. With the approach of a federal election in 1930 he sought the Conservative nomination for a Toronto constituency. When this was met with disgust and distrust, in desperation he had the nerve to appeal to Currie, of all people, for help and support! Currie kicked his emissary out of his office.

But the trial had taken its toll on Currie too; he was mentally and physically exhausted. A short while later he suffered a slight stroke and was hospitalized for several weeks. But now for the good news. His lawyers waived all compensation for their services, saying that the black eye he had given Preston was sufficient payment. His friend, Sir Edward Beatty, head of the CPR, passed the hat to collect $30,000 to defray costs of the trial as well as "providing you with a sufficient margin over those expenses to enable you to take a very much needed rest." On June 2, 1928, Currie and his wife set sail for a holiday in England and France.

Badly as he needed a vacation, it could never make up for the wear and tear Currie, in his 54 years, had endured, nor the punishing pace he insisted on setting for himself. Originally weighing in at 235 pounds he was now down to under 200. He had also become susceptible to a variety of illnesses. In France he contracted paratyphoid, a form of food poisoning. When he returned to Canada late in January 1929 he was subjected to bouts of flu, the grippe and tonsillitis. But despite his doctors' warnings and advice to take it easy, Currie rarely missed a day at the office and continued his relentless work schedule. It was fortunate that he was still able to summon that enormous extra energy with which he had been blessed. There were two great challenges — last battles — ahead, which he could not and, would not, ignore.

The first of these was the matter of pensions, one of Currie's greatest concerns. While he readily conceded that, "Pensions are not a reward for war service, nor are they given because of sympathy with a war veteran," he was aware that many veterans deserving of compensation were not receiving it. This was entirely due to the bureaucracy of the Pension Board which was ruled by such rigidity that the system was stacked against the individual. Legitimate requests from veterans entitled to pensions for a number of bona fide reasons were arbitrarily turned down. There was little, if any, attempt to examine the validity of such cases. It was much easier and less trouble to go by the book and turn them down. A crusade to right this wrong was, of course, a challenge Currie could not refuse. By lobbying, cajoling and insisting, Currie had the legislation governing pensions changed. But that still wasn't good enough for him; it remained wrapped in too much red tape for his liking. In the end Currie got his way. When the R. B. Bennett government took power in 1930, it acknowledged the complaints and appointed a committee to reassess the problem. It took three years but finally, in May 1933, the Pension Board and tribunal were replaced by the Canadian Pension Commission. Currie got his wish and had lived up to his promise to get "his boys" what they deserved.

His next, and last major "battle," was a crisis right in his own backyard. The Great Depression had left McGill University in financial jeopardy. Its future uncertain, Currie attacked the problem head-on by attempting to launch a fund-raising drive to rescue it. Given the temper of the time this proved impractical. Then, just when things looked blackest, along came Wilder Penfield. An American, Penfield, who was an acknowledged leader in the field of neurosurgery, had accepted a professorship at McGill because he loved Montreal and was enraptured with the medical academic atmosphere of the university. He had one proviso: that McGill agree to establish his dream of a neurological institute. Currie, immediately recognizing the stature this would give the school, pounced on this godsent opportunity. "It will mean," he wrote, "...an institution known and respected to the ends of the earth...."

The concept excited everyone Currie and Penfield approached. Through a series of negotiations, grants were obtained from the Rockefeller Foundation, the Province of Quebec, the City of Montreal, the nearby Royal Victoria Hospital and a number of individual wealthy Montrealers. McGill University was saved. On October 6, 1933, the cornerstone was laid to begin construction of the Montreal Neurological Institute, which at one time was recognized as the finest in the world.

In his final years, Currie regretted that he had not written his memoirs, complaining that he had never found the time to do so. He was also haunted with the spectre of another world war in which he visualized that, "not only the soldiers...will be killed...but the civilian population as well." As a result he became a strong advocate of disarmament — but only if all nations participated. Realistically he knew it was a pipe dream. The rise of Hitler in Germany and the Japanese invasion of Manchuria were omens that could only end in a new global conflict. And he had little faith in the League of Nations to solve those problems. "A spineless institution," he termed it. "We fought the last war," he lamented, "foolishly thinking that we were doing something that would end war, and we find war more and more likely today than it was 20 years ago."

On Sunday, November 5, 1933, Currie was working in his study on his annual Armistice Day message when he collapsed and had to be taken to the Royal Victoria Hospital. There, his condition was diagnosed as a blockage of a small vessel in the midbrain but after a week he was making a slow, yet steady recovery. Then on November 19, complications set in. He developed bronchial problems leading to pneumonia. At 2:50 on the morning of November 30, he succumbed to the illness.

Sir Arthur Currie's funeral took place five days later on the morning of December 5, at a joint civic-military service in Christ Church Anglican Cathedral. He was buried with full military honours in Mount Royal Cemetery to a 17-gun salute. On the same day, a memorial service was held in London's Westminster Abbey.

Many tributes were paid to his memory. The Sir Arthur Currie Gymnasium-Armoury is one such monument. A ski slope at the Laurentian resort of St. Sauveur is named after him. The Canadian Legion adopted as its motto a phrase from one of his Armistice Day speeches: "They served till death; why not we?" A plain granite cross in the military cemetery at Pointe Claire, west of Montreal was unveiled in his memory. The army barracks in Calgary bear his name. And, something was also tangible that the Canadian Cabinet had not seen fit to do in Currie's lifetime. On June 2, 1935 the Bennett government proposed a grant of $50,000 for his estate.

On December 5, 1936, the third anniversary of his funeral, a monument of unique character and heritage, was raised on Sir Arthur's grave. It features the Cross of Sacrifice, a design normally reserved for those killed or who died of wounds in the Great War. The two exceptions are Currie himself, and his old commander, Sir Douglas Haig. In Mount Royal Cemetery it was placed on an octagonal base containing earth from the sites of some of his famous triumphs — Vimy Ridge, the Somme, the Ypres Salient and Mons.

Walter Hose
1875-1965

Rollo Mainguy
1901–1979

5

SAVE OUR NAVY
Walter Hose
Rollo Mainguy

Mutiny! Small wonder! From a morale standpoint in the late '40s, the Royal Canadian Navy was in deplorable shape, a decidedly "unhappy ship." Insurrection lay in the wind, rough sailing loomed ahead, and not without some justification and sound reason. For the ordinary able-bodied seaman, life was barely tolerable. Working conditions under rigid Royal Navy, British-oriented standards were wretched and discipline unnecessarily harsh. Compared to civilian remunerations, pay and allowances were well below average. A leading rating trying to support his family on $120 a month was forced to moonlight and, when on sea duty, his wife — and children, more often than not, had to move in with the parents or in-laws. Inevitably this created marriage problems.

And time at sea was invariable for sustained periods, especially for skilled tradesmen who were overworked because personnel were not being trained to supplement their depleted ranks. In Halifax and Victoria, where most of the RCN was based, housing for families was inadequate. There were no married quarters except for senior officers. For the single man, the quarters were bleak and lacked privacy. The few recreational facilities that existed left much to be desired. On top of it all, the food, by any measurement, was a disgrace. Young men pondering their future careers with the navy had understandable doubts as to what lay in store for themselves and their families. This had two consequences. It seriously hampered recruiting and re-enlistments, particularly with old salts who knew the score. And, at the same time, it precipitated a widespread wave of requests for release or a transfer to more comfortable, less inhibited postings, such as on an air force station.

Compared to the real problem at hand, however, all this was purely the ground swell. Beneath the surface a tide churned that manifested itself in such discontent and dissatisfaction it could only have one result: open rebellion. No one characterized this lamentable state of affairs (or contributed to it) more typically than the starchy executive officer of His Majesty's Canadian Ship *Ontario*, Commander Jeffry Vanstone Brock. Though he had a fine war record, his time on loan with the Royal Navy had done nothing to improve his lack of rapport with those under him, officers as well as hands. His arrogant, distant and impersonal manner bred dissension where assurance, confidence, understanding and support were sorely needed. Unhappily Brock was not the only offender in this regard. There were other officers in command posts just as guilty for allowing and/or ignoring, the unrest spreading through the navy.

Ontario was on a shakedown cruise off Nanoose on Vancouver Island when it happened. A less insensitive individual than Brock might have foreseen and possibly averted the situation. The day was August 22, 1947. After dinner, some 50 disgruntled young seamen decided to express their indignation at the way they were being treated but, in as orderly a manner as possible, without actually committing an offense. They locked themselves in one of the mess decks and let it be known that they would not answer the usual pipe calling for all hands to "fall in." When word reached the captain, Jimmy Hibbard, who had taken command six weeks earlier, he wisely cancelled the pipe. He then cleared the decks and assembled all hands to hear their grievances. None were particularly serious; they were simply routine complaints like wearing night uniforms, unfair assignments and so on, but they were indicative of a general malaise seething among the lower decks not only aboard *Ontario* but other Canadian ships as well.

The incident was handled with discretion, ostensibly to everyone's satisfaction. Brock got the axe and was replaced by a congenial successor who kept the men happy. There was no investigation and no charges were laid. To all intents it appeared to be an isolated case. But it had sown a seed that would take root. Ironically, the officer who had given Brock his marching papers would be the one upon whose broad shoulders would eventually fall the responsibility to chair the commission appointed by Brooke Claxton, the minister of National Defence, "to improve conditions of service, the relations between officers and men, the machinery for ventilation of grievances and...the training of naval personnel."

He was Rear Admiral Rollo Edward Mainguy who, at the time of the *Ontario* incident, held the post of flag officer, Pacific Coast. A year and a half later, by which time he was flag officer, Atlantic Coast, three more mutinies had broken out. The first took place in February aboard HMCS *Athabaskan* while she was refueling at Manzanillo, Mexico when the junior hands refused to turn to. Two weeks later the destroyer *Crescent* had a similar experience in Nanking, China where she was guarding the interests of Canadian citizens caught in the Communist advance. A little later, *Athabaskan* joined the carrier *Magnificent* in the Caribbean after sailing through the Panama Canal. When the ships' companies met ashore, conversation naturally turned to the destroyer's recent mutiny. Next morning at sea after breakfast, 32 of *Magnificent's* aircraft handlers stayed in their mess deck to avoid falling in.

While all these incidents — and this included *Ontario* — were acts of insubordination, there was no violence, no breech of conduct on anyone's part. They were more like sit-down strikes but much more reasonable and orderly. Only junior hands were involved. Once they'd aired their grievances — and these were all of a pretty standard, routine nature — and were assured by their captains that all complaints would be addressed and given consideration, the men went back to work as if nothing had happened. No one was punished. But where there was smoke, and distress signals of concern quickly permeated the upper echelons of the military.

It was not so much the nature of the mutinies, which in any case were pretty tame, nor the fact that three of them had occurred in rapid succession. It was the timing that was scary. In 1949 the Russians had exploded the atomic bomb, and Communism became more of a threat than ever before. On April 4, Canada, along with six other nations, signed the North Atlantic Treaty in which all members were committed to pledge their armed forces. Under these circumstances, was it not logical to ask whether the mutinies were part of a plot to undermine those forces? That possibility could not, of course, be ruled out but indications seemed to point to a breakdown in discipline and morale, rather than subversion, to be the root of the navy's disorder. That is the way the Ministry of National Defence read it. It was an internal malady that called for a house cleaning. But Brooke Claxton's commission was not focused on disciplinary action. Rather, its mandate was to discover cause and effect and to make recommendations.

Claxton had chosen an impressive trio for the task. The senior citizen among the group was the venerable lawyer Leonard Brockington, the first chairman of the Canadian Broadcasting Corporation and wartime advisor to Prime Minister MacKenzie King. Ex-Navy Commander Louis de la Chesnaye Audette was also a lawyer as well as a member of the Maritime Commission. The chairman of Claxton's commission could not have been more suited for the job. Rugged and athletic looking (he in fact was the Maritime squash champion) the six-foot tall, 200 pound, Rollo Mainguy put the concern, comfort and welfare of those serving under him ahead of all other considerations, and went out of his way to do it. During World War II in 1942, as Captain (D)* Newfoundland, he started a recreation camp for the men as well as the famous Crow's Nest Seagoing Officers Club in St. John's. As captain of *Uganda*, serving with the Royal Naval Fleet in the Pacific in 1945, he inaugurated a regular series of talks to the entire ship's company. At these Town Hall sessions as he called them, he demonstrated a unique oratorical ability. Though he was soft-spoken, his delivery was always compelling, especially since it was always delivered off the cuff; he never used a note. This was deceiving actually. In reality he had a powerful faculty of concentration, and had carefully memorized every single word. Another outstanding quality which singled him out as a leader was his fair-mindedness. In the Mainguy Report, as the commission's official document became known, the admission was made that Mainguy's own decision to relieve Commander Brock of his *Ontario* XO (Executive Officer) command "without a complete investigation, appears neither completely wise nor completely fair." The words were Mainguy's very own.

Mainguy had been handed an enormous responsibility, an awesome assignment of monumental proportions that could be best summed up in three words: Save Our Navy. Perhaps it may have been of some consolation to him that in 1923, when he was a mere lieutenant taking a signals course apprenticeship aboard the renowned HMS *Victory*, one of his predecessors (as chief of Naval Staff) faced the identical challenge of saving the Royal Canadian Navy from extinction but for somewhat different reasons. Like his successor he too proved willing and able to cope with that ominous task.

Rear Admiral Walter Hose was no ordinary seaman, he was a sailor from the word go! He not only was *to* the sea born he was also born *on* it. His parents, the bishop of Singapore and his wife, were aboard the Pacific and Orient liner *Surat* in the Indian Ocean near Ceylon when the birth took place on October 2, 1875. It was an auspicious, fit-

---

*Destroyer

ting start for the man who would one day become the RCN's first chief of Naval Staff and would be forever remembered as "Canada's Father of the Navy." Twice during his long and distinguished career, which began in 1889 at age 14 when, as a naval cadet, he reported to HMS *Britannia* — an ancient Royal Navy wooden three-decker training vessel, moored in Dartmouth harbour — he had rescued the RCN from dissolution.

On both occasions, in 1923, and again in 1933, he faced massive naval budget cuts which threatened to scuttle the service altogether. But if the politicians thought they had a pushover in the handsome, wiry, wily director of Naval Service, they had another thing coming. In the first instance Hose cut costs by revamping the entire naval concept and structure in Canada. The second time around, he simply refused to give in to Treasury Board pressure by threatening to disband his force and take his ships out of service. At the same time, with sound logic acquired in 44 years of naval service — 22 of them with the RCN — he persuaded the Cabinet of the need for a permanent navy and argued that it would be impossible to maintain it under the proposed budget reductions. In the end he won the day. That was no surprise to those who knew him. From the start, his career had been a stormy one of ups and downs, excitement and frustration which through thick and thin, the short, wiry, five-foot-six, Hose, always managed to somehow scrape through and come out on top.

Ironically, while he was the one chiefly responsible for forging the RCN into the third largest navy in the world, most of his active service was with the Royal Navy. Following his training stint, in January 1892, he passed into fleet as a crew member of HMS *Imperieuse*, the very first armoured cruiser and the flagship of the China Squadron. On March 15 he was promoted to midshipman and exactly two years later, HMS *Centurion*, one of the world's most modern battleships, relieved *Imperieuse* as flagship and Hose was transferred accordingly. In 1895, he had his first view of warfare when *Centurion*, in a policing role, saw the Japanese Army, supported by gunboats, land on the Shantung promontory and capture the Chinese city of Wei-hai-wei. Some time later the battleship was also witness to the Japanese capture of Port Arthur.

Later in the year Hose was posted to Great Britain for further training attaining the rank of sub-lieutenant in August 1896 at which time he was given his first command, a torpedo boat. That September he joined HMS *Polyphemus* in the Mediterranean Station, then in April 1897 he was transferred to the torpedo boat destroyer HMS *Dragon* which was stationed off Crete during the Turko-Greek War. Here, Hose came under fire for the first time.

While on night patrol some 400 yards offshore, gun flashes could be seen at the top of a cliff. From experience, the crew knew that a party of Turkish Bashi-Bazooks were skirmishing with the Greek islanders. *Dragon* turned her searchlights full beam on the combatants to put an end to the squabble. It didn't. Instead, both sides opened fire on the meddlesome British warship which was forced to beat a hasty retreat.

In October, Hose was invalided to England with Mediterranean fever. On recovery he was promoted to lieutenant and assigned to the cruiser HMS *Bonaventure* back in the China Squadron. Then, in November 1899 he was given temporary command of the gunboat HMS *Tweed* which was employed in anti-pirate patrols on the Chinese West River. He then returned to *Bonaventure,* which by now was stationed in the Yangtse River to protect British interests during the Boxer Rebellion of 1900-1901. For his part in all these operations Hose received the China Medal.

Returning to Great Britain in 1901, he served for six months with HMS *Jupiter*, a battleship of the Channel Squadron, then joined HMS *Charybdis*, a cruiser with the North America and West Indies Squadron. Then and there his ties with Canada took root. One: a significant part of his duty was, as a lieutenant, to train professional Newfoundland seaman as members of the Royal Naval Reserve. Two: in Newfoundland he met the girl he would marry, Catherine Boone.

During this tenure, in 1904, *Charybdis* was sent to Venezuela to seize the country's navy ostensibly in response to the president of the republic's refusal to settle his debts with several British firms. Actually, what forced the issue was a so-called capture of a British ship whose crew he had taken prisoner. Hose, by now a first lieutenant, took charge of the assignment which turned out to be a total farce. The Venezuelan navy turned out to be nothing more than a pair of abandoned tugs manned by an old man and a boy. The president caved in on demand of payment. And there was no sign of any British ship or crew; it had been simply an idle threat.

That same year, Hose returned to England aboard *Charybdis* where he was commissioned as commander of the gunboat *Ringdove*. In April 1905, she set sail for Newfoundland and there in July, the trim, slim Hose with the twinkle in his blue eyes, married Catherine Boone. At the end of the season, the protection of the fishery was part of the RN's duties, and in October, Hose and his wife returned to England aboard *Ringdove*. The following January, he was given command of

HMS *Redbreast*, a gunboat in the East Indies Station, whose job was to prevent gun running from Muscat for the Afghans. She also surveyed the pearl fishery beds in the Persian Gulf, for which Hose received the thanks of the Indian government.

By 1908 Hose was back in England where he attended a course in combined naval and military operations at the Military Staff College in Camberley, as well as the war staff course at the RN College in Greenwich. It was here that the foundation was laid to pave the way for his career with the Royal Canadian Navy during which he would help to forge it into the major weapon that overcame the German U-boat peril. During his stint in Newfoundland he had become aware of plans for creating a Canadian naval service. He had come to the attention of Admiral Sir Charles Edmund Kingsmill, who, more than any other person, had been responsible for the formation of the staff college and had become its first director. This originated through Hose's connection with Sir Percy Cox, a leading politician of the day, whom he accompanied on visits to the Arab tribes while serving in the Persian Gulf. While at the staff college, Hose and Kingsmill had corresponded with a view to Hose taking a senior command in the new service.

On December 31, 1908 Hose was elevated to the rank of commander and took charge of HMS *Cochrane*, one of the newest cruisers of the fleet. That was his last RN appointment. In June, 1911, the British Admiralty placed him on loan with the newly commissioned Canadian Naval Service which had been given royal assent a year earlier. At Esquimalt Dockyard in Vancouver BC, Hose took command of the naval station itself as well as of HMCS *Rainbow*, one of two cast-off British cruisers in service with what had now officially become the Royal Canadian Navy (RCN). Not long afterwards, in January 1912, Hose voluntarily retired from the RN to join the RCN, the service he would serve so faithfully and vigourously for the next 22 years.

Hose had stepped into a difficult, yet challenging situation. The minute force of just over 300 men was having trouble getting recruits in the West. Hose quickly recognized that a large part of the problem stemmed from the fact that few people knew (or, for that matter, cared) about the newly formed service's existence. Here Hose's experience in Newfoundland training RN reservists in the early 1900s, stood him in good stead. Borrowing a leaf from the Royal Navy Volunteer Reserve (RNVR) log he proposed setting up a reserve of "local citizen navy" units right across the country to create national awareness. It was ambitious, far too ambitious for the likes of Admiral Kingsmill, who pooh-poohed the notion. "My dear Hose, you don't understand," he admonished. "It can't be done." But despite his objections, in 1913, by which time *Rainbow*, in effect a training ship, was cruising off the coast of British Columbia, the minister for Naval Service, Patrick Brodeur, granted permission to form a reserve and begin training along the lines of the British volunteer force.

It began in a small way. Four pioneer-spirited young men from Victoria, BC, who had served with the RNVR in England, approached Hose, volunteering their services part-time. With absolutely no support from Kingsmill, Hose enthusiastically welcomed them and placed the facilities of the Esquimalt Dockyard and of *Rainbow*, at their disposal. They received no pay, had no official status, nor even any uniforms, but with the help and support of Hose and the officers and men of *Rainbow*, in no time their numbers grew to 33. Proudly they called themselves the Victoria Company of Volunteers. This beginning was to play a significant role in saving the Canadian navy. The genesis was the Liberal government's allocation of funds — finally — for a country-wide Naval Volunteer Reserve Force on July 3, 1914, in view of the obvious threat of an approaching war.

Meanwhile, *Rainbow* had been assigned patrol duty in the Straits of Juan de Fuca. Then on August 4, the day the Great War broke out, she was ordered south to find, and escort back to Esquimalt, two virtually defenceless RN sloops, HMS *Algerine* and *Shearwater*. They were heading north from San Diego, and could be threatened by two modern, heavily-armed German cruisers *Leipzig* and *Nurnberg*, lurking somewhere in the same waters. *Rainbow* was poorly equipped for the task. Her fresh supply of ammunition in the form of high explosive shells had arrived in Vancouver after *Rainbow* was already at sea. That left her with old-fashioned gunpowder-filled shells. And that wasn't the only shortcoming under which the 20-year-old warship sailed either.

Hose put into San Francisco to refuel and also in the hope there might be news of the British ships. There wasn't any, neither sloop had a radio. But *Leipzig* and *Nurnberg* had been reported off San Diego heading north — about a day away. Hose steamed out of the bay stationing himself near the Farallones Islands right in the enemy's path. He had calculated that by this time his British charges were somewhere to the west, perhaps even north. The Canadians' prospects were bleak, even downright hazardous. *Rainbow*'s speed of 19 knots could not match the enemy's 25. Her gun range of 4,000 yards compared to the Germans' 10,000. Hose's salvation seemed to be the Pacific fog. His only hope was that he could use the fog banks as cover and fight an action at close enough to do some damage and force the enemy to withdraw for repairs.

But by August 10, with her coal supply dwindling, *Rainbow* had to return to Esquimalt to refuel. Unbeknownst to the crew, the very next morning, *Leipzig* was reported to have appeared off the Farallones. She had learned that *Rainbow* had berthed in San Francisco and was on her trail. Then, on August 12, *Rainbow* sighted a three-funnelled ship dead ahead, closing fast. Action stations! Fortunately, it was a false alarm. The "enemy" turned out to be SS *Prince George*, a British merchant ship. After refuelling at Esquimalt, Hose sailed south again. By this time, thankfully, *Shearwater* had reached the Juan de Fuca Straits. After escorting her safely to Vancouver, *Rainbow* set off again and this time encountered *Algerine* 60 miles to the south and brought her back home to Esquimalt, as well.

On August 17 on learning that *Leipzig* had arrived in San Francisco, Hose set sail at once but was almost instantly recalled when word was received that *Nurnberg* had joined her sister cruiser in the American west coast port. His orders were to wait until the RN cruiser HMS *Newcastle*, which was on her way from Japan, joined him. Then, almost simultaneously, a three-funnelled cruiser was reported off Prince Rupert and *Rainbow* steamed north. It was a false alarm; the truth was that *Nurnberg* and *Leipzig* had never even come within 2,500 miles of the BC coast.

By the end of the month, *Newcastle* finally arrived in Vancouver. But by then, with Japan's entry into the war on the side of the Allies, the danger in the Pacific had passed. The German Far East fleet under Admiral Maximilian Graf von Spee simply wanted to get home, but was hotly pursued by all available RN ships. Hose requested permission to join them but it was denied. Kingsmill was fearful that if *Rainbow* was lost in action, he would be criticized for sending such an ancient ship into battle to "engage modern vessels." Hose had to settle for patrols no further south than the coast of Mexico, where *Rainbow*'s crew did manage to capture two German schooners.

On January 1, 1916, Hose was promoted to the rank of acting captain, and in April 1917 was transferred to *Niobe*, RCN Headquarters in Ottawa. It was his first shore appointment after 25 years of continuous sea duty. In August that same year Hose was made captain of patrols with the responsibility of taking charge of the East Coast Patrols. It was a complicated business made difficult by the Royal Navy's insistence on always having the upper hand and its stand-offish refusal to properly cooperate. The RN ran the ocean convoys reporting directly to the Admiralty in London. Coastal convoys and shipping came under the jurisdiction of the RCN reporting to Ottawa. There was little liaison between the two navies, and yet Hose, in charge of patrols, provided escorts for all of them, including the first leg to seaward of the ocean convoys. On top of this the Robert Borden government was unsympathetic to naval matters and acted as if the service didn't exist. The concentration was on the army's requirements in France.

When Hose took over he had 12 patrol vessels for his undertaking. It took all his considerable powers of persuasion, his native ability to get along with others, his administrative skill and his determination, to make the enterprise work. By April 1918, now a full captain, he had 55 ships at his disposal. He needed 2,300 men to man them but had only 1,500. He picked up a few reservists from Newfoundland and some others from the Admiralty, but it still never made up the needed complement. He requested fast sloops, destroyers, even fast trawlers to meet the looming U-boat menace. The British supplied nothing. However, the United States Navy did everything it could by providing patrols of its own and even supplied airplanes to enable the RCN to start its own Naval Air Service, which everyone agreed, in a U-boat war, would be essential.

The first U-boat crossed the Atlantic in May. Early in August submarines sank 10 Canadian fishing schooners off Nova Scotia and, in an attack on a convoy out of Halifax, an oil tanker was damaged. Two weeks later, six more schooners had gone to the bottom. In little over a month, 28 vessels had been sunk in Canadian waters. The U-boat menace had arrived with a vengeance. But the resulting publicity overshadowed the fact that most of these victims had been fishing ships, not military or merchant vessels. The RCN East Coast Patrol had made convoy protection possible at a critical place and time. With what Hose had to work with, this was nothing short of a miracle. As he reported, "The officers and men of the vessels are untrained, not only in the technical knowledge required to handle the weapons, and offensive appliances on board the ships, but also in service discipline, being drafted to ships as hardly more than raw recruits."

By the end of the war in November 1918, Hose had a fleet of 130 patrol ships under his command and the responsibility for safeguarding 100,000 miles of water. Soon, the situation quickly reversed itself. On December 1, Hose was transferred to headquarters in Ottawa to oversee the demobilization of the Patrol Service.

Having completed that duty, on May 20 he became senior naval officer of the Halifax Dockyard where, for the next year he fought to keep what was left of the navy intact and attempt to modernize it. Following the cessation of hostilities, the RCN acquired two submarines, one cruiser and two destroyers from the Admiralty. Originally the British had tried to foist off an old coal-burning cruiser on the Canadians, but gritty little Hose dug in his heels. Under no circumstances would he agree to such a sale. The Admiralty, however, was insistent. It was that or nothing. Very well, Hose countered masterfully, in that case Halifax will stock only coal, no oil. And where would that leave the RN's new oil-fired cruisers wanting to refuel? The British backed down and Hose got his oil-fired cruiser, the HMCS *Aurora*.

In quick succession Hose, still as trim and slim as ever, was promoted to the rank of commodore, made assistant director of the Naval Service, as well as naval assistant to the minister for the Naval Service, Charles Ballantyne, then in January 1921, he succeeded Kingsmill as director of the Naval Service with headquarters in Ottawa. It was shortly afterwards that he faced the first of his two most severe crises in respect to the life, welfare and survival of Canada's navy.

By 1922, world temperament had changed dramatically and drastically since the end of the war, four years earlier. Military spending had given way to disarmament. That year, the newly elected Liberal government under William Lyon Mackenzie King had arbitrarily slashed the naval appropriation nearly in half, from $2.5 to $1.5 million. The navy's very existence was threatened.

Politically it should have come as no surprise and was probably as popular as any budget cut. With the change of government an incoming Cabinet minister told the outgoing minister of National Defence: "Now we'll sink your navy." The new defence Minister, Ned MacDonald, candidly admitted that "the truth is, the Navy is a damned nuisance."

It mattered little to the average Canadian who couldn't have cared less. The public probably had no idea what the navy had done, what it was doing, or even that there was one. It was this apathy, this lack of visibility, that motivated Hose's actions to save the navy. "I had long felt," he said later, "that the only way to make Canadians in the vast inland areas realize their dependence on the sea was to establish naval training centres across the country, and I realized that this was the time to make the change."

But first, how to judicially spread a limited budget to cover the navy's needs? A realist, Hose had no compunction about taking drastic measures to achieve it. He deliberately scrapped the Royal Canadian Navy as a force and, harking back to his pre-war days of training reservists aboard *Rainbow*, concentrated his efforts and spent every cent he could get his hands on to build and train the Royal Canadian Volunteer Reserve.

Hose returned *Aurora* and the two submarines to the Royal Navy. That left a destroyer and two trawler minesweepers each in Vancouver and Halifax and these would be devoted to training reservists. He cut back shore installations and reduced the RCN force to a mere 366 officers and men. At the same time, he made it abundantly clear that the main function of this diminutive permanent force would be to "foster, encourage and train the RCNVR." He closed the Youth Training Establishment for young sailors in Halifax and shut down The Naval College there. From now on junior officers for the RCN would be trained with the RN cadets in England.

With Hose's guidance and foresight, in 1923 the RCNR and the RCNVR came into being, and from that day forward a new concept in naval strength for Canada took hold. The Royal Canadian Naval Reserve was an organization set up to register trained and experienced merchant service officers and men from the country's ports who agreed to serve in the event of emergency.

The purpose of the Royal Canadian Volunteer Reserve was to recruit civilians who could be trained to form a nucleus from which men could be recruited in the event of war, and at the same time provide the machinery to handle that enlistment. Hose sent staff officers into towns and cities across the Dominion to speak to civic groups and service groups and headquarters were set up in 16 different cities.

A RCNVR rating was paid 25 cents per drill and given such uniforms as could be found. Officers were paid nothing and had to provide their own uniforms. A highlight was summer training on both coasts under the guidance of professionals — at sea. Hose regarded the formation of the reserve as his greatest accomplishment, and with some justification. By 1939, when the Second World War began, the RCNVR had some 2,000 officers and men (many of whom had never been to sea) which about equalled the number in the permanent navy.

But, back in 1922, Hose had to face yet another problem. The military economies exercised by the government, necessitated placing the air force, the army, and the navy all under one roof — the Department of National Defence. This meant that the chief of staff, Major General James MacBrien, was the chief adviser to the government — the minister of defence — for all three services. This, Walter Hose could not, would not abide. Sure the navy was small, but as its head, he demanded access to the government on naval matters. This created a precarious situation all round. But Hose held an ace card, an ally, in the person of the deputy minister, George Desbarats, who was sympathetic to the RCN and went to bat for him. The issue came to a head when MacBrien resigned as chief of staff in frustration, and that position simply vanished. Finally, Walter Hose was appeased — and pleased — when, in 1928, he became the first chief of Naval Staff. Then, in 1933, the axe fell again.

By that time the post of chief of the General Staff had been created and it was filled by Major General Andrew McNaughton, the brilliant artillery officer from the Great War. But he was certainly no military defence strategist. At the depth of the Great Depression it was only natural that the government would be forced to trim its operating costs. In 1933 it proposed a drastic budget reduction, cutting a whopping $14 million. This was particularly devastating for the navy. Its own appropriation was to be decreased by $2 million.

But McNaughton had an even brighter idea. Why not dispense with the navy altogether? His army experience led him to believe that the only defence needed was a standing army. This thinking extended to the air force too — with modern anti-aircraft weapons he was convinced the day of the warplane was doomed. His approach on the subject of the navy appealed to the economy-conscious Treasury Board. But they reckoned without the small, scrappy chief of Naval Staff.

Hose advised the Cabinet, the Treasury Board, the chief of the General Staff, and anyone else he could buttonhole, that a budget cut of $200,000 was the maximum the navy could stand to stay afloat. Contrary to McNaughton's reasoning, he argued, Canada needed a navy for several solid reasons. One of them was to prevent being drawn into a war between the United States and Japan, a not unlikely prospect at the time. Also if war came — and with Hitler becoming chancellor of Germany that year, that could certainly not be ruled out — the navy would be necessary to protect Canada's growing trade.

If the government persisted in slashing the appropriation as proposed, Hose stated flatly, he would have no choice but to take his last ships out of service, rather than cut down his precious, infant reserves. His reasoning was that, in the event of emergency, he could always beg, borrow, buy or even steal ships, but not trained personnel. To firmly emphasize and establish his point, he further contended that no navy could possibly operate effectively or economically, below a certain size. And it couldn't be improvised from scratch in the event of war. So, if the government passed its resolution, it would effectively destroy the RCN, with all its 900 men, and he, Hose, would be forced to resign.

In his outspoken, persistent and determined way, Hose had made his point and won the day. Since a navy without ships, or men — and above all — without Walter Hose, would be ludicrous, the government looked elsewhere for budget cuts. It had been a close call though. If Hose hadn't stuck to his guns the navy would have disappeared.

Hose had one more score to settle before he retired from the RCN on Dominion Day, 1934. Though McNaughton had failed in his absurd bid to abolish it, he wasn't quite through with the navy just yet. He now announced his intention to act as its inspector general. But Hose, with the support and help of the minister of defence, James Ralston, killed that attempt. Hose, who likened the development of the RCN to an ugly duckling transformed into a "splendid swan," held the defence minister in the highest esteem. "Under Ralston," he said, the usual twinkle in his eye, "the Swan's feathers began to appear."

At the same time that Walter Hose was hanging up his gold-braided rear admiral's cap, Rollo Mainguy, then serving with the RN's America and West Indies Station as a lieutenant commander on special radio duties, was well on his way to earning an admiral's headdress of his own. Like Hose he began his naval career at an early age.

The son of a farmer from Guernsey in the Channel Islands, Mainguy was born on May 11, 1901 in the Westholm lumbering town of Chemainus on Vancouver Island, BC where, as a young lad, he became a bell-ringer for Westholm Church. In August 1915, when he was 15 years old, he entered the Royal Naval College of Canada in Halifax. His training was cut short temporarily on the morning of December 6, 1917 when the French steamer *Mont Blanc* detonated alongside a jetty, creating the largest man-made explosion before Hiroshima. Damage to the city was devastating. It destroyed, among other installations, the naval college. Mainguy, who was aboard a vessel nearby at the time, was injured by flying glass.

Upon graduation in 1918, as a midshipman during the closing months of the Great War, he was assigned, first to HMS *Canada*, a battleship of the Grand Fleet and veteran of the Battle of Jutland, then to the HMS *Barham*, where he was promoted to acting sub-lieutenant and afterwards, to full sub-lieutenant. He then returned to Canada where, in 1921 he served aboard *Aurora*, the oil-fired cruiser the wily Hose had inveigled from the RN, and later aboard HMCS *Patriot*. That same year, Mainguy was promoted to the rank of lieutenant.

In 1923, Mainguy became very much a part of Hose's concentration on building and training the reserve. At the time his specialty was signals and, after completing a specialized long signals course at HMS *Victory*, he was appointed signal officer at HMCS *Naden*, the RCN naval establishment at Esquimalt, BC. His capacity for administration and the handling of personnel were soon recognized and his next appointment, in 1926, was that of supervising officer of the Western Division of the RCNVR with headquarters in Ottawa. At the time he married Maraquita Nichol and the couple eventually had three children: Daniel, who followed in his father's footsteps, a second son, Christopher, and a daughter, Quita.

Two years later, Mainguy was attached to the Royal Navy for additional training and experience, serving as signal officer and flag lieutenant to the vice admiral of the 1st Cruiser Squadron aboard HMS *Frobisher*. Then, in 1930, he was made executive officer of the destroyer HMCS *Vancouver* with the rank of lieutenant commander. The next year he joined the RN America and West Indies Station for special radio duties. Following that five-year stint he returned to Canada again where he served aboard the destroyer HMCS *Saguenay*. Then, in 1936, having attained the rank of commander, he was placed in charge of the destroyer on which he had earlier served as executive officer, the *Vancouver*. A year later, he was appointed director of Naval Reserves.

With the Second World War only eight months away, Mainguy took a staff course at the Royal Naval Staff College in Greenwich, England, and on completing it, in October 1939, he was given command of the destroyer HMCS *Assiniboine*. That winter he saw his first action at sea in the Caribbean when his destroyer joined forces with a British cruiser code-named *"Dash"* to capture the German steamer *Hannover*. It was more a case of saving the enemy ship than seizing it, but this turned out to be just as formidable a struggle.

When the British cruiser intercepted the steamer, the German crew did their best to try and scuttle it. They set fires on the decks and in the holds. They jammed the windlasses and steering gear and threw the anchors overboard before abandoning ship in small lifeboats. By the time *Assiniboine* reached the scene it was dark and a landing party from *"Dash"* had already gone aboard to do their best to salvage the situation with the eerie knowledge that explosive charges had probably been planted and set to explode. To make matters worse, it was a rough sea, and because the Germans had untied the ship's cargo, *Hannover* was pitching fore and aft as well as from side to side.

Smoke belched from every hold, and in the glare of *Assiniboine's* searchlights men could be seen scurrying about trying to put out the fires. *"Dash"* had gone off to hunt down the fleeing Germans in their lifeboats, leaving *Assiniboine* alone to try to help put out the fires by playing her hoses on the steamer. By dawn another problem presented itself. *Hannover* was drifting towards territorial waters where, under international law, the prize would be lost. Mainguy ran his destroyer alongside and had her lashed her to the steamer to push her out to sea. In his own words, "There was quite a sea, and we were bumping. We threw a wire aboard and made it fast and then the destroyer moved out to sea stern first. It was the easiest way to handle the problem — like an angry bulldog on the end of a rope."

By this time *"Dash"* had returned, and being the higher powered of the two warships, took over the towing chore, while *Assiniboine* got in as close as she dared to play her hoses on the burning steamer which had taken on a dangerous list. In addition, the wind had increased and the sea had turned rougher. Both destroyer and steamer were rolling heavily, *Hannover* lurching frighteningly. This is the way Mainguy described it: "It was a very ticklish business. Sometimes we were touching the *Hannover*, jammed right up against her side; sometimes we were a few feet away, but most of the time we maintained a distance of about three feet. We had to do that fire hose task a couple of times, when the fire blazed up again."

After six nightmarish days and nights of battling the elements — the wind and the sea — of fighting fires with the ever present danger of the enemy vessel being blown up, *Assiniboine* and *"Dash,"* with *Hannover* securely lashed between them, triumphantly, if a little wobbly, finally brought their prize into port at Kingston, Jamaica.

But Mainguy's chief duties during those early stages of the war were in the Atlantic as senior officer of some of the first convoy escort groups. In 1940 he transferred from *Assiniboine* to take command of another Canadian destroyer, HMCS *Ottawa* in which he directed the first ever Royal Canadian Navy sinking of a German U-boat. A controversial kill it turned out to be.

Shortly after midnight on November 9, in answer to a distress call from a merchant ship, Mainguy, the senior officer of the escort, together with a British destroyer, found a surfaced submarine blasting away at the cargo vessel. As they closed in, the marauding U-boat submerged. Both destroyers tried to set up a coordinated attack. In turns, one escort tracked the submarine while the other dropped depth charges. For three hours they relentlessly made nine different assaults in this fashion, unloading a total of 80 depth charges — 12 tons of explosives — with no apparent result.

However, later that night they heard several explosions. Then, as morning dawned, diesel oil was spotted oozing to the surface. Mainguy and his RN counterpart were certain they had a kill. The commander in charge of escort vessels in Liverpool agreed. But the Admiralty's U-boat Assessment Committee did not. Yes, they admitted, there were explosions, and fuel had leaked to the surface. But that was a common German trick. And there had been no confirmation that a submarine had been destroyed. Also, no wreckage had been sighted. Laconically, the committee members allowed the destroyers a "probably damaged," smugly satisfied that they had covered all the bases.

But they were wrong. Dead wrong. After the war, Italian officials firmly established and confirmed that one of their U-boats — *Faa di Bruno* — had indeed been sunk in the early hours of November 9. Its demise, and the fact that it had been the RCN's first submarine victory, had gone unrecognized all that time. If the U-Boat Assessment Committee had still been in existence when the truth came to light, would it have corrected its judgement? It certainly should have. Anyway, at the very least an apology should have been in order. However, the history of such instances would indicate that this would be wishful thinking at best.

In 1941, Mainguy was promoted to the rank of captain and given the post of captain (D) — in charge of destroyer escorts — in Halifax. Later that year, with the establishment of the Newfoundland Escort Group, he filled the same position in Newfoundland. It was his term there, during which he showed such intense interest in the welfare of his men, (such as founding the Crow's Nest Club for officers and inaugurating a rest and recreation camp for ratings in the interior of the Avalon peninsula) that inevitably led to his next appointment. In November 1942, he became chief of Naval Personnel headquartered in Ottawa. At the same time he was also made the third member of the Naval Board.

After holding that post for almost two years, in 1944 Mainguy was given command of Canada's first modern cruiser, HMCS *Uganda*. Original plans called for her to act as the vanguard of a fleet of 60 Canadian warships manned by some 13,500 men in the war against Japan in the Pacific. That never happened. *Uganda* was the only Canadian ship to take part in that fighting. On March 9, 1945, with the war against Germany in Europe still in progress, she arrived at Sydney, Australia, to join the British Pacific Fleet. On April 6, she set sail from Leyte in the Philippines to join the Royal Navy Task Force 57 which operated as part of the US Fifth Fleet, taking part in the struggle to capture Okinawa. Initially her only duty was keeping radar watch against approaching enemy planes — this was strictly an air show. Then on May 4 *Uganda* took part in a naval bombardment of Sukumu Airfield on Miyako Jima. Operation Iceberg saw the first sustained use of kamikazes by the Japanese. On May 9, the suicide planes concentrated their attacks on the British carriers *Formidable* and *Victorious*.

The *Uganda* escaped damage, and Mainguy and his crew had a ring-side seat from 3,500 yards away.

On June 12, after the conclusion of Iceberg, the force commander transferred his flag to *Uganda* and led his cruisers on a naval bombardment of Sakashima and Truk, shelling landing fields, shore installations and a seaplane base on Dublin Island.

By the first week of July, the naval war had moved into the home waters of Japan in preparation for an invasion. On the 16, *Uganda* sailed with the British Pacific Fleet to rendezvous with the US Third Fleet as the combined force bored in on the Japanese coastal waters to attack Honshu by air from the carriers. Moving in sight of land their planes bombarded Kure, Kobe and Nagoya. On July 26, the operation completed, the British fleet withdrew to refuel.

By this time Canada's policy for the Pacific War had finally been settled. Naval personnel could re-enlist for service in that theatre or not. Those who elected to do so were entitled to 30 days "Pacific Leave." As a result of this policy *Uganda*'s crew had the same option as everyone else and the cruiser was recalled to Esquimalt accordingly, where she arrived on August 10, the day after the Americans dropped the second atomic bomb, on Nagasaki.

Mainguy's wartime service earned him three awards, the Order of the British Empire "for gallantry and distinguished services before the enemy" as Senior Officer of Convoy Escort Groups, and two Mention in Despatches "for outstanding zeal, patience and cheerfulness, and for never failing to set an example of wholehearted devotion to duty."

During the early post-war months in 1946, *Uganda*, still under Mainguy's command, made a combined goodwill and training cruise around South America and became the first Canadian warship to round Cape Horn. On her return, in July, Mainguy was promoted to the rank of commodore and a month later was appointed Commanding Officer Pacific Coast with the rank of acting rear admiral. This was confirmed on July 1, 1947. Then, on October 1, 1948 he took up the post of flag officer, Atlantic Coast, making his home in the Admiral's House, the official residence of the FOAC.

About a year later, Brooke Claxton's commission to study and make recommendations concerning the current naval "mutinies," composed of Mainguy, as chairman, Louis Audette and Leonard Brockington, began work on what became widely celebrated as the Mainguy Report. It was a remarkable manifesto, truly a tour de force. The fine literary hand and mind of Leonard Brockington in the preface reflected the calibre of the entire document:

The times in which we live, like all post-war times, are full of restlessness, uncertainty and change. Wise men throughout the ages have observed that just as the sea after a great storm is troubled for many days and it is a long time before the winds are lulled and the calm settles upon the waters, so after every great conflict, there are turmoil and ferment in the affairs of mankind. The social and economic uncertainties and changes, which effect Canada as they do the world, and the general deterioration in the discipline of family life, which is one of the misfortunes of our times, press with particular intensity on the lives of young men. It would be a miracle if the comparative isolation of men within the walls of a ship at sea should protect them from the disturbing influences which harass their companions and contemporaries on shore.

In all, the commission conducted 238 in camera interviews ranging from the chief of the Naval Staff to the lowest rating, including 150 petty officers and ratings. Fifty men volunteered to come forward as a result of invitations run in the newspapers and on the radio. Witnesses included chaplains, medical officers, civil servants, as well as two journalists. The commission also went aboard the three ships involved — *Crescent, Athabaskan* and *Magnificent.* In addition, the commission visited the US naval establishment in Seattle, Washington to compare the modern American facilities with the outdated Canadian ones.

After reviewing the incidents and their causes, the commission found "no evidence of subversive or political activities," which was one of the chief concerns. A great deal of the trouble arose from the unpopularity of the three executive officers. "As a subject of criticism," the report stated, "he seems to be the equivalent of the proverbial Sergeant-Major…he is the pivot of the ship's routine and general discipline. If he fails to handle the ship's crew with tact, humanity, firmness and common sense, there is always the danger of trouble…we do not believe that sufficient care was exercised in the selection of Executive Officers."

The commission alleged that throughout the three ships — and indeed throughout the navy — changes in officers and men were made much too frequently to allow sufficient time to build a close relationship between them, which is needed to inspire confidence and establish mutual respect. In fact, there was found to be an absence of confidence, even between officers and petty officers, nominally the strongest link in naval discipline. As one high ranking officer put it:

I have heard several complaints — and that's the only thing I have heard — told to me by Chief and Petty Officers, that apparently they just don't matter, they are ignored, so there you have the middle of the string sagging; you have a void in your connection with the men. The backbone, you well know, is the Petty Officer. That is the only way you find out what is going on — Those fellows are useful, but not unless they get the support of the Officer.

All this had a bearing on what the commission termed an "artificial distance" between officers and men. The men didn't deny the officers their privileges but when the officers failed to live up to their responsibilities, resentment replaced respect. This amounted to a breakdown in discipline. As the report pointed out:

The only discipline which in the final analysis is worthwhile, is one based upon pride in a great service, a belief in essential justice, and the willing obedience that is given to superior character, skill, education and knowledge. Any other form of discipline is bound to break down under stress.

The report went on:

In Canada, many officers and men come from the same kind of home, and spend their boyhoods in playing baseball in the same lot, swimming in the same swimming hole and in playing "hookey" from the same school. With such a national background, it is more important that discipline should be based on the realities we have mentioned rather than on artificial distinctions.

The commission learned that one of the most serious factors in relation to the mutinies was the lack of effective communication and grievance procedures. In fact *Magnificent* did not even have one. As the report stated, these are "the most useful and proper safeguard against insubordination resulting from mass grievances." In all three cases there was no adequate method, in fact, no method at all of communicating mass grievances to the captain of each ship.

One of the main grievances from men interviewed was the lack of Canadian identity in the navy. The Mainguy Report had this to say:

There was amongst the men a very real and almost universal opinion that the Canadian Navy was not sufficiently Canadian.

The absence of identification on the uniforms of the Canadian ratings gave rise to many unpleasant incidents in which American sailors were present. While the incidents often resulted from ignorance, ill manners, and unfortunate national prejudices, there is no doubt that the relations between Canadian, American, and British sailors were greatly impaired by the continual mistaking Canadian ratings for British sailors…the men were vehement in their demands that they be identified as Canadians.

Recruiting methods also came in for harsh criticism from almost every witness interviewed. It was charged that advertising had been left to professional agencies who knew nothing about the navy. Furthermore the advertising contained false promises, misleading claims; "THE NAVY'S THE LIFE - Travel and Adventure in Fast new ships - Financial security Now, and a Pension for the Future," was a typical message. This, both men and officers agreed, was the wrong approach. The hardships of the sea, the manliness of the service and the appeal of practical patriotism was rarely, if ever, mentioned.

In the same breath navy public relations was judged unsatisfactory. The commission noted:

> There is the occasional suppression of stories of public concern with a result that exaggerated versions and incorrect rumours appear in the Press. The Navy is traditionally the "Silent Service." The result of this tradition is that many senior officers, not aware of the change in conditions which have been brought about by the war, are not sufficiently conscious of the necessity of good relations with the press and public. In peacetime, at least, a prompt statement of the plain truth is in the public's interest and right.

The Mainguy Report concluded its findings with 30 recommendations. As a starter it emphasized training. "It is our opinion," the commission asserted, "that the navy should be given breathing space for essential training and the strengthening of its men and ships." It suggested the establishment of one or more training ships and that these be commanded and staffed by officers specially selected for "both for teaching and learning."

The report recommended that the "bed of roses" or "beer and skittles" approach to recruiting be eliminated, and that naval officers be encouraged to take part in recruiting campaigns. It also stressed that neither the design nor the content of the publicity should be left to commercial advertising houses.

The commission also dealt with the education of recruits. They should be taught the traditions and customs of the Naval Service, and efforts should be made to make them understand their own importance in the navy, no matter how humble their tasks may be, and to realize what patriotism and service to one's country means. To this end it recommended that a booklet be published on the history of the Royal Canadian Navy and issued with the *Seamanship Manual*.

The report went to great pains to recommend vast improvements in living conditions for both single and married. These had been found to be inadequate, in some cases to the extreme. This extended to overhauling and broadening recreational facilities ashore and afloat.

One item that came in for attention was the showing of films at sea. There had been complaints that poor calibre movies were the usual fare. That put it mildly. A glaring example was a film featuring venereal disease, that was "shown over and over again!" The commission recommended that negotiations be made at the highest level with film distributors.

The serious question of identity was also given strong consideration. The report recommended that a "Canada" or "Royal Canadian Navy" shoulder badge be issued to all ranks. At the same time it advised that the Maple Leaf insignia on the funnels of RCN vessels identifying the ships as Canadian during World War II, be reinstituted.

The report tabled the commission's conclusions by summarizing that, while the incidents were indeed mutinies, apart from barring the doors aboard *Athabaskan* and *Crescent*, no force was used, nor was there any open defiance of higher officers' orders. However, there was no justification, and could be none for any form of mass insubordination, and in future, insubordination should be most severely punished. It also pointed out that had the various captains and executive officers been fully informed, and if there had been proper welfare committees in place, the incidents might have been prevented. The report ended by urging that the "legitimate grievances which we have outlined in our report should be promptly and sympathetically investigated and remedied."

The Mainguy Report was a Masterpiece! It was a classic example, a lesson, of how an inquiry into military wrongdoings should be properly conducted. It was the legacy of Admiral Mainguy — who liked to entertain his friends by strumming on a banjo — to the navy — and indeed to Canada's armed forces.

On December 1, 1951 Mainguy became the seventh chief of the Naval Staff of the Royal Canadian Navy, with headquarters in Ottawa. At that time he was promoted to the rank of vice admiral. In 1956 he retired and took over the presidency of the Great Lakes Waterways Development Association until he retired in 1965 to Qualicum on Vancouver Island. On April 29, 1979 he died in hospital at Nanaimo, BC. He was 77. Because he did not approve of funerals, his body was donated to science. He is commemorated by the Maritime Headquarters building in Halifax which was named after him.

Upon retirement, the first chief of the Naval Staff, Walter Hose, and his wife returned to England. During World War II, he offered his services to the Royal Navy but was turned down because of his age. However, he worked vigorously in the Air Raid Precaution Division of the Civil Defence. In 1945 he and Catherine moved back to Canada and settled in Kingston, Ontario, and later in Windsor. Hose continued to take a lively interest and pride in the navy. "If it had not been for the Canadian Navy the battle of the Atlantic could not have been won," he liked to say proudly. He became honourary president of the Windsor branch of the Naval Officers' Association of Canada, and was later appointed honorary president of the Naval Officers' Associations of Canada.

Hose's services to Canada's navy did not go unrecognized. He was awarded the Companion of the British Empire and the Royal Military College conferred upon him the degree of military science. In 1960, at age 84, he took the salute from the RMC graduating class. At the Dominion Council held in Windsor in 1965, he became the first officer honoured by the Naval Officers' Associations of Canada by being presented with their Gold Medal, the highest honour it can bestow, for his outstanding contributions to the association and the RCN.

Still slim, trim, ever the sailor, Hose was a regular visitor to HMCS *Hunter*, the reserve division in Windsor, where he continued to live with one of his two daughters, following the death of his wife in 1956.

Hose passed away suddenly on the night of June 21, 1965 at age 89. Probably as he would have wished, the "Father of Canada's Navy" was carried to his grave by six petty officers from the Royal Canadian Naval Reserve and buried with full military honours. On October 4, 1967, plaques honouring his memory were unveiled at the naval establishments on both coasts, as well as at *Hunter.*

Clifford MacKay McEwen
1896–1967

6

BLACK MIKE
Mike McEwen

On Monday, August 8, 1967, Bruce West of the *Globe and Mail*, began his daily column in his inimitable way:

> Yesterday morning, just as the first rays of the sun were reddening the eastern skies, as they had done during those dawn patrols of long ago, one of Canada's most illustrious fighting airmen departed on that mysterious journey which must be made by all men.

He was writing of the passing of the legendary Clifford MacKay McEwen. He was known as Black Mike for his swarthy complexion. "Nothing sinister," he liked to say. "I tan very easily to a dark shade." He had been a fighter ace in the Great War who had revolutionized combat tactics, took charge of flying instruction in peacetime, and became one of the greatest of all the bomber group commanders in World War II. The crowning point in his career was his arrival at Allerton Hall in Yorkshire on February 29, 1944, only three months before the Normandy invasion, to take charge of 6th Group Bomber Command of the Royal Canadian Air Force. It was about time. It had developed a sorry reputation and badly needed shaking up. A firm hand on the throttle had been long overdue.

Losses in the "chop group," as the airmen lamentably labelled it, were consistently higher than in any other. It also had the highest percentage of crews abandoning their sorties and failing to reach their targets. Excuses ran the gamut from mechanical failures to airsickness. Morale was at an all time low. Maintenance was shocking; 6 Group had the record of being the group with lowest percentage of aircraft ready for operations.

To the tall, stern-looking air vice-marshal with the dark moustache, it was obvious where the problem lay, just as it was to Air Chief Marshal Sir Arthur "Bomber" Harris, chief of RAF Bomber Command also, who had picked the brook no-nonsense, no-excuses McEwen for the job. There was a severe lack of both group leadership and discipline. Six Group was about to experience a vigorous change in each. From then on things around the Yorkshire airfields would never be quite the same again.

McEwen was born in Griswold, Manitoba on July 1, 1896. He received his education at Moose Jaw College and the University of Saskatchewan with aspirations of one day going into the ministry. But, upon graduation he enlisted in the Western Universities Battalion of the Canadian Army in 1916. On arrival in Great Britain, like so many other Canadians, he despaired of the idea of fighting in the trenches and, in June 1917, transferred to the Royal Flying Corps as a pilot.

On completing his flying training on Sopwith Camels at Reading, McEwen was posted to 28 Army Co-operation Squadron at Drogland in the Ypres Salient in France and was assigned to C Flight, commanded by the famous Captain Billy Barker, one of three Canadian airmen to win the Victoria Cross during the Great War.

McEwen did not fly his first patrol across enemy lines until November 29, 1917, by which time the squadron had been transferred to Gossa in Italy. This flight marked the very first RFC aerial offensive on the Italian front against the Austrian air force. McEwen learned fast. On February 18 of the new year, he scored his fifth enemy kill, qualifying himself as an air ace. The fight took place at 15,000 feet over Rustigno, but it was some time before the victory was confirmed. During the encounter, McEwen's goggles frosted up and he was unable to follow his victim, who was spinning down out of control, below 4,000 feet. Some weeks later the wreckage of the enemy plane was found near the Italian village where the combat occurred and McEwen was duly given credit.

In the meantime Barker had left the squadron to be replaced by Captain Stan Stanger and he and McEwen quickly became an inseparable Damon and Pythias type of aerial combat team. On the morning of May 2, 1918, the pair took off on an "OP" — Offensive Patrol —

across the Austrian lines in search of reconnaissance planes that had been hovering above the British positions. Over the town of Valdobbiadene, they sighted ten Albatros D-5 scouts shepherding a two-seater Aviatik observation plane. The two Canadians peeled over in a dive, McEwen playing the decoy to draw off the fighters, while Stanger concentrated on the two-seater. But the Aviatik pilot refused to play. Pushing his nose down to gather speed he streaked for home.

Now "Damon and Pythias" found themselves amid a horde of Albatroses which, no longer needing to protect their ward, came at them from all sides. But, all the while, Stanger kept his eyes on the fleeing Aviatik. Ignoring the fighters, he chased after it. It was, after all, the main prey. To bring it down meant putting an end to its photographic prying of Allied positions. Angling in from the port side, Stanger took a deflection shot that ripped into the two-seater. The Aviatik flopped onto its back then, pointing straight down, crashed to earth.

Stanger now returned to help out his teammate who, by this time, had got onto the tail of the closest Albatros and sent it into a dive spewing flames and smoke. By this time both pilots were nearly out of ammunition and decided to beat a hasty retreat. They dived to the deck and hedge-hopped their way home.

Another mission assigned to British scout pilots at the time was close escort to bomber formations, as well as reconnaissance planes. This placed the fighter on the defensive when essentially its role was an offensive one — to take the initiative. This gave the enemy every advantage. He could choose the best position from which to attack (such as, from above, preferably hidden by cloud) and the exact moment to execute it. To McEwen this seemed all wrong. Borrowing a leaf from the wars in pioneer times in North America, when scouts were sent out ahead, he initiated the idea of assigning part of the escorts to sweep ahead and search out the lurking enemy patrols. At the time this seemed radical. In fact, it was this very tactic used in World War II in daylight operations that won the Allies fighter supremacy.

On June 19, 1918, McEwen successfully but quite accidently proved his theory, and it almost cost him his life. He and two other pilots had been assigned close escort duties to cover a pair of Bristol two-seater reconnaissance planes. At 15,000 feet above the Austrian lines, six Berg scouts appeared above, closing in on the Bristols from behind. When one of the two-seater observers spotted them, he fired off a Very pistol warning flare. Only McEwen saw it, and he immediately turned into the attack. On their first pass the enemy fighters missed the Bristols completely. They wheeled away to reform behind a cloud bank unaware that McEwen was right on their trail. As soon as he came within range he opened fire and, for the first time, realized he was all alone. However, he had no choice but to attack. A burst from his machine-guns sent one of the Bergs plunging down in flames. Then he sighted on a second enemy fighter and it, too, fell to his guns. Now the remaining four Bergs closed in on the lone Camel.

McEwen decided to make tracks. He dived to the ground hotly chased by the four Austrians. Deftly he steered his nimble little Camel into the Astico valley. The high hills on either side made it impossible for the lumbering Bergs to follow him. It had been a risky venture but McEwen had come through with flying colours and had made his point. His initiative in attacking the marauding enemy fighters had destroyed the advantage they thought they had and had robbed them of their objective of interfering with the Bristols' mission of carrying out their photographic reconnaissance work. These tactics, inaugurated by McEwen, soon became standard procedure and carried over to the next generation of Allied fighter pilots.

On October 4, 1918, together with Stanger, McEwen was able to demonstrate his tactic again. The two Canadians had been picked to escort two bomb-carrying Camel fighter squadrons for a raid on Campoformido airfield. This was a long-range sortie through airspace infested with Austrian fighters. Fighters had been chosen to carry the bombs because once they had dropped their loads they could fight their way back to their own lines. McEwen and Stanger flew top cover for the formation. As they neared the target they saw six Albatros D-5's below them poised to attack the bomb-carriers. Wasting no time, they plunged down sending two of the enemy fighters crashing into the ground.

The attack completely broke up the remaining Austrians who high-tailed it for home. McEwen and Stanger chased after them. Stanger opened from long range but his aim was true, shooting pieces off the Albatros, which splashed into the marshes of the Taliamento River. Finally the Canadians were forced to give up the pursuit and returned to join the bomber formation.

That was Black Mike McEwen's last operational flight. He finished the war officially credited with 24 1/2 enemy planes destroyed and was decorated with the Military Cross, the Distinguished Flying Cross and Bar, the French Legion of Honour, as well as the Italian Medaglio Valori and Croce de Guerra.

Following the armistice, McEwen transferred to the newly organized Canadian Air Force which had been formed on August 5, 1918, and became a member of No. 1 Squadron stationed at Upper Heyford in Oxfordshire flying Sopwith Dolphin and SE 5 fighters. But, in June 1919, the British government cut off all further financing and the CAF was disbanded, the last of its members, McEwen among them, returning to Canada in February 1920.

That same year the Air Board resurrected the CAF in Canada by setting up a training establishment at Camp Borden, Ontario, a former RFC training field. The service's main duties were fishing patrols and forestry work. McEwen was engaged in forestry photo surveying, mapping and testing. Then, on April 1, 1924 as one of a force of 66 officers (along with 194 other ranks) he became a member of the Royal Canadian Air Force.

By this time McEwen was an instructor who had developed an ability, as one of his superior officers put it, "…to stimulate the enthusiasm essential to good work among the junior officers." This led to his appointment as commanding officer, with the rank of wing commander in the mid-1930s, of the newly constructed Trenton air station on the shore of Lake Ontario. It gradually replaced Camp Borden as the RCAF's principal flying training station. It was there that McEwen earned his reputation as "a stickler for discipline." In fact he was the only officer in the entire air force entitled to carry the swagger stick of a trained and graduated disciplinarian. He proudly wore it on ceremonial and special occasions.

But if McEwen could be stern on the parade square and was equally insistent that flying rules and regulations be strictly obeyed, as an individual it would be hard to find anyone more amiable, gracious and courteous. A family man with three daughters, he had a courtly manner in the company of ladies and would rise to his feet when a padre entered his office.

With the advent of the Second World War, Trenton became the hub of the British Commonwealth Air Training Plan and the home of the Central Flying Training School. It maintained such high standards due to the groundwork and administrative ability of McEwen's tenure as CO. His next command, in 1942, was that of air officer commanding RCAF Coastal Command in Newfoundland but his real yearning was for an overseas appointment and he constantly hounded his superiors for one. Eventually he got his wish but it was not quite as he had hoped. He had his heart set on a Tactical Air Force command where he would be among fighter pilots. Instead, with the rank of air commodore, he was given command of one of the 6 Group bomber fields in Yorkshire. This experience served to provide him with first-hand knowledge of the weaknesses that permeated the entire group of the six four-engine bomber squadrons command.

To begin with 6 Group had its own peculiar set of circumstances, one being geographic, and another atmospheric. Its Yorkshire location was the most northerly of any group in Bomber Command. This was not exactly suited, or even conducive, to the group's operational role of long-range night bomber sorties. Its crews had to fly further and were in the air longer than any other. The rolling, hilly countryside created its own set of problems. Of necessity, fields were located in the one suitable area of the county and this placed them close together—too close. Frequently landing circuits overlapped and as a result, on returning to land in the dark, even with navigation lights turned on, there was the inevitable risk of collision. This danger was intensified by the smog from nearby industrial complexes, which, combined with the low clouds that persisted in that part of the country, seriously reduced night visibility. This hazard, coming at the end of a nerve-racking distant flight, deep into enemy territory and back, often in a damaged aircraft with wounded aboard, did nothing to inspire confidence. As a result the quality of the group's flying had suffered seriously.

Just like Gregory Peck in the Hollywood epic *Twelve O'Clock High*, in which a US Flying Fortress bomber commander took over a group that had lost confidence in itself, as the new air officer commanding (AOC) RCAF 6 Group Bomber Command, McEwen focused on the key element that was at the heart of all the group's failings — its flying! He immediately ordered an intense schedule of training. Including cross-country runs, fighter affiliations, bombing practice, link trainer blind instrument exercises, drill and lectures too!

McEwen's next target was morale. The group lacked pride and team spirit. McEwen took aim on the dress code. There would be no more "operational" floppy hats. Pilots had to put the hatbands back in, act, dress, and look like officers and NCO's, not like a bunch of prima donnas. And that applied to ground crews as well as aircrews.

They didn't like it — at first. The flight training irked them, particularly those with 20 or more operational flights (ops) under their belt. They scoffed at all that spit and polish bullshit! Who was this guy? Who the hell did he think he was? But the attitude quickly changed — literally overnight.

A few days after assuming command, McEwen demonstrated that he hadn't earned those two rows of gongs under his wings for nothing. He established conclusively that he was no swivel-chaired AOC, no pukka parade paragon. Late one afternoon he called Bill Swetman, the CO of 426 Squadron over at Linton-on-Ouse, and told him to save him a seat in his Lancaster for that night's show. Somewhat taken aback, Swetman replied "Certainly sir," then wondered what that was all about. The Old Man going along for the ride? There was a superstition among aircrews about carrying brass along on ops. It was asking for the chop. But Swetman had no choice.

The mission was a hairy one, buffeted by strong winds and a bomber-stream so crowded that some of the aircraft, much to McEwen's ire, turned on their navigation lights. It was one way to reduce the risk of collision, but also a sure way to attract enemy night fighters. It was a long, uncomfortable, seemingly endless flight to and from the target, and flak had been unusually heavy. Thankfully cloudy weather prevented interference by night fighters. Swetman's Lancaster was one of the last to return to base and his problems weren't over yet.

On his landing approach, he had to dive to avoid ramming another Lancaster that suddenly loomed directly ahead. Then, once on the ground he was forced to swerve abruptly to prevent piling into another aircraft taxiing in the wrong direction towards him. After bringing his Lancaster to a stop, and switching off the engine, Swetman climbed down, thankful that the AOC's first ride bomber raid had gone off without serious incident. McEwen, who had been totally unperturbed throughout the sortie, reached forward to shake the bomber captain's hand, not only to commend him for masterful display of combat flying but also to congratulate him in completing his second tour of operations.

McEwen's regular presence on operational flights was soon taken for granted by his aircrews, the superstition long forgotten. In fact, it had became a good luck symbol to have the "man with the moustache" along as part of the crew. Furthermore, it won their respect for an AOC who was willing to share their dangers with them. But it could not last. When Bomber Harris heard of these capers, he grounded McEwen from further operational flights. He was relegated to having to sweat it out on the ground, a commander unable to sleep at night when his men were out on a raid without him.

The crews began to realize that the flying practice was paying off too. Losses due to flying accidents were reduced sharply, and bombing was more accurate. Shortly after McEwen took over, 6 Group made an incredible 11 raids without a single casualty, at a time when the RAF groups suffered the loss of a total of 114 bombers. Morale began to soar. They even took pride in the dress code. *Time* magazine reported: "They scorn casual attire. The wire is in their caps...and they appear ready for a dress parade...men of all squadrons [in the group] consider themselves the cream of the RCAF." These were "Black Mike's Boys" now.

During the period of just over 14 months until the end of the war on May 8, 1945, under McEwen's leadership, 6 Group, which had grown from six squadrons to 15, had performed a variety of tasks, and performed them magnificently. The main concentration, of course, was bombing industrial Germany. Despite Bomber Harris' protestations, he was forced to support the invasion of Normandy with what was called the "Transportation Plan" to paralyse all railway movement in the occupied countries. Following the invasion itself there were tactical targets to be bombed, and other attacks were on naval installations, coastal batteries and submarine pens. Sea mining, or Gardening, as it was known, became an important assignment. Six Group was considered so "experienced and advanced" in the technique that its methods were studied by the Australians for application in the Pacific.

The risks involved varied with the type of operation. For instance, there was a big difference between a raid on Nuremburg deep into Germany and an attack on the Lille marshalling yards in northern France. During a sortie against Nuremburg, the bombers would be hounded by night fighters all the way from the German border to and from the target with losses as high as 94 aircraft lost, 13 of them crewed by Canadians. The only danger in a raid on Lille would be sporadic heavy flak which caused negligible damage or loss to the attackers. Recognizing this, McEwen, ever alert to the need for updating, initiated a point system to determine the length of an operational tour. Under the revised method, instead of arbitrarily "screening" aircrews after completing 30 sorties, the yardstick applied was 120 points computed at four points for an op over Germany, but only three points for a raid on occupied territory or a lightly defended target. The final decision as to whether or not a target was considered heavily defended, rested with Black Mike himself, who advised the various bases on the day of the raid.

Six Group flew its last op, a daylight operational sortie, on April 25, 1945, two weeks before World War II ended. The target was two coastal batteries on Wagerooge Island, at the eastern end of the Frisian Chain (three points). Twelve Canadian squadrons — 100 Lancasters and 92 Halifaxes — participated in the raid. No enemy fighters were encountered, thanks to a Spitfire fighter escort, and flak was negligible. However, four aircraft from 6 Group were lost in mid-air collisions.

By that time, the group had dropped a total of 126,122 tons of bombs, destroyed 116 aircraft and sunk or damaged 438 ships. It had also received 2,230 awards for gallantry. Under McEwen's command it had the lowest casualties while flying the highest number of sorties and delivering the greatest amount of destruction of any other group in Bomber Command. Arthur Harris, its commander-in-chief, had high praise for McEwen's leadership:

> I regard this officer's contribution to the efficiency and effect of the bomber offensive as invaluable. In ability as in personality he stood out amongst his fellows. He is a great commander and the value of his work was a major contribution towards the success that was achieved. I cannot speak too highly of him or of his share, and his Group's share, in the common effort.

Eight squadrons from the group, under McEwen's leadership, were earmarked for combat duty in the Pacific. But this special "Tiger Force," as it was named, was disbanded with the Japanese surrender. On November 1, 1945 it was officially taken off active service.

For his World War II service, McEwen was made a commander of the Bath and awarded the US Legion of Merit (degree of commander). He was also awarded an honorary doctor of law degree from his old alma mater, the University of Saskatchewan. Following his retirement from the air force, after 40 years of military flying service, he still retained his interest in aviation. Living in Toronto, he became a consultant to aircraft manufacturers. He also kept up a close association with veterans' groups, serving as vice-president of the Canadian Legion and of the Dominion Council of the Last Post.

McEwen never lost his zest in flying, and between 1959 and 1961 served as a director of Trans Canada Air Lines (Air Canada). Whenever he travelled he always talked his way into the cockpit. Don Lamont, one of his wartime bomber pilots and later a TCA captain, recalled that whenever McEwen joined him on the flight deck he liked to chat, not about the airline's business but about the "good old days" at 6 Group.

Air Vice-Marshal Black Mike McEwen, the "man with the moustache," passed away peacefully after a brief illness on Sunday, August 6, 1967 at Sunnybrook Hospital in Toronto and was buried with full military honours. May his legend live long after him!

Guy Granville Simonds
1903–1974

7

MILITANT MASTER OF COMMAND
Guy Simonds

Picture Guy Granville Simonds in his Royal Military College cadet uniform, pillbox cap worn at a jaunty angle to one side, or astride his horse in full dress as a battery officer with the Royal Canadian Horse Artillery. You can see him next wading ashore off the coast of Sicily in summer khaki shorts as a major general commanding the Canadian First Division. In Italy, wearing battledress, as CO of the Fifth Armoured Division, he is seen conferring with British Eighth Army commander Field Marshal Sir Bernard Montgomery. Then, during the Battle of the Scheldt in Holland, he is photographed while complaining bitterly to the Canadian minister of National Defence, the Honourable James Ralston, of the shortage of trained replacements. To complete this pictorial essay, Simonds is seen with the British prime minister, the Right Honourable Winston Churchill, among others, while viewing the Allied airborne crossing of the Rhine in Germany.

All these form a composite caricature of a handsome, athletic, domineering, elegant figure, neat and orderly, impeccably turned out, immaculately groomed, his jet-black hair with a trace of grey, worn short, bushy black eyebrows framing icy-blue eyes and the inevitable military moustache curled up at both ends. He is a man completely confident, composed, self-possessed and in absolute control of himself, a perfectionist, perfectly at ease with those in high places, a military professional through and through. And, depending on where you stood, a perfect prick.

Montgomery called Simonds "the most brilliant general Canada produced...a first class soldier." Of that there was no doubt. General Sir Harold Alexander echoed that appraisal when he wrote, "I know of no Canadian other than Guy Simonds in whom I should have confidence..."

Gifted with a driving ambition, as a leader, Simonds was an ardent student — and teacher — of military history, strategy, tactics and weaponry. A master of manoeuvre, he knew how to coordinate and make effective use of all the elements — air, land and sea. A clear thinker, blessed with an extraordinary memory, he could explain operations precisely, without notes. Innovative, flexible and tireless he succeeded at every step of his career. As his responsibilities increased and he was promoted in rank, his performance improved. He was a better corps commander than he was a division commander and a better army commander, than a corps commander and probably the best chief of staff the army ever had.

But there was a price to pay. He was as friendless as he was unfriendly. It didn't matter. What counted was his military career and how best that could serve his country. Simonds was a very private sort who refused to share his feelings with others. If fact, he made it a rule never to allow himself to develop a friendship with those upon whom he depended, and he always kept his subordinates at arm's length.

Cold and remote, he was aloof, arrogant, opinionated and devoid of a sense of humour. He took himself so seriously that his tense, clinical, unfriendly manner made him highly unpopular. He had no time for small talk and in the mess when the conversation turned to subjects other than military he did nothing to disguise his boredom and disgust.

Simonds set punishing standards for his staff and had an uncanny ability for sizing up their character and capabilities. He would not abide dishonesty, lack of energy and mistakes that cost men's lives. He ruthlessly weeded out the inefficient and ineffectual. Any officer who did not contribute to success did not last long under Simonds. He was known as a "good butcher," for giving people the sack when he had to. Many a subordinate trembled at the thought of one of his tongue-lashings for incompetence or breach of conduct or disobeying orders. As one staff officer put it, "When Guy became angry he was icy." Oscar Lange, a chief clerk on his staff, remembered him as, "A strict disciplinarian. He expected no less than excellence from everyone under his command. He looked like a soldier, he acted like a soldier. He was stern and he was clever. He stood for no nonsense."

Simonds was intolerant of malingering, straggling and absenteeism under the guise of "battle exhaustion." He drove himself so hard he had little sympathy for the hardships of others. As one of his divisional commanders, Major General Chris Vokes, said of him, "when it came

to dealing with personnel, Guy wasn't worth a pinch of coon shit!"
Vokes was both right and wrong. Simonds, in fact, was a very shy,
lonely person, and when away from his command, on leave in London,
for instance, could be witty and good-natured. And even in the field,
he did have a human side, as we shall see.

In the fall of 1944 all Simonds' qualities, pro and con, were put to
the acid test in what was to become his finest hour in the field: the campaign to free the Scheldt Estuary of the Germans and allow Allied
shipping into the port of Antwerp.

Following the Battle of Normandy in August, by pulling up short of
Antwerp, the British 11th Armoured Division had allowed three German armies to escape. By September 6, they had manned the key
fortress of Flushing on Walcheren Island north of the estuary and had
begun to mine the river. It now fell to the Second Canadian and the
First British Corps under General Harold Crerar, to capture Antwerp
and clear both sides of the estuary. Initially Montgomery, commander
of the 21st Army Group, had given priority to clearing the channel
ports, but by September 12 he had changed his mind and switched the
emphasis to opening Antwerp. Instead of changing direction at once,
Crerar continued to concentrate on mopping up the channel ports
much to the disgust of Simonds, then commander of the Second Corps.

However, planning finally got underway for a seaborne assault on
Walcheren. Simonds proposed that the dykes in West Copelle be
bombed to flood that part of the island and make an assault from the sea
practical. But Crerar, on the advice of his First Army engineering staff,
rejected the idea on the basis that the flooding would be insufficient for
the operation. Simonds insisted that an attempt at least be made. "If it
failed we had lost nothing," he urged. "If it succeeded we stood to gain
much." Crerar finally relented and on September 26, requested bombing
assistance from 84 Group of the Royal Air Force Tactical Air Force.

Next day Crerar flew to England to undergo medical tests for a
severe case of anaemia stomach disorder. This was a most fortuitous
turn of events for Simonds. Taking over command of the First Army,
he was now in complete charge of the Scheldt campaign — and of his
own destiny. It was as if his whole life had been in readiness for this
moment and this opportunity. And no one had better trained or prepared himself for it.

***

The erratic behaviour of his parents had a decided influence on the character and ambition of Guy Granville Simonds. Descended from a long
line of British army officers dating back to his great-grandfather who had

served in the army of the Honourable East India Company, his father, Cecil Simonds, had been commissioned in the Royal Artillery and had served in the Boer War shortly before Guy was born on April 23, 1903 in London. His mother was the former Eleanor "Nellie" Easton, daughter of a wealthy Virginia racehorse breeder and trainer who moved to Suffolk near Bury St. Edmunds where he rented Ixworth Abbey.

Both families were well connected and the Simonds children, Guy, Peter, Eric and their sister Cicely, enjoyed frequent visits to Windsor. Here and at Ixworth, Guy learned to ride and shoot and would soon excel at both. In 1909 Nellie's father, William, died and she inherited her share of the family fortune. Spoiled and flighty, she had never learned to live within her means nor, with her father always bailing her out, had she needed to. But now, with that back-up gone, her inheritance quickly dwindled to nothing. With his major's pay their sole source of income, in 1911, Cecil, with strong urging from his wife, decided to leave the army and seek his fortune in Victoria, BC, as a surveyor, taking the family with him. At the time Guy had reached the impressionable age of eight. He regretted his father's decision. The Simonds were army and he felt that his father was turning his back on family tradition. And he blamed his mother, who had been behind it all.

In Victoria things did not work out as Cecil had planned or been promised by the province's agent-general in London. Though he qualified as a surveyor in the army, provincial regulations prohibited him from setting up his own firm of surveyors in BC, until he had passed the necessary examinations. In the meantime, he took employment on the survey of a new railway for Vancouver Island. The pay was far from adequate and the family scraped by as best they could. In some ways the breakout of the Great War in 1914 rescued the Simonds's from destitution when Cecil was recalled to the colours. But at the same time it had a marked influence on the children. His departure left the family in Nellie's hands — something with which she was unable to cope, nor for the most part, did she even really try.

The onus fell on an aunt, Vera, Nellie's sister, and Cicely, the daughter, to keep things on an even keel. Nellie continued to spend money with total disregard for the family's limited resources though this was partly offset by selling some of the paintings inherited from Ixworth Abbey. But Nellie did play a part in the children's education even though, to supplement the family income, Guy gave up school for two years to take a job. Far from feeling disgruntled about it, as the eldest son, the situation seemed to stir a sense of responsibility in him and a pride at being able to cope and solve a family problem on his own.

As a scholar, Guy proved to be a star at mathematics and his writing was well above average. He had a knack of making himself easily understood smoothly and succinctly. He also became a prominent member of the Victoria School Collegiate cadet corps. Athletics — football, soccer, field hockey, track — came easily to him; he seemed to excel with little effort. And he was also an excellent shot with both the rifle and the shotgun.

In 1919 Cecil, having been wounded a year earlier, returned from the war with the full rank of colonel and was able to arrange for his sons, Guy and Peter, to attend a private school, Ashbury College in Ottawa. Guy now had his sights set on a military career. In his second year he took the entrance exam to the Royal Military College in Kingston and passed second in merit.

Guy Simonds' class at RMC was the last to be selected from a competitive national exam and the first after the war to enter a four-year course. At this time the public and the press were fed up with war and they looked upon the cadets whose purpose was to train for a career in the permanent force of the Canadian army, as a bunch of swaggering, upper-class snobs strutting about in fancy uniforms, and the college itself as a snooty institution.

The chief criticism from the press was the tradition known as "recruiting," a system of fagging, in which a first classman was assigned to a senior to do his bidding, shine his buttons, polish his shoes, make his bed and any other chores he could dream up. This was accepted by the cadets themselves as part of the drill, though outsiders considered it degrading. But it was the abuse of the discipline that came under fire. It extended to harassment of a downright bullying nature. One example was forcing recruits to run several laps around the grounds at a brisk pace in cold weather. Another was the "shit" meeting in which recruits were herded into a confined space, made to stand at attention, their fingers stretched down, while seniors hurled verbal insults at them. Worst of all was the cruelty of "arse fanning," repeated caning by a swagger stick for what was sometimes the slightest infraction, or the whim of a sadistic senior. Inevitably these incidents leaked to the press. Simonds was to play a key role in redressing the practice. That came as no surprise to his classmates or to the college faculty.

From the start, he had demonstrated a capacity for leadership and organization, one that was quickly recognized by the Cadet Battalion sergeant major who appointed him class senior only two weeks into his first term. At the same time he berated him for the conduct of his class. They were late for parades, absenteeism had gone unreported, the saluting and dress were shameful. Simonds was told to smarten it up. This he did quickly and efficiently and would brook no argument. He also, much to the expressed annoyance of some of his classmates, put an end to stealing exam papers and selling them. Nicknamed "Count" for his fastidious attention to his dress and appearance, he was not popular nor did he try to be. He never lost his British accent and among his classmen, this heightened his air of aloofness.

The question of recruiting came to a head, and made headlines, after a series of runaways and injuries sustained by recruits, with what became known as the Arnold affair. Arnold, a recruit had run away across the ice over Lake Ontario to Cape Vincent on the American side, then joined relatives in New York City. There, he was interviewed by the press to whom he announced that he had been unmercifully and illegally bullied at RMC. The story was subsequently reported in the Canadian newspapers with the direct result that the commandant, Major General Sir Archibald Macdonnell, who had commanded the First Canadian Division on the Western Front, placed the entire senior class under arrest and promoted Simonds, who was in his third year, and Jack McMahon, his deputy, to take battalion parades. Simultaneously he issued a statement to the press denying Arnold's accusations.

In light of this, Simonds and his class felt that the commandant's actions against the seniors were too severe and unfair. They were of the opinion that the staff was shielding the facts from their commandant. It was decided that Simonds and McMahon should interview Major Eric Greenwood, the staff adjutant, and request that he communicate their views to the commandant.

When so confronted, Greenwood turned purple with rage. Macdonnell accused the pair of mutiny, then explained that when he had asked the senior class for the facts, they had told him less than the whole truth and what he had learned he had communicated to the press. When Arnold and his father had been able to refute his statement, he had been placed in an untenable position before the public and he placed the blame squarely on the shoulders of the seniors. They were accordingly deprived of their authority for the remainder of the year. From then on, recruiting softened dramatically. But Simonds and McMahon suffered the consequences. When they entered their fourth and final year as seniors in which they were expected to be made senior under officer and senior company commander respectively, they were passed over and appointed senior company commander and senior platoon commander instead.

However, upon graduation, Simonds was awarded the Sword of Honour and also received the Victor Van de Smissen Award given to the cadet adjudged by his peers, through secret balloting, to be best all-rounder, morally and physically. In addition, he also received the Governor General's Silver Medal and the artillery prize. And, although he received no award for it, he was generally acknowledged to be the best horseman in his class.

The majority of RMC graduates in 1925 went into civilian life, though a few joined the Royal Canadian Air Force or the Royal Air Force. Simonds, however, was determined to pursue a career in the Canadian Army. He was commissioned in the Royal Canadian Artillery and duly appointed to the Royal Canadian Horse Artillery (RCHA) as a subaltern, first with B Battery in Kingston, then with C Battery in Winnipeg, Manitoba.

The function of the army at this time was to train the militia, which in the event of war, would provide the manpower needed to raise an expeditionary force. Military life consisted of training, sports associated with horses, which in those days provided the means to haul field guns, and social activities in the garrison towns of Winnipeg, Kingston and Halifax, which went hand in hand. But the small size of the service, limited to a few thousand officers and men and the lack of opportunities to serve in operational theatres curbed enthusiasm and made for slow promotion which called for an exercise in patience.

Simonds time with the RCHA was divided between training horses, men and, both simultaneously. One of the main exercises was military rides — a dangerous form of entertainment. This required precision, split-second timing, discipline and control. These exhibitions were of paramount importance in winning public esteem and prestige during a period when military budgets were cut to the bone. In this field Simonds was a master trainer. In addition, Simonds spent time training the militia at practice camps, in drill halls and classrooms.

He also won the reputation of being an accomplished polo player, and his wealthy friends in Winnipeg welcomed him on their teams and provided him with ponies that would otherwise have been beyond his means. In 1929, the year his parents separated, he met the girl he would marry. She was Katherine Lockhart Taylor, known as "K," the daughter of the prominent Winnipeg stockbroker, Charles Taylor. The hitch to their relationship was that, as a subaltern, Guy could not get married without the permission of his commanding officer. The couple had courted for two years when, in June 1932, Simonds' application to marry was turned down on the grounds that he would not attain the age of 30 until April of the following year and that it would be detrimental to a junior (he held the rank of captain) officer's training to be married and living out of the mess. Also, he would not derive the full benefit of the Long Gunnery Staff Course he was scheduled to attend in England that September. However, when he appealed to the district officer commanding on the basis that other officers who had taken the course were under 30, the order was countermanded. On August 17, 1932, Guy and K were married in All Saint's Church in Winnipeg and on September 2, sailed from Halifax for England aboard the *Duchess of Bedford.*

During the year they spent in England, they were not only roundly entertained by friends of Simonds' father, but by both the British Army authorities and the Canadian high commissioner. The service clubs, the army, navy and cavalry accepted them as honorary members. In June 1933, K gave birth to their first child, a daughter, Ruth. In 1934, the Simonds were back in Canada where Guy served as a qualified gunnery instructor at The School of Artillery in Kingston. There, their son, Charles, was born.

It was during this stint at Kingston that Simonds earned the reputation of being a patient and thorough teacher. Even commanding officers were struck by the manner in which the young officer, with the red band of a instructor gunnery, presented his lectures about the strengths and weaknesses of their regiments. Junior officers too were taken with his easy methods of teaching them gunnery. What he lacked, as usual, was warmth, understanding and fellowship, all sadly missing in his make-up.

In 1936 Simonds returned to England to attend a two-year course at the Camberley Staff College which Winston Churchill once referred to as "the most exclusive institution in the British Empire." This was a turning point in Simonds's military education, and his career. He credited any success he later attained as a senior officer to that curriculum and its instructors. While he had established himself as an expert in gunnery, it was at Camberley that he began to think more broadly in terms of all weapons and all the services, as well as the roles of their commanders and staffs. Equally important to what he learned during his training, were those students and members of the directing staff he met, many of whom he would become associated with during the war and afterwards.

The Staff College concept was "not to indoctrinate officers with preconceived ideas, but to make them think and come up with solutions to the problems of war." Each section of the course was introduced in lecture form, followed by a demonstration in the form of a light-hearted skit using humour to establish the various points. A forum technique was used made up of a hybrid of ten students, from the various services. A member of the directing staff acted as moderator while all questions were thrashed out by the participants who were given various theoretical ranks. Each session culminated in the writing of an order or appreciation. Another exercise was to give each student a subject at nine o'clock in the morning on which he had to deliver a paper by noon.

The first year of the course, after dealing with each phase of battle, attack, advance, defence, pursuit and withdrawal at the divisional level, ended with interservice exercises such as assault landings, defence of airfields, tactical air support and moving expeditionary forces overseas.

The second year of the course dealt with the theory of war and political considerations, particularly those involving the defence of the Empire and relations with the Dominions, and entailed a great deal more essay writing.

Simonds proved to be a star pupil. His excellent memory for facts enabled him to shine, as did his clear thinking and organizational ability. He was obviously destined for high rank. He eagerly participated in the debates among students about how the curriculum was taught and this did not escape criticism. Some thought there was too much paperwork — written appreciation and orders — arguing that in a mechanized battle, events would move much too fast to allow time for written instructions. Orders would have to be transmitted by radio. Simonds had reservations on that point.

He did not disagree with the use of radio for sending out specific orders, but argued that location, codes, times and other minutae had to be recorded in writing, not verbally. But, at the same time, he was a strong advocate of reducing the amount of written instructions and red tape from the command level when time could be saved by giving orders verbally and action taken much more quickly.

Simonds put his finger on another factor in the formula of modern warfare: armies no longer needed to rely on attrition to break through defences as had been the case in 1914-18. Air power and the use of airborne troops could isolate the battlefield by destroying communications — railway lines, roads and bridges — and prevent rapid reinforcement. Bombardment could stun the defenders into insensibility and reduce their effectiveness if not obliterating them entirely. The speed and mobility of mechanical vehicles had increased to the point where an attack could be quickly decisive.

However, at this time, the Staff College was still wrestling with the role of the air force. The foundations for tactical air support had been laid in 1918 — Billy Mitchell's use of it at St. Mihiel was a prime example — but Simonds was not made aware of it. Nor was he apprised of the differences of opinion concerning RAF priorities, such as, defence by fighter aircraft, observer corps and anti-aircraft guns versus strategic bombing. This indecision ruled out army cooperation, at least for the time being.

Another point open to question, and it was one that Simonds would mull over long after the course ended, was the disparity in the speed of the tanks and the infantryman. Did this mean that the infantryman was obsolete, that tanks would fight tanks like naval battles? For a start this theory seemed to ignore the effectiveness of the anti-tank gun which had already proved itself on the Western Front during the last year of the war.

With uncanny foresight, Simonds concerned himself with the problems surrounding invasion, such as the landing of ships on a hostile shore. His examination, in one of the study forums, of the Gallipoli expedition, had paved the way for his intense interest in the subject. His principle proposal was that for any amphibious operation, a command ship from which the commander of the landing forces, with proper communications equipment, could control the army staff, the supporting aircraft as well as the naval ships, was an absolute must. He eventually won his point in the debate that followed but not without strong opposition from both the air force and the navy types.

During the same forum Simonds recommended production of special troop landing craft and, by showing aerial photographs of the Yangtze River, demonstrated that the Japanese already possessed such boats. His presentation so impressed the directing staff member in the chair, that he asked him to repeat it the next day when the first lord of the Admiralty, Duff Cooper, and the secretary of state for war, Hore Belisha, visited the college. Obviously great things could be expected of the neat, trim, young Canadian officer with the British accent, who so clearly expressed himself in clipped, quick phrases.

The final exercise of the course was a theoretical war with Germany on the premise, as accepted in those days, that Britain would not participate in the fighting on the Continent. Simonds's "syndicate" deployed its French forces echeloned back from the Maginot Line with a concentration of armour in the centre to counter an attack on either flank. The German "syndicate" attacked through the Ardennes which, ironically, the member of the directing staff ruled as improbable and impractical. (Oh, the lessons lost!)

Simonds's two years at the Staff College rekindled his love for the country of his birth and reinforced friendships with friends of the family. It was not a sentiment shared by his wife, K. She did not enjoy the social life particularly and, with two young children to look after, was left at home by herself most of the time. The downside to their stay in England was the death of Guy's brother Eric, who was killed in July 1937 flying with the RAF, and whom Guy had been seeing regularly.

All the students in Simonds's class left the college sensing that the outbreak of war was merely a matter of time and were astounded at the complacency of political leaders and high government officials in the face of what was going on in Germany. By the end of his term, Simonds learned that he was to be posted to RMC with the rank of major, to teach tactics, strategy and international affairs under the commandant, Brigadier Harry Crerar. With war imminent, he was disappointed at first, at what he considered a static appointment, but when he was told that his duties would include revamping and reorganizing the RMC curriculum, he approached the challenge eagerly.

On their departure from England aboard the *Duchess of York*, Simonds received a telegram from the Canadian High Commissioner, Vincent Massey, which read: "To wish you and your family a pleasant crossing and success in your new appointment in Canada. My warmest congratulations also on your wonderful results at Camberley. You were a credit, indeed to the service."

At the outset Simonds wanted plans for RMC in the event of war clarified but none had even been considered. In 1914-18 the college had remained open, which Crerar considered a mistake. In the event of another war, he favoured closing it and having all officers selected from the ranks and given similar training in officer training units. Simonds wanted RMC to stay open on the basis that a two-year course for cadets, aged 16 with junior matriculation, would give them a good grounding in general education, mathematics, science, the humanities and social sciences. When they reached military age at 18, they could be quickly trained as junior officers and would provide an invaluable additional pool of officers. And, after the war they would be qualified to enter college. As it turned out Crerar got his wish. RMC was shut down in 1942, a decision that appalled General Andrew McNaughton, who had come out of retirement to command the Canadian contingent, when he learned of it.

During the year prior to the war, Simonds wrote three articles in the *Canadian Defence Quarterly* propounding his views to anyone who cared to digest them. In these he disagreed with his commandant, not for the last time. He took the British and European view of tactics and strategy in his lectures and articles, opposed to Canadian government policy, which was to avoid committing itself to Imperial strategies, let alone becoming involved in another land campaign in Continental

Europe. This inevitably led to a clash with the politically oriented Crerar who disdained officers who contradicted the manuals because it confused the cadets and created discord among his instructors.

After the war started, as general staff officer II, with the rank of major on the operations staff, Simonds sailed aboard the Cunarder *Aquitania*, on December 9, 1939, with the First Canadian Division, under Andy McNaughton, for the United Kingdom. There, the contingent moved into the army barracks at Aldershot. His wife, K, who had been living in Kingston, moved to an apartment in Winnipeg with the children to be near her own family in Guy's absence. As GSO II, Simonds's responsibilities included organizing divisional courses, procuring training areas, maps and range allotments. He borrowed instructors to train those new to the division who were unfamiliar with weaponry and procedures. He also studied local defence schemes and tended to other divisional duties.

In those salad days, the Canadian Active Service Force, composed of the Permanent Force, the Non-permanent Militia and the other volunteers who were neither, had its work cut out for it to coordinate the division into a cohesive unit. McNaughton's Canadian Military Headquarters Staff under the former RMC commandant, Harry Crerar, who was promoted to major general, dealt with the British Army, the British government, as well as army headquarters in Ottawa.

Because of McNaughton's insistence on Canadian rights, this was ticklish. He was highly unpopular with the British. As was his GSO I, Lieutenant Colonel George Turner who made friends with no one and ran a decidedly unhappy ship. Here Simonds was at a distinct advantage that would later serve him well. As a result of his Staff College days he had made many friends in England in high places. Also he thought like the British, hell, he *was* British. Because of Turner's unpopularity with those under him and his constant indecision and refusal to take initiative, the junior officers turned to Simonds for leadership. They were not the only ones who came to rely on him.

In April 1940 the cold war turned hot when the Germans invaded Denmark and Norway. A Canadian contingent comprising the Princess Patricia's Canadian Light Infantry, the Edmonton Fusiliers and the Saskatchewan Light Infantry, under the command of Colonel Ernest Sanson, formed part of a group code-named Hammerforce, which was ordered to seize and man the forts covering the port of Trondheim in central Norway.

Fully aware of his excellent mind for detail and his remarkable energy and drive, McNaughton entrusted the logistics of organizing the three battalions on short, last-minute, notice for embarkation, to Simonds. In this the latter succeeded with characteristic thoroughness overlooking nothing — sleeping bags, heavy underwear, extra socks, boots and other clothing. But the force never got further than Scotland before the operation was cancelled after the Germans overran Norway. However, for the First Division the exercise had been far from wasted. It had provided a useful experience in functioning efficiently and effectively under pressure on the spur of the moment. McNaughton was highly impressed with Simonds's performance and marked him down for rapid promotion from that day on.

By this time the British Expeditionary Force in France was being driven back to the sea. A plan underway for the Canadian First Brigade, followed by the rest of the division was, to re-establish road and rail communications between Calais and Dunkirk in case evacuation became necessary. But first McNaughton began shuffling between Calais, Dunkirk, Dover and London to try and sort out what was happening on the ground. Holed up in Dover Castle, Simonds kept in contact with McNaughton by radio, reporting the latter's findings and recommendations to the director of Military Operations at the War Office. At the same time he supervised the loading of troops and anti-tank guns into ships in the harbour, staying in close liaison with the Royal Navy. It did not exactly inspire him with confidence to discover that explosives had been laid against the cranes on the docks as if the navy expected a German invasion at any moment.

Because the situation in France had become so hopeless, McNaughton convinced the chief of the Imperial General Staff, Field Marshal Sir Edmund Ironside, that sending over the Canadian troops would simply be sacrificing them for nothing. The brigade was disembarked and returned to Aldershot.

In July 1940, Simonds was given command of his old regiment, the First Royal Canadian Horse Artillery. Before he arrived at Beckenham, to where it had been moved, his reputation as a harsh disciplinarian, a *staff* officer, if you will, had preceded him. They were in fear and trembling and expected the worst. They were in for a pleasant surprise. The unit was in somewhat of a shambles. They had been part of the contingent sent to Brittany, a venture that turned into a fiasco, then promptly ordered to re-embark having lost most of their equipment. Morale was at rock bottom. Simonds gave the men encouragement and restored their *esprit de corps* with his efficient, no-nonsense manner of getting things done.

His officers were impressed with his knowledge of gunnery and tactics, and the concise, easy-to-understand way in which he expressed himself. His writing on even the most complex subjects was clear and simple to digest. This rubbed off on his subordinates. But he was intolerant of those without the proper qualifications to do the job or others who failed to learn quickly enough. They were sent packing. The regiment was handicapped because of the constant interruptions caused by the threat of imminent invasion and the shortage of vehicles. But the experience of taking his first regimental command was a useful and rewarding one for Simonds.

In November, McNaughton, who was keeping a close watch on his protégé, and, mindful of Simonds's huge success at the Camberley Staff College, named him commandant of the newly formed Canadian Junior War Staff College. This was a manifestation of the decision to increase the army overseas to five divisions and two armoured brigades making necessary the need to train more staff officers. Camberley could not accommodate the overload, thus the need for a Canadian college.

It opened at Ford Manor in Surrey in January 1941, and lasted 14 weeks. The curriculum was a condensed version of the British first-year course based on an identical style of instruction. The course proved highly successful, producing a number of bright young staff officers, many of whom would later serve under Simonds. At the end of it, in April, McNaughton wrote him a note, "I want to express to you my very deep appreciation for the way you have made a very substantial contribution indeed and I thank you for it." That was symptomatic of McNaughton's interest and support which was responsible for Simonds' meteoric rise over the next two years.

Soon after the completion of the course, he was appointed GSO I (senior operations staff officer) of the newly arrived Second Infantry Division with the rank of lieutenant colonel. After a brief stint in that capacity, McNaughton promoted him to brigadier general staff (BGS) of the Canadian Corps, before returning to Canada on sick leave. In the fall of 1941, Harry Crerar, who had earlier relinquished his post as chief of staff of CMHQ to become chief of the General Staff in Ottawa, returned to England, to take command of the corps.

On April 6, 1942, the First Canadian Army headquarters was established and, by this time, McNaughton had come back to Great Britain to command it. Meanwhile, Simonds had been promoted to the rank of brigadier and remained as BGS to Crerar until mid-July 1942, when he became McNaughton's chief of staff of the First Canadian Army.

Simonds's two masters were a couple of very different cups of tea. Crerar was fully aware that his self-assured chief staff officer overshadowed him and the jealousy showed, according to Crerar's biogra-

pher, Dominick Graham. In fact Crerar had not chosen Simonds for his
BGS himself and, from the outset, made no secret of the fact that he
wanted to replace him. The ease with which Simonds handled himself
embarrassed him. His BGS's ability to explain operations clearly without notes, compared to his own dull, uninspired speaking style rankled
him. It went deeper than that. In truth, Crerar did not know how to handle staff. A nice enough fellow in most ways, he lacked originality and
tended to waste a lot of his time on trivialities. Regretfully, he avoided
responsibility whenever and wherever possible. This was the very
antithesis of Simonds's strict sense of discipline. It did not help either,
that to outsiders it was abundantly clear who was actually running the
show. When Montgomery congratulated Crerar on the performance of
his corps during a certain exercise, it was his BGS whom he singled
out for praise. In short, Simonds regarded Crerar as a political animal,
for which, in terms of military conduct, he had no time. Ironically, both
men suffered from the same common symptom. They lacked the common touch, so necessary at times to inspire the loyalty and support
from those directly below them.

On the other hand, up to a point, Simonds and McNaughton got along
like a house on fire. Simonds recognized his chief for what he was — a
brilliant eccentric. As head of the National Research Council before the
war McNaughton had proved to be a proper whiz at developing radio
and aerial communications in Canada's north, just as he had perfected
artillery techniques on the Western Front. But he was much more inter-
ested in the science of war than in strategy and techniques. Consequently
he left those activities, such as the logistics of the Norwegian operation,
in which he had little interest, to Simonds whose ability for organization
he admired so strongly and upon whom he was so totally dependent.
Personally, he liked him as well. Alike in many ways, they shared, at
times, the same gruff, soldierly manner. However, their divergent points
of view were bound to place them at loggerheads sooner or later.

Inevitably it came to a head. In Simonds's own words:

> From the beginning, I had a running argument with Andy…I told
> him I would serve him in any capacity he wished, except that I
> would not remain as chief of staff at Army HQ unless he would
> accept my advice on the matter of organizing headquarters to
> fight a battle and concentrating on the training and operational
> aspects…He kicked me out of his office and within 48 hours I
> left on attachment to 8th Army. In all fairness I must add that he
> never held that interview against me.

The German attack on Russia and the entry of the United States into the war in 1941 had dramatically altered the pattern of behaviour of the armies in Great Britain. Invasion was no longer a threat and the Chiefs of the Imperial General Staff now turned their attention to the offensive. And it was Montgomery, who had command of the Southeast Army, who led the way. And Montgomery had taken a shine to, and was highly impressed with, Simonds, whom he had watched very carefully during the anti-invasion exercises. The fact that Simonds had earned the "outstanding grade" at the Camberley Staff College didn't do him any harm either. Montgomery also admired him for his insistent, outspoken manner.

When Montgomery ordered all officers to attend certain courses, Simonds took issue because the Canadians were fed up to their teeth with courses ever since arriving in England. What they needed was practice and he told Montgomery so in no uncertain terms. Monty agreed. "Quite right!" he responded. "Do it your own way."

In August 1942, McNaughton gave Simonds command of the First Brigade of the First Canadian Division under Major General Harry Salmon. After an initial period of familiarization, in December the brigade moved to Inverary in Scotland for combined operations training. Then, at the turn of the year, McNaughton brought Simonds back once again as his BGS of the First Canadian Army.

Simonds realized he would gain little more, if anything, in the way of field experience or knowledge from McNaughton than he had learned from Crerar and knew that he would have to look to the British for guidance. With this in mind, in April 1943 he visited Eighth Army headquarters in Tunisia where he met Corps commander General Sir Brian Horrocks and Montgomery's chief of staff, Major General Sir Francis Guingan, both of whom were highly impressed with the Canadian officer with the British accent. When McNaughton recalled him from his two-week sojourn, Simonds tabled a report on his study of the Eight's tactics.

He was convinced that the day of the blitzkrieg was over because of improved defences, anti-tank weapons, mines, wire and centralized mortar and artillery control. He predicted that a shortage of infantry would result and recommended the need for panzer-grenadier type of divisions with a ratio of infantry to armour of two to one. The fact that infantry divisions would frequently need the support of armoured brigades suggested the use of army tank brigades. He also recommended that armoured regiments ought to be standard in equipment and organization.

Simonds was surprised to learn that the air force and army head-quarters were so far apart. The RAF wanted its HQ near its airfields, which was some distance from the forward Army HQ. But Simonds agreed that air support left little to be desired and noted that the US Army Air Force was quickly integrating itself with RAF tactical air operations.

Immediately upon his return on April 20, McNaughton gave Simonds command of the Second Division, replacing General Hamilton Roberts, who had commanded it at Dieppe. Four days later the decision was made for the First Canadian Infantry Division to replace the British Third in Operation Husky, the invasion of Sicily. On April 27, the commanding officer, General Salmon, and other staff officers bound for Cairo, were killed when the Hudson bomber in which they were flying, crashed in Devonshire. That afternoon McNaughton gave Simonds command of the First Division.

Next day the Canadian press hailed the appointment: "BOY GENERAL TO SUCCEED DEAD LEADER." The story went on to say, "In normal time it [his hobbies] includes riding, polo, writing. At present it is participating in beating the German army." Another report from an interview with one of his staff, read,

> By the amount of work he gets through and the military study he does in his spare time, you might say Guy Simonds is a slave to his job were it not [for] the fact that the way he does it, it doesn't look like work. He reads through any memorandum put before him no matter how complicated, and at once has the whole thing summed up in his mind. Officers associated with him say it is a joy to work with such quick reactions, such a precise brain. There's never any humming and hawing.

After a few days needed for reorganizing, Simonds and his staff took off in two four-engine Liberators for North Africa, stopping off at Gibraltar on the way, to refuel. One of them then proceeded directly to Cairo, the other, with Simonds aboard, to Algiers to confer with General Sir Harold Alexander, commanding both armies in Operation Husky, Montgomery's Eighth and General George Patton's Seventh United States.

Simonds learned that plans for Husky had still to be finalized. His party then took off for Heliopolis airport at Cairo where they were met by their British counterparts and taken to Shepherds Hotel. Over the next few days the staffs went over the last-minute details, the logistics for loading the invasion fleet and the final preparations.

Simonds and Rear Admiral Sir Philip Vian, who commanded the naval operation, agreed to sail together aboard the command ship, an old coal burner, HMS *Hilary*, formerly employed in the Atlantic listening for U-boat signals. Because intelligence about the condition of the invasion beaches was sketchy and unsatisfactory, they ordered a submarine reconnaissance. Unfortunately, they would not learn the results until the convoy was nearing the beaches. Montgomery gave the final briefing using a sand model in Kasr el Nil barracks. The plan laid down called for the First Canadian Division to assault the beaches in a single brigade front. Simonds stood firm. When it came his turn to speak he said, "No, sir, I'm not going to do it that way." Heads turned. But Montgomery was all ears as Simonds explained that because he

could not be certain of the depth of the water behind the sandbanks offshore, or the exits from the beaches, he did not intend to place all his eggs in one basket. Also he wanted to penetrate inland as quickly as possible which required a much broader front. So his plan was to attack with two brigades and four battalions. Montgomery agreed to the modification, provided the extra craft were available.

After five days in Cairo, Simonds and his Divisional Quartermaster General, Ab Knight, flew back to England. Due to a navigational error, the pilot lost his bearings and very nearly landed the plane in Cork, Ireland, where they would have been interned, since Ireland was neutral.

From his headquarters in Norfolk House, Simonds had his work cut out for him, making frequent trips to and from the west of Scotland where the division was going through last-minute training and from where it would embark. The logistics of organization were multiplied by the way the division had to be re-equipped. Up until it had been assigned to Husky it had been treated as an auxiliary or reserve, bastard force armed with outdated, cast-off British army equipment, most of it not even standard. All this had to be sorted out and quickly.

In June the division was given embarkation leave. It now became obvious that an overseas operation was in the offing. But a masterful deception plan had been devised to disguise it. Proposed landings in Greece, Crete, the south of France, Corsica and Sardinia were leaked to the Germans through a masterful fraud coded "Mincemeat." This was the "Man Who Never Was," in which a cadaver taken from cold storage and dressed as a marine major carrying a briefcase with the false documents and floated off the coast of Spain. When British intelligence revealed that the enemy had been taken in, Churchill signalled Roosevelt, "Mincemeat swallowed whole."

At 2043 hours on June 28, the convoy carrying the "Red Patch" division made famous on the Western Front under Sir Arthur Currie and Archie Macdonnell, weighed anchor and set sail down the Clyde. Next morning off the north-west coast of Ireland, a naval signal to all ships read, "We are on our way to the Mediterranean to take part in the greatest combined operation that has yet been mounted."

Sometime later at sea on July 1, Dominion Day, the word went out that the target was Sicily. This was followed by briefings so that every man knew the specific part he would play in the overall operation. The men learned too the nature of the land over which they would fight. Sicily was hot, dusty and mountainous. Here the mountain training the Third Infantry Brigade had received at Glenfishie would come in useful. Everyone was given a pamphlet about Sicily which included simple Italian phrases and suggestions on how to behave with the inhabitants. They were warned that malaria was prevalent and were issued mepacrine pills to be taken daily. Only boiled or treated water was to be drunk. Each man carried a 48-hour ration that had to last two days. Sunburn would be treated as a self-inflicted wound.

In one of his pep talks, Simonds gave his commanders some idea of what they would face in the way of resistance once ashore. They could expect to meet stubborn opposition from the Italian coast defence. But once outflanked, the Italians would probably surrender, as they had in Tunisia. The Germans on the other hand, would fight bitterly even when surrounded; they needed to be severely badgered and pummelled.

Besides the briefings and practices, time at sea was taken up with activities such as physical exercise, shooting at targets in the water, weapons inspections and ammunition cleaning. In their spare time the troops amused themselves with musical entertainment and playing cards. On the night of July 4, when the convoy was passing through the Straits of Gibraltar, German submarines torpedoed the *City of Venice* and *St. Essyl.* Six 17-pound anti-tank guns, 25 field guns, engineering stores and signals equipment were lost. Next day the U-boats sunk the commodore's ship, *Devis,* sending transport, signals and office equipment for divisional headquarters to the bottom. These incidents brought the war into focus, for real.

On D-Day minus 24 hours, a heavy westerly storm threatened the landings. But both Simonds and Vian, aboard the command ship, agreed that the weather would abate somewhat and that the landings should proceed as scheduled for 0245 hours on July 6. Simonds knew that failure to put his troops ashore would affect the other landings. Surprise would be lost allowing the two defending German divisions, the Hermann Goering and the Fifteenth Panzer Grenadier, to move eastward and oppose Lieutenant General Sir Oliver Leese's Thirtieth

Corps. But, the storm itself, poor navigation, and anti-aircraft fire from their own fleet, utterly wrecked the airborne side of the operation. Parachutists and gliders were scattered all over the island and in the sea. Some even landed back in Tunisia where, thinking they were in Sicily, they began to take on their own airfield defences.

This threw a monkey wrench into Montgomery's original plans for the Canadians to fight on the left flank of the Eighth Army under the Thirtieth Corps. They, and the Americans, on their left, were supposed to engage and hold German formations they met.

As a result of this fiasco, Montgomery had to transfer the weight of his attack from right to left where the Thirtieth Corps was in action. Alexander, in overall command, decided to cut the island in two with a drive through the centre through Enna. As a consequence, the Canadians were in for some tough slugging, a long stiff struggle to accommodate Montgomery's plan to turn the western flank of the German position on the slopes of Mount Etna on which hinged the Catania plain defences. At the same time Alexander planned to release the Seventh US Army and push up to Palermo to the north-west corner of the island while its Second Corps, under Lieutenant General Omar Bradley fought for town and road junctions en route to the east-west road between Palermo and Messina on the north coast.

The initial landings lasted three days and went without incident for the Canadians. Although this had been expected to be the most hazardous part of the operation it turned out to be by far the easiest. Thanks to the prelanding bombardment, Italian resistance was minimal. But Simonds, his headquarters staff, and his brigade commanders, were acutely aware that the equipment losses at sea would hamper them in the long struggle, most of it on foot, in the days ahead. By this time Simonds was a national figure, his picture on the front page of the Canadian daily newspapers, taken wading ashore. He received a letter from his wife K dated July 31.

> Guy darlingest, yesterday I got such a nice photo of you from the *Free Press* [Winnipeg]. Coming ashore in Sicily in the water. I love it, darling, but it makes you feel so far away and another man. You have on a beret and it looks as if it would be becoming. I love looking at you as I know your arms so well and I can see that they are really you. And your moll [*sic*] on your cheek too. Guy darling, I miss you so and I do hope that you can come home and be an ordinary man again and not so famous and super. I don't know how I'd behave if you were too public for the rest of your life....

By the time Simonds had set up his headquarters ashore, in a hovel, 12 by 16 feet, previously occupied by an "old woman, eleven guinea pigs, four dogs, a goat, and four bottles of wine," he had already swung into a rigid daily routine. He rose early, received an early-morning briefing on events overnight, had breakfast, and by 0630 hours was on the road in a jeep with his aide-de-camp, Stuart Graham, who also acted as his signaller and driver. Most of his day was spent in front of the different brigade headquarters and, because the division fought most of the Sicilian campaign with open flanks, he frequently came under shell fire. He was generally asleep by 11:00 p.m. and was not woken until 6:00 a.m.

In Sicily the First Canadian Division was unique. None of its commanders had any experience under fire. They were battle novices, as in fact were most all of those serving under them, though the division itself was better trained than any previous Canadian one. Simonds, who tended to breathe down the necks of his subordinates, had no experience at the lower levels of command and, of course, had never been under fire before. He had to rely on his own rigorous standards of analysis and study, generally brilliant and usually correct, but decidedly theoretical. He lacked patience, understanding and above all sympathy for those commanders serving him. His menacing manner was decidedly unnerving and often caused friction, not to mention, open argument. Few understood that his stony silence did not necessarily signal disapproval, but it could be just as disturbing as his cold, icy stare when he became angry. And, he was intolerant almost to a stage of distemper.

A case in point was a contretemps between Simonds and his First Brigade commander, Howard Graham, on the eve of the Battle of Grammichele where the brigade was to face the vaunted Hermann Goering Division for the first time. It had been boiling for some time, going back to the Norfolk House days. A basic friction lay between the two, though it was one Simonds would never admit to. Graham was a militia officer while Simonds was strictly PF, Permanent Force. Before there were other things to worry about, such as fighting the war, for example, there were always underlying differences between the PFers and the militia.

In Sicily, Simonds and Graham had already argued over the landing procedure. Graham consolidated his bridgehead before going on to his second objective, Pachino Airfield. Simonds ordered him to get on with the objective at once and stop wasting time consolidating. Graham maintained that his was the correct procedure and that the former was simply picking on him. But Simonds was right, it was essential to move inland as far as possible in the very first hour. However, Graham resented Simonds interference.

That was only the warm-up. The climate was ripe for a showdown, and that took place on the early morning of July 15 at a roadside before Grammichele. Simonds took issue over the fact that Graham had failed to pass his brigade through the village of Vizzini quickly enough after a British division had cleared it. Whether the tongue-lashing Graham received as a result was justified was beside the point. But Simonds was certainly out of line delivering it in the presence of Graham's and his own drivers and signallers. Yet, it must be remembered that this took place on the eve of the Canadians first real battle and that nerves were stretched to the breaking point. In any event, Graham lost his command — but only temporarily.

When this incident came to Montgomery's attention he had these words of advice for Simonds:

> I hear you have had a row with Graham. I have seen Graham at Corps H.Q. The Corps Commander will tell you my views about it, and my general views on the whole question of command in war. I want you to do the big thing and take Graham back, giving him a warning and a last chance. Difficult subordinates have to be led and not driven, and the higher commander has got to keep calm and collected and not be too ruthless. Good luck to you and once more I congratulate you on how you are handling your division and how they are fighting.

The upshot was that Graham not only got his command back, but, perhaps with a twinge of conscience, Simonds recommended him for the Distinguished Service Order.

Simonds was a strong advocate of the firepower plan, as if he had inherited his artillery mindset from Sir Arthur Currie's successes during the Great War; and perhaps, Andy McNaughton, an artilleryman's artilleryman, had some influence on him also. In any event, Simonds believed that the delay needed while waiting for the softening-up bombardment before the attack was insurance and well worth it. Critics, and there were some right in the division itself, argued that the battles of Grammichele, Valguaneri, Leonforte, Assoro and Agira could have been won much quicker and at less cost with less dependence on firepower. In the latter battle, which lasted for six days between July 23 and 28, en route to the village of Agira, the Canadians encountered a collection of stone hovels surrounded by low hills and ridges from which the Germans offered some of the stiffest resistance of the entire

Sicilian campaign. Three successive attacks were beaten back. Finally, Simonds ordered massive artillery support along with air strikes and the town finally fell. His dependence on artillery had been vindicated.

By mid-August the First Division's part in the Sicilian campaign came to a close. Looking ahead to the approaching assault on the Italian mainland across the Strait of Messina, on a August 20 visit to the Canadians' camp, Montgomery told them, "We shall soon be packing again, I expect. Wherever I go, I would like to have you with me." Earlier, an Associated Press dispatch quoted him as saying that the advance of the Canadians from Pachino to Etna had been "simply wonderful — quite amazing." They had travelled "farther in Sicily, and fought longer, than any division in the Eighth Army...with the most frightful conditions and terrain to contend with...We all knew that 1 Canadian Division would deliver the goods."

From the First Canadian Corps Headquarters in London, Harry Crerar, soon to arrive in the Mediterranean with the corps, sent his congratulations. "You can well imagine the consuming interest and intense pride of all ranks here in the reported exploits of your command," he wrote. "I should dearly love to see you and your command. Perhaps wishes may become facts."

On September 22, by which time the First Division, as part of General Miles Dempsey's Thirteenth Corps, had been fighting in Italy between Potenza and Calabria, Simonds was laid low with jaundice. Several days later he learned he had been awarded the Distinguished Service Order. He was also informed by secret signal from an associate in Great Britain that Crerar was on his way to the Mediterranean with the First Canadian Corps and that he, Simonds, was to take command of the Fifth Armoured Division getting ready to embark for Italy from the United Kingdom. This move was part of Operation Timberwolf which met with strong disfavour from Alexander, commanding the Allied armies in Italy, and Montgomery in whose Eighth Army the Canadian Corps would become a part. They didn't need, or want, another corps headquarters and any more armour in the mountainous Italian country. They rightly suspected that the Canadians, by including an armoured division in Timberwolf, had the pretext they needed to foist off a corps headquarters on the British and at the same time give Crerar an opportunity of gaining field experience he needed to qualify as a replacement for McNaughton as chief of the First Canadian Army. Given this set of circumstances, Montgomery would have much preferred to have seen Simonds command the First Corps and later, hopefully, the First Canadian Army.

Montgomery managed to delay Crerar's arrival by keeping him in Sicily until room could be found for him in Italy. When he finally did join the Eighth Army Crerar's manner was quite hostile; he was aware that no one wanted him.

Simonds was quite disgruntled over the entire affair. First of all, he didn't trust Crerar whom he blamed for the resurrection of the Dieppe raid after it had been cancelled. Simonds also resented the fact that he had received word of his appointment from a Canadian lieutenant colonel at Allied Army headquarters in Italy. He felt McNaughton should have advised him personally. He interpreted his transfer from the First Division to the Fifth Armoured Division as a type of demotion, an indication that his superiors were dissatisfied with him. Montgomery reassured him on that score, pointing out that the experience of commanding an armoured division would qualify him for command of a corps. That mollified him to some extent but when he learned that his armoured division was to inherit the dated, cast-off equipment from the Seventh Armoured Division, the Desert Rats, which was returning to Great Britain, he was purple with rage. When Crerar appeared, taking over as senior Canadian commander as well as becoming Simonds' military superior, the latter felt he had been treated in cavalier fashion.

What upset him most was his conviction that the First Corps, which had no combat experience, would be run on bureaucrat grounds compared to the easygoing manner in which the Eighth army operated, with paperwork kept to a minimum, and commanders, at all levels, liking and understanding each other. Simonds did not disguise his dislike for the entire set-up and his behaviour towards Crerar was less than cordial. Unfortunately by throwing his weight around in the company of battle-hardened veterans, Crerar did nothing to make himself popular. Simonds was not even cordial to him and that was a mistake.

What astounded him was that Crerar appeared to ignore the proven principle of creating armoured divisions with more infantry and infantry divisions with some armour. In reference to the new Canadian organization, Alexander wrote, "As to manpower, a corps HQ for two divisions is very extravagant. Saving it might allow [them] to find the extra infantry brigade." Crerar dismissed this as a typical British view "that God is an Englishman."

Things came to a head between the two when Crerar visited Simonds in his caravan. It was a particularly unfriendly conversation. Crerar accused Simonds of "thinking of nothing but [himself]" and "wanting to go home to bask in [his] newly won glory." But, taken by the design of the caravan, Crerar asked if he could send off some of his staff to copy it. Of course, Simonds agreed. On December 2, Simonds returned from a field trip for a meeting with Defence Minister James

Ralston to find a Captain Kirk and his assistant busily taking measurements, without the courtesy of having notified him first. Simonds was incensed. He gave them 15 minutes to finish up and clear out. Several days later he received a letter from Crerar:

> Although this might be regarded as an unimportant incident, and one which I could afford to ignore, there are certain implications which disturb me sufficiently to cause this letter.
>
> The least important aspect, which I will discuss first, is that this intolerable treatment of a junior officer dispatched to you on my initiative was, in effect, an indirect act, on your part, of personal discourtesy to me. I cannot bring myself to believe that this was intentional because I am aware of no grounds for this attitude on your part and I know of a good many reasons, extending over a number of years, which should induce in you feelings for me, of loyalty and appreciation. All the same, whatever your actual intentions, the result has been to convey to a number of personnel on [sic] your own headquarters and to a number at present directly under me, a very regrettable impression. The much more important effect of this episode is that it tends to indicate that your nerves are over-stretched and that impulse, rather than considered judgment, may begin to affect your decisions...Although it is difficult, I would like you to undertake a self-examination and give me a diagnosis of your own mental and physical condition.

This missive arrived at a time when Simonds was busy sorting out the commanders he had inherited with his armoured division, some of whom he considered unsatisfactory and, for one reason or another would have to be replaced. This placed him on even more precarious ground with Crerar who believed that an officer should not be removed from command until he had been tested in battle. Added to that was the fact that it was Crerar who was responsible for their appointments in the first place.

Simonds did find time, however, to reply to Crerar's letter. He concluded with the following two paragraphs:

> I can assure you quite honestly also, that you can rely on my loyalty in carrying out your policies. I have worked for senior officers whom I neither liked nor respected, but I have never had one complain of my loyalty, honesty or usefulness of the service rendered...

> I would welcome an opportunity for a perfectly frank talk with you. Your letter reinforces the feeling that you are looking for an opportunity to "take a crack" at me…If you cannot express full confidence in my judgment and ability to handle my command in battle, I shall have to ask to be relieved.

Crerar responded by calling in a psychiatrist as well as his deputy director of medical services to judge whether Simonds was fit to command. Their evidence did not support Crerar's belief that he was overwrought or incapable. Meanwhile Crerar had written to Montgomery:

> A number of reactions on the part of Simonds since I arrived in this theater of operations, nearly two months ago, have given me serious cause to doubt his suitable ability for higher command…My present judgement is that while he has all the military brilliance for higher command in the field, with his tense mentality, under further strain through increased rank and responsibility, he might go "off the deep end" very seriously indeed.

Monty — who had earlier written to Simonds advising him to ignore Crerar if he attempted to order him about — came right to the point:

> I have the highest opinion of Simonds…Briefly my views are that Simonds is a first class soldier. After a period with an armoured division he will be suitable for a corps. He will be a very valuable officer in the Canadian Forces as you have no one else with experience; he must be handled carefully, and be trained on.

This letter obviously made an impression on Crerar, who recommended Simonds as commander of the Second Canadian Corps. But underlying it was Montgomery's low opinion of Crerar, evidenced by the fact that he ensured that the latter had little responsibility in the early days of the Normandy campaign. In December 1943, both Montgomery and Simonds were recalled to England. Montgomery was appointed to command the Anglo-American Twenty-First Army Group, and Simonds was assigned the Second Canadian Corps under him.

The Second Canadian Corps consisting of the Second Infantry Division, the Fourth Armoured Division and an artillery group, was to fight in the breakthrough phase of Operation Overlord once the bridgehead had been firmly established in Normandy. The Third Canadian Division and the Second Armoured Brigade would join the corps after fighting in the assault phase under the First British Corps. Later, the First Polish Division would come under Simonds's control.

By the end of the first week of July 1944, Harry Crerar had arrived in France as commander of the First Canadian Army but it would be some weeks before headquarters would be officially operational. Relations between Crerar and Simonds were frostily formal.

Of the four battles that Simonds directed in Normandy, two of them were battles of attrition, the other two were breakout battles coincident with the American breakthrough in the west. The open countryside in which the corps fought these encounters favoured the Germans. Fields of fire were extremely long whereby, and at a range of 2,000 yards, enemy 88-millimetre and 75-millimetre guns frequently destroyed as many as 60 advancing tanks of an armoured regiment. The Canadians were badly outgunned in this open country. Their own 75-millimetre guns mounted on Sherman tanks, and their 17-pounders were no match for the superior firepower of the Panzer divisions. Yet casualties to Canadian tank crews were remarkably light. They bore out Simonds contention as early as 1938, that less men are lost in tank battles than infantry ones.

Ironically, Simonds's first battle was an infantry action. On July 18, 1944, Operation Atlantic, fighting on the British Eighth Corps' right, in the built-up area of the port Caen, the Canadian infantry suffered heavier casualties than the British. The objective was to secure the industrial suburbs of the city, Vaucelles and Colombelles south of the River Orne, and at the same time force a gap through the German armour. They were unsuccessful in opening the gap, but the Germans had been pushed out of the industrial suburbs of the city. Next day rain hampered air support and, the attempt to seize the villages on and behind Verrieres Ridge and Tilly-la-Campagne beyond Bourguebus proved to be a disaster. The Essex Scottish lost 300 men killed and wounded, the Fusiliers Mont-Royal had two companies wiped out. Total casualties were over 1,200.

Simonds blamed the ineptitude of the commander of the Second Infantry Division, Major General Charles Foulkes, for the failure. Among the flaws he found were: insecure start lines, failure to follow-up artillery support fire, insufficient mopping up and lack of success in establishing a firm base to withstand counter-attacks. He had also come to the conclusion earlier that Foulkes "did not have the qualities to command." Simonds might well have sacked Foulkes, had it not been for the latter's close friendship with Crerar which made such a move impossible.

Simonds's next task, Operation Spring, had as its objective the high ground on either side of the Caen-Falaise road at the crossroads of Camesnil. This was to act as the springboard for a drive on Falaise in a double encirclement, with the Canadians pressing from the north and the Americans, after breaking out in the west, closing the gap from the south.

After the failure of operation Atlantic in broad daylight, Simonds decided to attack at night. Here, he demonstrated his talent for innovation. He devised "artificial moonlight" by beaming searchlights against the cloud base to lead the way.

At 3:30 a.m. on July 18 the North Shore Regiment supported by the Fort Garry Horse tanks, attacked Tilly-la-Campagne, but by dawn only half the town had been taken. Most of the tanks were destroyed and the North Shores were cut off. In the centre Lieutenant Colonel John "Rocky" Rockingham managed to capture Verrieres village on the crest of the slope, the only success of the entire operation. The Royal Regiment had failed to reach its objective of Rocquanfort. On the right flank the Calgary Highlanders reached the outskirts of May-sur-Orne but were driven back in the face of severe German resistance. Before it even reached the start line, the Black Watch lost both its commanding officer and the senior company commander. Reorganization threw the advance towards its objective, the village of Fontenay-le-Marmion, badly off schedule. By 9:30 a.m., unaware that the Calgary Highlanders had been driven back, the Black Watch marched up the slope into a trap. Furious German tank, anti-tank, mortar and machine-gun fire from all sides ripped them to pieces. That morning the regiment lost 123 killed, 100 wounded and 83 taken prisoner, the worst single day's losses in its history.

At this stage it was the commander of the Third Canadian Division, Major General Rod Keller, who came in for criticism, not only from Simonds, but from Crerar and some British commanders as well. Crerar had already warned Keller that a senior British officer had shown him a letter, "to the effect that it was too bad Keller, who was an excellent commander, drank too much and made an objectionable fool of himself on social occasions." Simonds considered sacking him but demurred on the grounds that "his qualities…are unimportant at the moment in comparison with the bigger problem of maintaining morale of 3 Canadian Division." Embarrassment was saved all round when, a little over a week later, Keller was wounded when American aircraft mistakenly bombed the division, and was replaced by Major General Dan Spry.

On July 25, Omar Bradley's US First Army broke out of the bridge-head at St. Lo. To try to stop the American spearheads pushing south and to isolate General George Patton's Seventh Army plunging into Brittany, Hitler ordered a counter-attack forcing the Germans to move west towards Mortain. But with the help of RAF rocket-firing Typhoons, they were stopped in their tracks and, with Montgomery keeping up the pressure around Verrieres Ridge, the Germans in Normandy were trapped. Now the blow was ready to fall in the direction of Falaise. Montgomery ordered Operation Totalize to begin on August 8, fittingly, the anniversary of the great Canadian victory before Amiens in 1918.

Simonds Second Canadian Corps on the British left flank was in the best position of any to attack towards the objective and was logically, therefore, given the assignment. Once again, Simonds preferred to attack at night. At 11:00 p.m. Simonds again used his "artificial moon-light" preceded by heavy air bombardment directed by red and green flares fired by the artillery. The dust churned up by the armoured personnel carriers and the tanks made the advance difficult, but by daylight most objectives had been realized including the capture, at last, of Verrieres Ridge. The Canadians now paused to regroup, but in the meantime the Germans brought up reserves, as well as a number of assault guns and their vaunted Tiger tanks.

That evening, due to a mix-up in communications, or a lack of them, the US Eighth Air Force scattered its loads on the First Polish Armoured Division as well as the Canadian Third. The Sherman tanks of Major George Kitching's Fourth Armour Division suffered heavily at the hands of the Tiger tanks' 88-millimetre gunfire. And the British Columbia Regiment got lost. For their efforts the corps had gained a paltry seven miles.

By August 10 the Germans were still in the Mortain area. Patton's XV Corps had reached Le Mans and was wheeling north toward Argentan. Montgomery now wanted Falaise captured as quickly as possible before the Germans could escape. Simonds drew up a plan for the final operation — Tractable. After several changes in schedules and other details, the Canadians were to take the high ground north and east of the town, then thrust south-east to Trun. Kitching's armoured division was assigned to attack on the left flank, the Third Infantry Division and the Second Armoured on its right. The date set was August 14. George Kitching remembered the briefing well:

It was a very tough and unpleasant briefing of all the armd regt CO's and bde comds [*sic*] on Aug 13. Simonds blasted armoured regiments for their lack of support for infantry — he quoted the heavy infantry casualties of the past month compared to armour. He demanded much greater initiative from armd regts — drive on — get amongst the enemy etc. Forget about harbouring at night — keep driving on. Arrange your resupply accordingly. Don't rely on the infantry to do everything for you! It was a real blast and it shook everyone up. I was upset because apart from the Cdn Green Gds ops [*sic*] and harbouring on August 8 I felt our commanders of regiments did not deserve such treatment. Worthington had shown great dash on the night 8/9 and had captured one of the Polish Div's objectives with the BCR and Algonquins…but it is important to remember that up to that occasion none of our armd regts had to operate in the dark — it was policy to harbour and refuel etc.

Low-flying medium bombers laid down a carpet of bombs with the artillery firing off smoke shells, another Simonds' innovation, to blind the German gunners. Nevertheless, when the attack began, they fired point blank into the advancing Canadians, inflicting heavy casualties and damaging a number of Sherman tanks. The infantry had covered a lot of ground but the principal objective, Point 195 on the Caen-Falaise road, remained in enemy hands until August 16. That same day Falaise fell to the Canadians.

Montgomery now ordered the American XV Corps, which by now had come under his jurisdiction, to advance north. But it was too late to complete the encirclement of all the German forces, thousands of which were fleeing through the ten-mile gap. To shrink it, Simonds ordered Kitching's Fourth Armoured Brigade to thrust south to Trun, while the First Polish Armoured Brigade made for Chambois. The Fourth reached its objective on August 18 but the Poles did not take Chambois until the next day, the date the first contact was made with the Americans. As the Germans tried to flee through the narrow gap, Allied fighters and fighter-bombers harassed them continuously, taking a horrendous toll in dead and wounded, as well as destroying tanks, transport and horses.

On August 21, after three days of bitter fighting at St. Lambert Dives, the key escape route between Trun and Chambois was slammed shut by a detachment of 175 men of the South Alberta Regiment commanded by Major David Currie who was awarded the Victoria Cross for his gallantry and leadership under fire.

In Normandy, the Canadians suffered heavier casualties than any others in the Twenty-first Army Group: 18,444, of which 5,021 were killed. Totalize and Tractable alone accounted for a loss of 5,679 men. The significance of this high casualty rate was not lost on Simonds, though other Canadians in high command and the Cabinet itself turned their backs on it. Simonds was looking ahead, concerned about reinforcements. As early as August 7, he had briefed Crerar on the situation as it applied to the Second Corps. The Second Division alone was deficient by 1,910 infantry and other ranks and would probably be 2,500 short by the end of Totalize. "No definite information is available to this headquarters," he went on, "concerning further arrivals of infantry general duty reinforcements and it is felt that for one reason or another, the system for the supply of reinforcements to this theatre is not functioning satisfactorily and that reinforcements in sufficient quantities to take care of actual and probable losses are not immediately available."

Next day, Simonds reported that reinforcements were taken off ships and sent straight into battle. On another occasion a draft advertised as 1,600 strong arrived two days behind schedule and consisted of 690 infantry and 160 for other arms. "I feel," Simonds complained, "that field units should be relieved of any anxiety concerning the availability of reinforcements when an operation is required to be undertaken...nor does there appear to be any reasonable reassurance of an improvement in the situation."

Crerar was well aware of the need for reinforcements — particularly for trained infantrymen, but, in a sense, because it had political over- and undertones, he could not change the situation, he could only request. The ball landed squarely in the court of Lieutenant General Kenneth Stuart, Chief of Staff at Canadian Military Headquarters in London. Stuart faced a thorny situation, one that dated back to June 21, 1940, when Parliament passed the National Resources Mobilization Act (NRMA) providing for universal conscription for the defence of Canada. This was Prime Minister Mackenzie King's wily way of appeasing Quebec by avoiding a repetition of the conscription crisis that took place during the Great War. A NRMA conscript would not be sent overseas but could volunteer to "go active" — be transferred to the Canadian Active Service Force — if he so chose.

At this time there was a general feeling that the war would soon be over so that, while there was still a need for reinforcements, only a short-term solution seemed to be required. In other words, make do with what you've got by reshuffling and reallocating personnel. Stuart took the line of least resistance. Take a cook, and remuster him into an infantry battalion, send the wounded back into battle as soon as they were well enough to walk. As the war moved into Holland and the Americans advanced on a wide front to the German border it became obvious that the war would continue for some time longer. Sooner or later the situation of the Canadian shortage of reinforcements had to come to a head. It did. The catalyst was Simonds.

On September 27, 1944, when Crerar fell ill and Simonds took over command of the First Army, he had to face the problems of inferior equipment, high casualties and insufficiently trained replacements. Meanwhile, on September 18, Major Conn Smythe MC arrived on a stretcher in Halifax and in a signed statement to the *Globe and Mail* said that the "large numbers of unnecessary casualties" had resulted from the fact that "reinforcements received now are green, inexperienced, and poorly trained." His remarks made headlines and caused an outcry from coast to coast. Defence Minister Ralston had earlier declared in Parliament, "If we cannot maintain the army overseas with volunteers and it is necessary to send NRMA men, there can be no alternative for me to recommend action under the act and I shall do so." Now he hastily announced he would visit the overseas commands to learn the truth.

His first interview was with the battle-hardened, outspoken Chris Vokes, commander of the First Division in Italy, who emphasized the need for properly trained replacements. Ralston promised Vokes that if, after talking to Simonds in the Scheldt, the latter corroborated what Vokes had told him he would advise the Cabinet to release *trained* NRMA men for service in Europe. Simonds confirmed exactly what Vokes had said, as well as providing the minister with similar reports from his own divisional commanders. When Ralston returned to Ottawa, Mackenzie King accepted his resignation over the issue and replaced him with McNaughton. In the long run, however, NRMA men — known as "zombies" to volunteer service men and women, and practically everybody else — *were* sent overseas.

In Holland, as acting commander of the First Canadian Army, Simonds faced the responsibility of opening the port of Antwerp to Allied shipping. This was vital to supplying the Allied armies in the field facing the German border. The situation had become so critical that General Dwight Eisenhower, the Supreme Allied Headquarters Expeditionary Force commander, called a halt to any further offensive until the situation had been alleviated.

This task had been made formidable after the British and Canadians allowed the Fifteenth German Army to escape. On September 4, the Eleventh British Armoured Division had captured Antwerp intact then pulled up short, ostensibly to rest and refit. The Canadian Second Corps was wasting time and energy freeing the channel ports, no longer a threat to anyone or anything. Meanwhile the Germans had made for the port of Breskens on the south shore of the West Scheldt River. By September 6, having crossed the river north to Walcheren Island, they had manned the key fortress of Flushing and were heavily mining the Scheldt Estuary.

Shortly after taking command, Simonds issued operational orders to his two corps commanders, Lieutenant General Sir John Cocker and Major General Charles Foulkes, who had replaced him as head of the Second Corps. His formula involved four operations. The first objective was to clear the area north of Antwerp and close off the South Beveland Isthmus to the west. The second was to clear out the Breskens pocket between the south bank of the Scheldt, the Leopold Canal, and the Canal de Deriviation de la Lys. The third stage was to reduce the Beveland Peninsula and the final operation was the capture of Walcheren itself.

Simonds set up his headquarters on the grounds of the Chateau den Brandt on the south side of Antwerp, well hidden by trees covering the trailers and marquees. This afforded protection from air attack but not necessarily from the German V-1 flying bombs and V-2 rockets that began falling on the city soon after the Allies liberated it. At the height of the Battle of the Scheldt, King George VI visited the chateau to confer the Companion of the Order of the Bath upon Simonds.

As an army commander, Simonds was even further removed from the actual fighting than before, but now he could influence it and also control the battle. On October 3, thanks to his persistence with the RAF 84th Group of Tactical Air Force, the bombing of the Walcheren dykes was carried out by 243 heavy bombers dropping 1,263 tons of bombs. They left a gap 75-yards wide and the sea flowed in virtually "sinking" the island. The flooding created beaches in the breach and inside the island itself and severely disrupted German communications and ammunition supplies. Montgomery was highly impressed with the accuracy and success of the operation. By the third week of October most of the island lay under water.

Simonds had begun to experience the military politics that went with high command. After the failure of Market Garden, the attempted airborne assault to breakthrough the Ruhr, Montgomery's prestige had fallen. He was not the useful ally to Simonds that he had once been. Furthermore the vendetta existing between Montgomery and the RAF and the Royal Navy going back to Normandy, inhibited Simonds plan for heavy bombing and airborne support to take Walcharen Island.

Clearing the Breskens pocket on the south shore of the Scheldt was done under the most arduous conditions — swampy, half-flooded land, cold and rain. One of the most spectacular feats of this entire mopping-up operation was conducted on October 9 by the 9th Infantry Brigade led by Brigadier John "Rocky" Rockingham. At three o'clock in the morning, a flotilla of 97 Buffalo LVTs (Landing Vehicle Tank), under cover of heavy artillery fire, left the port of Terneuzen, made its way west across the Braakman Plaat (inlet), to land 2,000 men with their vehicles, equipment and supplies at the backdoor of the Breskens pocket, on the south shore of the Scheldt. This flanking assault eased the pressure of the 7th Brigade fighting on the north of the Leopold canal and paved the way for the eventual capture of Breskens.

By contrast, it took less than a week to clear the South Beveland peninsula. Simonds's plan for the capture of Walcheren Island at the west end of the peninsula called for a three-pronged attack. The British 4th Special Brigade was to land near Westkapelle, on the western tip of the island, while the British 4th Commando, accompanied by the 52 (Lowland) Division, was to storm Flushing from Breskens. From the east on the South Beveland peninsula the 5th Canadian Infantry Brigade was to attack across the long and narrow Walcheren causeway.

The west end of the causeway was heavily defended with German mortar and artillery. The salt marshes on either side were not deep enough to allow for assault craft and too muddy to support men or vehicles. There was only one way across and that was straight down the exposed causeway in the face of murderous enemy fire.

For Vitality, as the operation was coded, Simonds had relied heavily all along on RAF bomber command to take out the German coastal guns, particularly around Weskapelle. But on the eve of the assault, October 31, the weather had so deteriorated that the bombers in England were grounded. Next morning, November 1, the sky had cleared sufficiently to allow tactical air force rocket-firing Typhoon fighter-bombers to plaster the gun emplacements. The firepower was not enough to destroy them but it did take them out of action.

Earlier, at 8:40 on the evening of October 31 on Beveland, the Black Watch Regiment sent three companies in pelting rain forward across the Walcheren causeway. German shelling forced them to hit the dirt. Luckily many were fortunate to be able to take cover in brick-lined slit trenches abandoned by the Germans. There they remained until dark before pulling back. But it had proved to be chaotic. The regiment was down to 60 men.

Next, it was the Calgary Highlanders' turn. Just before midnight they started across the narrow route to the island. By 9:30 the following morning, November 1, they had established a small bridgehead about the midway point on the causeway, where a crater blocked it, and hung on grimly. The following morning Le Regiment de Maisonneuve were to form a toehold on the island itself where the French Canadians would be met by the 1st Battalion of the Glasgow Highlanders of the British 52nd Division. Relieving the Calgarians, by dawn one company of Maisonneuves had established themselves at the Walcheren end of the causeway, but the regiment was down to 40 men.

Later in the morning, the Glasgow Highlanders moved in to consolidate the position. By that time the amphibious assaults at Flushing and Westkapelle had landed the British commandos and infantry. It was all over except for mopping up. A week later, Middleburg, the capital of the island, finally surrendered. By that time the mines had been cleared from the river and on November 28, the first convoy sailed into Antwerp — led by a Canadian merchantman.

During the Scheldt campaign from October 1 to November 8, 41,043 Germans had been taken prisoner and another 30,000 were casualties. The First Canadian Army suffered 12,873 casualties, half of them Canadians. At least half of those might have been spared but for Mackenzie King's shameless political pandering to Quebec over Conscription. On November 4, Simonds issued a congratulatory note to all those who had fought in the battle:

> The fighting has had to be conducted under the most appalling conditions of ground and weather. Every soldier serving in this army — whether he has fought along banks of the Scheldt or in driving the enemy from the northeastern approaches to Antwerp — and every sailor and airman who has supported us — can take a just and lasting pride in a great and decisive victory.

Montgomery had written to Simonds the day before to say:

> It has been a fine performance and one that could only have been carried out by first class troops. The Canadian Army is composed of troops from many different nations and countries. But the way in which you have all pulled together, and operated as one fight-

ing machine, has been an inspiration to us all. I congratulate you personally.

Even Crerar sent his congratulations. In a signal from the United Kingdom he wrote, "My sincere congratulations to you on the great ability and drive which you have carried through your recent very difficult responsibilities to a most successful conclusion. As a result the reputation of [the] First Canadian Army has never stood higher." The inventive Major General Sir Percy Hobart who had created vehicles for mine sweeping, crossing boggy ground, filling ditches and demolishing obstacles, known roundly as "Funnies," had these words of praise:

> I would like to say myself how much I enjoyed working with you. You are always ready to discuss ideas: you have provided a whole series of new techniques and methods and have succeeded in surprising the enemy on many occasions; and it has been a great relief to be able to get firm decisions from you and feel sure they would remain firm. I hope very much that I shall have the satisfaction of working with you again.

The Scheldt had shown Simonds to be an army commander without peer. It had elevated him as an international soldier to be admired, respected and trusted with troops of all nations, British, Polish, Czech, French and American, as well as Canadian. After the battle, along with Lieutenant General Sir Brian Horrocks, Simonds became Montgomery's favourite corps commander.

By the beginning of February 1945 the Allied armies were ready to bring down the curtain on the Second World War in Europe. The first objective was to clear the Germans west of the Rhine then cross that river and drive into the heart of the Third Reich, joining up with the Russians advancing from the east. The First Canadian Army, once again under the command of Harry Crerar, was charged with the job of capturing the Reichwald Forest, breaking the Siegfried Line and seizing the Hochwald Forest defences. It was a slogging, inch-by-inch battle fought on mud and flooded ground and through water sometimes three feet deep.

The first phase of the attack, code-named Veritable, opened at 5:00 a.m. on February 8 with an overwhelming artillery barrage. Montgomery had correctly reckoned that the Germans would not suspect that his major offensive would begin on the Canadian front. The initial objective was the area between the Dutch-German border and the Hochwald, a forest reserve guarding the approaches to the crossroads of Xanten, the key to the Rhine crossings at Wesel. By nightfall of the first day the Reichwald Forest reserve defences had been broken and the Siegfried Line which ran through the western part of the forest, taken. As well, the defending German 84th Division had been smashed.

But there were problems. An attack north-east by the US Ninth Army had to be postponed when the Germans blew up the Roer Dam flooding the river and inundating the countryside. In the centre of the front an early thaw had turned the dirt roads into a muddy morass, forcing the British armour to use the few paved roads available. The destruction of Cleve and Goch by Allied aerial bombing hadn't helped either. The wreckage made both towns virtually impassable. On the night of February 19-20, the Germans counter-attacked inflicting heavy casualties on the Royal Hamilton Light Infantry and the Essex Scottish. And the initial objective, the Hochwald Forest, was still in enemy hands.

The second stage of the offensive, code-named Blockbuster, began on February 26, in which Guy Simonds' Second Corps would play a major role, with Brian Horrocks's Thirtieth British Corps guarding the Canadian right flank. The plan was simple. The Second and Third Infantry Divisions would take the Hochwald and the smaller Tuschen-wald and Baibergerwald forests beyond, separated by a gap through which ran the Goch rail line to Wesel. The Fourth Armoured Division was to sweep through this gap south of Xanten and then towards Wesel.

But, in front of the Hochwald Forest there was a belt of strong defences backed by nine German divisions, known as the Schlieffen Position. It was a tough go. Although the Second and Third Infantry Divisions penetrated the Schlieffen Position on the very first morning of the attack, the forest was so well defended it took another six days to clear the Germans out of it. At one point, impatient at the delay, Simonds jumped into his Staghound runabout vehicle and drove foward by himself. Encountering no enemy troops or hostile fire, he shouted to the foremost company, "Come on you bastards, there's no one here!"

Three days later came the news that the US First Army had captured a railway bridge across the Rhine at Remagen between Bonn and Coblenz. On March 11, the Germans evacuated Wesel. The campaign west of the Rhine was all over. By that time, Simonds had been given command of the Thirtieth Corps' divisions giving him a total of nine, equivalent to that of an army.

The crossing of the Rhine — Operation Plunder — marked one of the last acts of the war. Simonds's Second Canadian Corps was ordered north-west from its Rhine bridgehead to push the Germans out of eastern Holland, secure the Dutch coast along the North Sea, and move into north Germany on the left flank of the Second British Army moving toward Leeuwarden. Meanwhile, the Fourth Canadian and First Polish Armoured Divisions on the corps' right flank, advanced northward towards the Dutch-German border.

It was not until April 13 that the corps ran into enemy resistance at Groningen within sight of the North Sea defended by fanatical Dutch Nazis and the SS. It was a bitter battle, made more difficult by Simonds's order not to use artillery for fear of harming Dutch civilians. It took three days to force a surrender.

At noon on May 4, Simonds's corps was preparing to enter the port of Wilhelmshaven when he received a phone call from Crerar telling him that the Germans had agreed to meet with Montgomery. Next evening, at Bad Zwischenahn, Simonds accepted the surrender of the Germans in north-west Germany.

At the end of July Simonds, now 41 years old, assumed command of the Canadian forces in the Netherlands. In September he was charged with the repatriation of Canadian troops in Europe. During that time, Charles Foulkes, who had been subordinate to Simonds, was appointed chief of the General Staff. Simonds was disappointed at being overlooked, and he began to consider retiring from the army. Then, at the end of 1945 he was accepted as a student at the Imperial Defence College for the 1946 course. Early in the new year, he took leave and returned to Canada to see his family for the first time in six years.

Shortly after his arrival, he was honoured by the Ontario Legislature. Premier George Drew introduced him as "one of the war's most brilliant leaders." Simonds responded by urging universal military training. "I think in a democracy," he declared, "we must recognize the principle that, with equal rights must go equal, shared responsibility, and that when the nation is engaged in a life-and-death struggle, the whole effort must be put into the pool of victory."

Simonds was naive and way out of step with reality. His speech was hardly likely to endear him to the Liberal Party which had avoided conscription and was busy dismantling the armed forces. Nor would the government favour an advocate of universal military service as chief of the General Staff in peacetime. And none of the other political parties would want to pick up such a hot potato. After five years of war, the public was thoroughly apathetic. To hell with any more military. Get on with the peace.

But with characteristic lack of political instinct or sensitivity, Simonds continued his crusade with speeches and press interviews. At the end of the month he returned to England with his wife K and his son and daughter, to begin the course at the defence college.

After a year in England it was clear the Simonds's marriage would not last. The war, the years, the distance, had created an inseparable gulf between them. K went back to Winnipeg where she became seriously ill with cancer. After an operation and treatment she was cured and when Guy returned to Canada to take command of the National Defence and Staff Colleges, a joint command at Kingston, Ontario, in 1949 they tried a reconciliation. It didn't work. Their marriage was over.

During Simonds's tenure in Kingston, the defence minister, Brooke Claxton, had conceived the idea of creating a "super chief of staff," a military chief of the Defence Staff to match the defence minister. This came into being in 1950 with Charles Foulkes filling the position of chairman of the Chiefs of Staff Committee. Simonds, at the defence staff colleges, became the logical person to fill Foulkes' shoes as chief of the General Staff.

It was as if his arrival in Ottawa on January 2, at A Building on the corner of Elgin Street and Laurier Avenue in Ottawa had been perfectly timed to suit his military temperament and outlook. On January 31 Canada agreed to return to Europe under the North Atlantic Treaty Organization. The Korean War, which broke out of June 24, stopped the dismantling of the forces. In both cases Simonds had the job of organizing, mobilizing and reconstructing the ground forces.

Apart from their personal differences, there were bound to be a divergence of views between Simonds and Foulkes on these matters as well as others. Simonds was rigid and uncompromising; to him, everything was black and white, right and wrong. Foulkes had the government to consider, he was also in the position of having to satisfy all three services, not just the army.

From the outset, there was a fundamental difference in Simonds's view of Canada's military role and that of Foulkes and the Cabinet. Simonds considered it essential to maintain the Commonwealth and British connection, while Foulkes thought it more realistic to rebuild the forces on American lines with American equipment. He did not share Simonds's consternation at becoming more dependent on the

United States and falling under its influence. Paradoxically, Simonds expected Canada to join the US wholeheartedly in the struggle against Soviet Communism.

Simonds also opposed the estrangement of the RCAF from the RAF because it steered the former into the American sphere. He did not seem to consider or appreciate the shabby treatment accorded the Canadian air force by the RAF both during the war and after it. Foulkes wanted the RCAF to join the Air Division in Europe which meant it would serve in the American area. He also favoured the adoption of American aircraft, such as the Sabre — as the RCAF eventually did — on the grounds that American equipment was better and more readily available.

Simonds also deplored dependence on ballistic missiles armed with nuclear warheads. He correctly foresaw that this would lead to a mutually assured destruction between east and west and that this would lead to the reliance on conventional forces once more. Foulkes shrugged off the subject as a political responsibility not a military one.

As chief of the Defence Staff, Simonds was looked upon as a storm petrel, a thorn in the side of politicians. His critics accused him of not realizing that the Second World War was over and that military matters had to give way to the Canadian economy, of being ungraciously militant in his dealing with the government. But Simonds was a soldier, a military man who saw his duty as guarding the nation's interests and not being pushed around in the interest of satisfying voters. And the army praised him for it. The *Vancouver Province* editorialized, "he [Simonds] has demonstrated initiative and drive such as the defence department has not seen in a long time providing army forces for our commitments in Korea, Europe and at home." Internationally no other CGS had gained such respect. He was right most of the time, too. Reinstatement of conventional forces as the main bulwark of Western defence is one example.

In August 1955, after four and a half years as CGS, Simonds resigned and left the army. Prime Minister Louis St. Laurent expressed the grateful thanks of the nation when he wrote:

> I feel I should be remiss if on this occasion I did not express to you something of the admiration and regard with which we all look back over your long and distinguished career, including your brilliant and courageous leadership during the last war. Your great contribution to the defence of our native land and the preservation of the principles for which it stands will long be remembered.

Simonds had decided that he could do more for his country's defences outside the department than inside it. He thus became a self-appointed watchdog of how the defence department was run. This ran the gamut from the issue of nuclear weapons, enlistment, the unification of the services and the building of the Avro Arrow. By this time Simonds had developed other interests in civilian life as well. Retirement had changed the man. It had also changed his life.

Shortly after his retirement, Simonds met Dorothy "Do" Sinclair, a Toronto widow whose husband had been killed at Dieppe. After a six-year courtship, Guy divorced K and married Do. It was a happy union, Guy became more relaxed — and tolerant.

Simonds joined the Halifax Insurance Company as a director and took an active part and interest in the company's affairs. At the same time he took over the directorship of the Canadian branch of the Royal Life Saving Society as well as the chairmanship of the National Ballet. His hobbies were chiefly hunting and fishing — in that order.

In October 1962 Simonds was made an honorary colonel of the Royal Regiment of Canada at the time of the unit's 100th anniversary. Later, he was elected an honorary member of the Royal Canadian Artillery Association. On October 29, 1971 he was made a Companion of the Order of Canada.

In his last years his health deteriorated steadily. Guy Simonds died on Wednesday, May 15, 1974, at age 71. The funeral took place in Toronto's Grace Church-on-the-Hill. His coffin was carried to Mount Pleasant Cemetery where he was buried with full military honours — a 400 man honour guard and a 15-gun salute.

Keith Louis Bate Hodson
1915–1961

8

KEITH
Keith Hodson

When, on the morning of July 6, 1961, I opened the *Globe and Mail*, the front-page headline that stretched across the full width of paper hit me like a cannon shell from a Messerschmidt.

LEAPS FROM STRICKEN JET TRAINER

OWN CHUTE KILLS TOP RCAF MAN

Colorado Springs, Colo., July 5 (AP) - Air Vice Marshal Keith J. B. Hodson of the Royal Canadian Air Force, deputy chief of staff for operations at the North American Air Defense Command here, was killed late today parachuting from a disabled T-33 jet trainer 12 miles south of here.

Once I got over the initial shock, memories surged back with a rush.
D-Day + 39, July 15, 1944, Beny-sur-Mere, Normandy. East of the River Orne it had been a dicey-do. Ten German Messerschmidt 109 fighters had bounced our section of four Spitfires spread out in figure-four formation at 1,000 feet under a thick, grey cloud base. As each of us broke around and upwards into the attack, we became split up and it was every man for himself.

197

My evasive manoeuvre lifted me right into the cloud layer. We had been headed west towards our airstrip at the end of an hour-and-a-half of an air-to-ground sortie when the Huns caught us. I found myself trying to get my bearings on instruments, faced in the opposite direction. A quick check of my fuel supply told me I was flying on empty. Shit! Only one thing to do. Get home — fast!

I dropped down out of the cloud and made a sharp 180-degree turn starboard, took a quick lookout left, right and above, banking to either side for a glimpse below. All clear, thank God! But my worries were far from over. The Merlin engine started to sputter. Jesus! If it quit on me now I'd come down east of the Orne where the goddam Germans could grab me and take me prisoner — the bastards! I was sweating, priming the fuel pump for all I was worth. C'mon! Over the bloody canal at last. Engine still spitting like a son-of-a-bitch. Then mercifully, finally, the field came into sight on my left. If only I could keep that engine going. As I lined up on the north-south wire-mesh runway, it started to cough intermittently. I jammed the undercarriage lever into place, heard the wheels come down with a reassuring clunk. Then it happened. The Merlin conked right out on me. Another problem. I had too much height. That's when I should have pulled the undercart back up and pancaked, belly flop in and shorten the landing distance. But I didn't. I panicked. I shoved the stick foward to put the nose down, the propeller windmilling in front of me and, conveniently, I forgot to lower my flaps to induce drag. I hit the ground at around 100 miles an hour, 30 m.p.h too high for a normal landing speed. The Spit bounced once, then hit the ground again. The port wheel root broke right off. The aircraft spun around at right angles, bending the prop blades and the left wing-tip, before it jolted to a stop. And as if that wasn't bad enough, I noticed I'd failed to take the normal procedure of turning off the gun button. Luckily the prang failed to trigger either the machine-guns or the cannons which might have added murder of bystanders to my clumsy performance. Christ!

I quickly redressed that oversight, flicked off the engine switches, unfastened the safety and parachute harnesses, and climbed out of the aircraft feeling like an absolute idiot. A piss-poor show. After nearly two years on ops, I should have been capable of a lot better. But, perhaps after all, that was the problem. I'd been at it too long. I thought I knew it all; had become a complacent smart-ass. I was tired too, maybe. But at least the only bit of me that was hurt was my bruised ego.

Having watched the whole sorry spectacle from the operations trailer right across the strip, the tall, impressive figure of the airfield commander came bounding over. A paternal pat on the shoulder "You OK?" I nodded. "You have a knack for picking up flak, don't you?" he grinned sympathetically, referring to two days earlier when I got clobbered by ground fire and barely made it into a field wheels up. I shook my head. "No sir." I replied "This time it was finger trouble, loud and clear," a lewd term we used for a proper screw-up.

Several days later, the handsome Keith Hodson said goodbye to me as I hopped a transport for England on my way home, my tour of operations ended, probably not a day too soon. I did not see Keith again until May 19, 1960 at the first Canadian Fighter Pilots reunion in Toronto. He had not changed all that much; he seemed much younger than his 44 years even though as deputy chief of staff he was well on his way to becoming RCAF chief of the Air Staff and was shouldering enormous responsibilities. He still had that warm personality and assurance that made him such a popular station and field commander. Tragically, that was the very last time that we ever saw him.

Keith Louis Bate Hodson was born at St. Martin on the British Channel island of Jersey on September 12, 1915, the second of three sons of Vernon and Jeanne Marie Hodson. When he was a year old his parents moved to London, Ontario where his father enlisted in the Canadian Army (Royal Canadian Regiment) rising to the rank of brigadier. Keith attended London Central Collegiate Institute where he proved to be a star athlete in track, basketball and tennis. He was also a diligent student who worked hard to earn a $1,000 scholarship that allowed him to enter the University of Western Ontario. There he won a place on the tennis team which won the inter-collegiate title, as well as becoming a punter for the football team. When his father's regiment was transferred to Halifax, Nova Scotia two years later, Keith attended Dalhousie University where he graduated with a Bachelor of Science Degree in 1937. Because he needed a degree in engineering to join the RCAF, with which he had decided to make his career, he simultaneously — through evening classes — enrolled at Nova Scotia Technical School, receiving both diplomas at the same time. He had also become a member of the Canadian Officers Training Corps. On January 3, 1938 he joined the air force.

Exactly a year to the day later, he had completed his flying training at Trenton Air Station, received his wings and was promoted from provisional pilot officer to full flying officer. With the war clouds darkening on the horizon, half the graduating class was posted to the permanent RCAF squadrons, while the rest, including Hodson, were sent to No. 112 Detachment in Winnipeg for further training to qualify them as instructors. In May 1939, Hodson was posted to the Central Flying

School at Camp Borden. In November when the CFS was transferred to Trenton, Hodson was promoted to the rank of flight lieutenant.

The following month the British Commonwealth Air Training Plan came into being and Hodson became one of its artisans. The first of the many airfields and schools springing up across the country was No. 2 Service Flying Training School at Uplands, just six miles south of Ottawa. When Keith arrived there at the beginning of 1940 as examining officer, the buildings were still in the process of construction and there were not even any living quarters. Hodson and others had to find accommodation in town. At the end of the year Hodson was posted to Moncton, New Brunswick, to help organize No. 8 Service Flying Training School. Shortly afterwards he was made chief flying instructor.

Hodson proved to be not only a first-class instructor but an able administrator and organizer as well. But he yearned for an overseas posting. That opportunity presented itself in November 1941 when he became attached to RAF Ferry Command as the second pilot of a B-24 Liberator in which he made the flight to England via the northern route.

On his arrival in Great Britain, Hodson was marked for leadership and was immediately posted to an operational training unit for fighter instruction. He then became apprenticed to 602 Fighter Squadron equipped with Spitfires and commanded by the famous Irish ace, Paddy Finucane. At this time, in early 1942, British fighter command was engaged in fighter sweeps over occupied France against the German Messerschmidt 109 and Focke-Wulf 190 single-engine fighters, as well as providing escort to medium bomber daylight raids, and flying cover for Hurricane-bombers on coastal shipping strikes.

In June, having acquired the experience he needed, Hodson was promoted to the rank of squadron leader and given command of 401 Squadron RCAF based at Gravesend in Kent. In 1940, as No. 1 Squadron, the unit had been the first Canadian fighter squadron to go into action. By 1942, the veterans of the Battle of Britain had long since been replaced by graduates of the BCATP, some of whom Hodson had instructed himself.

The pilots liked him. As one of them said, "The first impression was that he was a very, serious dedicated type, but this mask of seriousness hid a very warm and ready smile that came easily and endeared him to everyone from the erks [ground crew] up."

July marked a turning point for 401 and other squadrons re-equipped with the improved Mark IX version of the Spitfire, more than a match for the hitherto dominance of the FW 190. On the 17 of the month Hodson scored his first victory by shooting one of them down. This occurred on the first raid in which the Canadians played escort to American B-17. "Flying Fortresses made their first appearance," Hodson noted in his log book. West of Rouen at 24,000 feet, 20 Focke-Wulfs dived out of the sun to attack the bombers on the port side. Hodson led his formation of 12 Spitfires, three sections in line astern, into the Germans' midst. Hodson zeroed in on the nearest one to him, closing to 300 yards. A three-second burst struck the port side of the 190's fuselage just ahead of the plane's tail. It went into a spiral dive from which it never recovered. In that same mêlée, the squadron accounted for another enemy aircraft destroyed, four probably destroyed, and one damaged; a cost of two pilots lost and one wounded.

One of the squadron's most spectacular successes under Hodson's leadership took place on August 19 during the Canadian ground assault at Dieppe. Three times Hodson led his pilots from Lympne airfield on the English coast over the blood-soaked beaches, enabling them to destroy one Focke-Wulf 190, probably destroying three others and damaging five more. Hodson accounted for one of them, a twin-engine Dornier 217 bomber.

The day after the Dieppe raid, the squadron moved back to Biggin Hill, Britain's most famous fighter field. On September 15, Hodson was awarded the Distinguished Flying Cross. The citation read:

> This officer has participated in a large number of sorties. He is a skillful pilot whose personal example has inspired the squadron he commands. Much of the success it has achieved can be attributed to S/L Hodson's excellent leadership.

In fact, during his tenure as CO from June 3, 1942 to January 21, 1943, Hodson had flown 85 sorties with the squadron, which had run up a record of 12 enemy aircraft destroyed, 11 probably destroyed and 28 damaged. With the rank of wing commander, Hodson now took over the Kenley wing comprised of four Canadian squadrons including 401. During the five months he commanded it his leadership shone through as he exhibited his qualities as a master strategist. Teamwork and discipline were his métier which he demanded of everyone who served with him. Bud Malloy, one of his squadron commanders, said:

> Keith was one of the greatest wing leaders. His objective was to achieve the aim set out for the operation, get as many enemy as possible, and protect the pilots in his wing. The tactics he devel-

oped greatly reduced our losses. He would position the wing for the attack and then cover the squadron he assigned for the target. It was excellent teamwork which enabled us to operate as a well-trained team. Unless we were very heavily engaged, we returned to base as a wing...Keith was an outstanding leader in the air, and on the ground as well.

Around about this time Hodson had been smitten by an attractive blond on the London Stage, Edna Smith (stage name Edna Harvey), a graduate of the Royal Academy of Ballet. When they were first introduced by a night club owner, who catered to airmen, the romance did not exactly get off to a flying start. When Keith asked Edna for her telephone number she replied: "look it up in the phone book." In the end love triumphed, however, and the couple were married on September 11, 1944, at St Luke, Chelsea in London. Eventually they had two children, a son, Michael, and a daughter, Suzanne.

Hodson was posted to RCAF headquarters at Lincoln's Inn Fields in London and later attended the RAF Staff College. Meanwhile he was awarded a bar to his DFC. In August 1943, he was given command of 126 Airfield of the Second Tactical Air Force, stationed in Kent where we lived under canvas. Later, as winter approached, we moved to permanent quarters at Biggin Hill where the airfield was redesignated 126 Fighter Wing RCAF. Though his duties were administrative he never missed an opportunity to join in on operational flights when time and circumstances permitted.

Two days before Christmas 1943 I was called into Hodson's office and told that we would be driving over to Kenley next day to have lunch with George Drew, then Ontario Conservative leader of the opposition and a friend of my family's. This was customary. When they visited overseas, VIPs frequently took the time to look up sons of their friends. This happened to me frequently though I always felt a little uneasy in the company of my buddies. On this occasion I missed out on a sweep. I watched the squadron take off before it was time to go.

During the lunch — I recall there were two others in the same boat as myself — Drew asked us what we expected when we got home. All of us, including Hodson, were from Ontario. Hodson alluded that he thought he spoke for the rest us — and he certainly did — when he said, "After experiencing the civilized fashion in which the British serve drinks in their pubs over here we'd like to see an improvement in the drinking laws." At the time Ontario, except for beer parlors, most of them lamentable, many of them disgraceful, was dry. Drew took it all in with good grace. On the way home, Hodson started to laugh. "Give him something to think about," he smiled. "Not a bad guy for a politician though."

When we got back to our own aerodrome the wing had not yet returned from their sweep. We knew they had to stop at Manston on the coast to refuel but they were still long overdue. We went into his office where Keith made a phone call. "They're socked in with the weather," he said. "But they say it should clear soon." He didn't sound convinced. He looked worried. It was mid-afternoon and it would soon get dark, as it does in that part of England in the wintertime. We went back outside and peered down the runway. "I want my boys home for Christmas," he said almost in desperation. I said nothing, there was nothing I could say. An hour and a half went by, then an orderly ran up, saluted Keith and set "They're on their way, sir." Keith's face was wreathed in smiles. It was an incident I have always remembered — his concern for his "boys."

I have a memento of my time serving under Keith Hodson which was typical of him also. It is a clipping from *The RCAF Overseas* which I pasted in the back of my logbook. It was reprinted from the daily Wing Routine Orders which Keith issued in Normandy, on July 1, 1944.

> Today is Dominion Day. Some of us have been away from home so long we forget temporarily what it means…Canada is a good place to live where a man of limited means can enjoy life and independence. Today all over the [Commonwealth], men will be paying tribute to Canada. While here in France you and I will be working to keep Canada the way we want it…If we doubt the urgency of our work, think what will happen if the Army between us and the Hun is pushed back in our laps…There will be no letup this summer…But with our resources and our good heart, we will one day send aircraft which will have no target so that next Dominion Day we can walk down our own main street and say "I am one of the Canadians who really worked to finish that War."

I have one last anecdote in connection with Keith that I'll always remember. It has to do with the fact that our own ack-ack gunners were pretty edgy and quite often mistook our own planes for German ones. The usual complaints were filed through official channels. This is one occasion when they went right to the top, *un*officially. At Beny-sur-Mere, General Montgomery kept the Flying Fortress that Eisenhower had given him on our field. It was well guarded, camouflaged and hidden by trees. One rather wet and dreary day in July, Montgomery appeared with his entourage. The motorized cavalcade of three vehicles had stopped at the entrance off the road close to the officers mess tent. Hodson must have got word he was coming because he was on hand to greet him, saluting all round with the usual pleasantries. I was within earshot, able to hear most of what was said. Montgomery asked how we were getting along and so on. Hodson smiled, "Well, we'd appreciate it if you could stop your gunners from shooting our planes down. We've got enough trouble with the Huns as it is!" Montgomery, who I had always pictured as being a rather stern character, broke into laughter. With a salute and a wave he was off towards his "Fort."

At the end of July, Hodson relinquished his command of 126 Fighter Wing and became attached to the United States 9th Air Force as liaison officer. In January 1945, he was appointed a commander of the Order of the British Empire, received the American DFC and was awarded the Croix de Guerre with Gold Star. In June 1947 he was promoted to the rank of group captain. He successively held the posts of chief instructor of the RCAF College in Toronto, chief staff officer of No. 1 Air Division in NATO with headquarters at Metz, in France, chief staff officer of Air Defence Command at St. Hubert, Quebec, and commandant of the RCAF College.

During his tenure at Metz with NATO, Hodson demonstrated how perfectly he understood the ramifications of the cold war. He had this to say:

In the final analysis, however, the use of the A-bomb means world war and the certain retaliation by US Strategic Air Command. In such case the situation in North America is equally critical to that of Europe and the entire world is at the mercy of the horrors of the hydrogen bomb. There will be no winner of that one. But the importance of German rearmament and subsequent strengthening of the Allied defences in Western Europe is that Russia could no longer win in Western Europe without embarking on a world war. With a German contribution, Western Europe should be in a position to withstand the shocks of the cold war, national governments should be safe from Communist coups d'etat from within, and the stabilization...should obtain. The major contribution of NATO then, is to political and economic stability in Western Europe, a stability which should allow Western leaders to negotiate with the East from a position of strength. The RCAF is proud to be contributing to that position of strength.

On July 1, 1952 Hodson had been promoted to air commodore. In 1958 when NORAD was formed he was given the post of deputy chief of staff and was promoted to the rank of air vice-marshal.

On July 5, 1961 Hodson was being checked out in a T-33 jet trainer by Colonel Harry Allen, a routine familiarization flight, when at 13,000 feet the aircraft's engine failed. Both men managed to jump out and their parachutes opened. But gusty winds hampered their landing. Hodson was dragged along and broke his neck. He was dead by the time Allen, who suffered cuts and bruises, reached him. His funeral was held at Canadian Forces Base Rockliffe Chapel and he was buried at the Beechwood Military Cemetery at Rockliffe with full military honours.

The library at the Canadian Forces Staff College is named in honour of A/V/M K. L. B. Hodson, OBE, DFC & Bar USA DFC, Croix de Guerre, whose memory stands as a monument to everything the RCAF stood for. In the library are two displays showing his officer's mess kit complete with miniature medals, his cap and his logbook, fittingly commemorating him.

John Meredith Rockingham
1911–1987

9

FATHER OF THE SPECIAL FORCE
John Rockingham

He was deep in conference with company union officials when the telephone rang. The caller was Lieutenant General Charles Foulkes, the Canadian general chief of General Staff, with a special request. At precisely the same moment that Prime Minister Louis St. Laurent was announcing over the radio that by an Order in Council the government had decided to recruit a Canadian special army force to meet its obligations to the United Nations forces in South Korea, Foulkes was asking John Rockingham if he would come out of retirement to head up that special force.

On that date, August 7, 1950, Rockingham had been out of the army for five years and held the position of superintendent of Pacific Stage Lines in Vancouver, British Columbia. Before reaching a decision, he told Foulkes he would have to discuss matters with the president of his company as well as his family. By the following evening, Foulkes had his answer and was able to advise the minister of National Defence, Brooke Claxton, that Rockingham had accepted the command. Within 24 hours, recruiting for the force had already begun and Rockingham was in Ottawa.

The army was looking for fit young men, particularly veterans and the sooner the better. The situation in Korea was desperate. On June 26, when the army of the Democratic People's Republic of Korea drove south across the 38th parallel of the northern latitude to invade the Republic of Korea, their troops within days captured the southern capital of Seoul and pushed the South Korean Army (ROK) back into a perimeter around the port of Pusan at the south-eastern foot of the peninsula. General Douglas MacArthur, commander of the Allied powers in the Pacific, reinforced it with the United States 8th Army.

In Canada it had been decided that to fulfil her United Nations obligations, the country would contribute an infantry brigade made up of three infantry battalions with a minimum of supporting arms and services to operate within a Commonwealth division. However, at this time the Canadian Army Active Force strength was down to 20,369; all ranks and formation of a new brigade would take every trained infantry soldier the army had. Charles Foulkes therefore recommended that consideration be given to recruiting a special force for combat in Korea. This would leave the Active Force intact for its joint role with the United States in the defence of North America. The minister agreed but doubted whether a special force could be raised quickly enough, in view of the existing employment rate — the country was flourishing — compared to 1939 at the tail end of the depression. But he was wrong, a lot of veterans had had a hard time adjusting to civvy street and they welcomed the opportunity to enlist with a sense of mixed relief and excitement. Claxton was both surprised and pleased with the quick results that the recruiting campaign had produced. After a visit to No. 6 Personnel Depot in Toronto, on April 11, Claxton reported to the CGS and the adjutant general:

> Altogether I must have seen four or five hundred [recruits]. They are young, generally between 18 and 25, exceptionally fit, (out of 253 examined, only 3 were rejected), generally with good background and fair intelligence. About 50% were veterans...In the two days they had fully processed something like 50 per day, whereas up to Wednesday they had 657 applicants...this depot will be dropping steadily behind.

In fact, by the end of the month that recruiting station alone had enlisted 2,075 personnel. In the final analysis, Dominion-wide, 45 per cent of those who enlisted had seen some sort of service during the Second World War and of that group 20 per cent were former non-commissioned officers. As for specialists, 20 per cent had trades of use to the army. The Special Force was off to a healthy start with a solid rank and file base. And its leader, John Rockingham fit the mould (veteran-civilian-re-enlister) to a "T." He was the logical man for the job. "Rocky" had been an outstanding brigade commander in north-western Europe during World War II and Foulkes was confident that he would get along well with the US military authorities. In 1945 Rockingham had retired after 12 years of service to go into business in Victoria, and later in Vancouver, BC. He certainly had the right outlook with what the CGS and the minister of defence had in mind for him. He left no doubt about his philosophy when he wrote:

> There is no peacetime job that you can compare with the demands of wartime command. If you're really conscientious and really think about what you're doing, you're exposing the lives of thousands of men in everything you do. And they've got to follow you; they have no choice. So you better be right...In business, if you take a wrong decision, you lose your money or you get fired. But that's pretty easy compared to losing a lot of lives.

He was the ideal choice — he'd worked both sides of the street.

John Meredith Rockingham was born on August 24, 1911, in Sydney, New South Wales, Australia. He first attended grammar school in Melbourne, then, after his parents emigrated to Halifax, Nova Scotia, went to school there, and in Barbados. In 1933 he joined the Canadian Army and was commissioned in the Canadian Scottish Regiment. Three years later, on January 11, 1936, he married Mary Carlyle Hammond. The couple had two children, a son, John Robert Meredith, and a daughter, Audrey Vincent.

When the Second World War broke out in 1939, Rockingham went overseas with the 1st Canadian Scottish Regiment as a lieutenant and was later given the rank of captain. In 1942 he was transferred to the Royal Hamilton Light Infantry as a major, and he served in this regiment with distinction in Normandy. By July 1944 he had been given command of the unit with the rank of lieutenant colonel.

On July 18, the 2nd Canadian Corps commander Major General Guy Simonds, launched Operation Spring with the objective of seizing the high ground on either side of the Caen-Falaise road. The attack took place at night using artificial moonlight — beaming searchlights against the cloud base to guide the way. But the assault ran into such stiff German resistance it proved to be a total failure. There was one notable exception. Under Rockingham's determined leadership the RHLIs managed to capture Verrieres village on one of the slopes and hung on desperately against fierce enemy counter-attacks. It was the only success of the entire venture.

Shortly afterwards, in August, Rockingham was given command of the 9th Infantry Brigade. Initially this was not a popular appointment with those who would serve under him. He had been ordered by Simonds to replace a commander who had objected to an order to commit his men to what he considered an impossible and unfair assignment. Padre Jock Anderson, who had landed in Normandy on D-Day with the Highland Light Infantry, described the situation:

> They fired our brigadier and the COs of the Novas and Glens [the North Nova Scotia Highlanders and Stormont, Dundas and Glengarry Highlanders], and as well our CO had been badly wounded. Everyone on the ground in Normandy...knew we couldn't possibly regroup to make a night attack. So when Rockingham was appointed brigade commander, we felt this was a slap in the face to us. The men were resentful. Then, one Sunday evening as I was finishing a service, he stepped up and asked if he could say a few words. He told those men in no uncertain terms that orders were orders — he would obey any order he was given and he demanded the same from the men.
>
> The fellows were really mad, but after a while they respected him. He was always seen where the battle was toughest, and everybody thought the world of him then.

Following the German defeat in Normandy, in September the 9th Brigade was assigned the capture of Boulogne where Rockingham accepted the German surrender of the garrison. In October the brigade was engaged in clearing the Breskens pocket on the south shore of the Scheldt Estuary, part of the operation to rid the river of the enemy on both sides and allow shipping to enter Antwerp.

On October 6, the 7th Canadian Infantry Brigade had successfully established a small bridgehead on the north side of the Albert Canal. However, the three regiments came under intense enemy fire, even from the heavy guns at Flushing across the river on Walcheren Island. But Rockingham had conceived a masterful scheme to relieve them.

At three o'clock in the morning of Sunday October 7, a flotilla of 97 Buffalo LVT's (Landing Vehicle Track, amphibious carriers capable of transporting 30 infantrymen), brought north from Ghent to the Scheldt, left the port of Ternuezen and began making its way across the mouth of the Braakman Plaat (inlet) under heavy artillery cover to land 2,000 men with their vehicles, equipment and supplies at what Rockingham called "the back door" of the Breskens pocket. By mid-morning, all three battalions of the brigade, the Highland Light Infantry of Canada, the Stormont, Dundas and Glengarry Highlanders, and the North Nova Scotia Highlanders, had reached a point just east of the fishing village of Hoofdplaat.

The Germans were taken completely by surprise. But, although he faced the Canadians on two fronts, General Knut Eberding, commander of the German 64th Infantry Division, was determined to drive them out of the pocket. An equally resolute Rocky Rockingham was just as determined to roll up the pocket as quickly as possible.

The Germans quickly pulled their defences together as Eberding rushed over reinforcements from Walcheren Island. Now a raging battle developed over the dykes and polders with ground gains measured in yards at a high cost in casualties to both sides.

While the HLIs and the Novas consolidated their position at the enemy's rear, the SD&Gs were assigned to "kick out the front." Operation Switchback called for them to breakout of the bridgehead, advance west along the coastal seawall and capture Hoofdplaat. After a bitter struggle, the village fell the next day but the regiment found itself surrounded. The Novas, who were to have advanced on the left flank were unable to do so, while the SD&Gs had outrun the range of their own field guns and were without artillery support. For the next three days they took a frightful battering from the heavy coastal batteries at Flushing. Finally on October 11, the Novas arrived on the left flank to relieve them; then they were ordered to capture the port of Breskens itself. Rockingham's flanking assault had greatly eased the pressure on the 7th Brigade and by the middle of October the Strooiburg bridgehead had been considerably enlarged. The 9th Brigade now received orders to advance west along the south shore of the Scheldt.

On October 31, Rockingham's SD&G and the HLI regiments had established a bridgehead at Retranchment near the Dutch-Belgian border. This enabled the North Shore Regiment from the 8th Brigade to pass through and force the Germans to surrender at the coastal resort of Knocke. Thanks to Rockingham's daring and ingenuity, the Breskens pocket was closed. The south shore of the Scheldt was in Canadian hands.

His leadership style and behaviour during the Scheldt campaign was typical of Rockingham. To those under him he was a big, burly, handsome figure, omnipresent, intrepid, flamboyant and always cheerful. Although it was an infraction of procedure at the brigade level, he insisted on spending most of his time at the front with his units, conducting the battle from his scout car, usually under fire. He inspired confidence in the ordinary soldier, aroused enthusiasm, even affection, probably more than any other Canadian brigade commander.

Before an engagement he would reconnoitre the battleground himself; he would never commit troops to ground he hadn't looked over first.

One junior officer described it: "Rocky would come to our forward positions (he seemed so huge sticking out of that little scout car of his) and he'd pop off a few shots, stir things up. After he left, we'd get the hell pounded out of us with counterfire. But the men loved it. They thought he was God."

Rockingham justified his actions in this way:

Maybe I differed from a lot of other guys, but I didn't believe you could get the feel of the battle, the smell of the battlefield unless you were up at the front line where the troops were, where you could see how their morale was, whether they were happy or unhappy, why they were unhappy, why they were happy. So I believed that the front line was where a brigade commander belonged, at least part of the time.

I used to take the little armoured car I rode around in, it had a big 52 radio set and I could talk for thirty miles back, so I could relay messages directly from the front to my headquarters and my battalions.

When the war in Europe ended in May 1945, Rockingham had been made a companion of the British Empire and had been decorated with the Distinguished Service Order and Bar, the Belgian Order of Leopold with Palms, and the Croix de Guerre with Palms and was given command of the 2nd Infantry Brigade of the Japanese Canadian Force slated for service in the Pacific. When the war with Japan ended in August, the force was disbanded and Rockingham took his discharge from the army with the rank of brigadier.

The family settled in Victoria where Rockingham took a job as personnel supervisor with the BC Electric Railway Company. Then, in 1949 when he became staff assistant to the general manager of transportation, the Rockinghams moved to Vancouver. He subsequently became assistant general superintendent of the Vancouver and Intercity Lines before being appointed superintendent of Pacific Stage Lines.

On August 10, 1950, two days after accepting the appointment as commander of the Canadian Army Special Force, Rockingham arrived in Ottawa to begin selecting officers from the applications pouring in since the prime minister's speech. He and the Command and Staff Selection Committee put a top priority on wartime service. In view of the lack of time to train the new brigade to fight, this was sound. Leaders with qualifications to teach the fundamentals in a hurry were mandatory. Two of the three commanders of the infantry battalion were volunteer veterans. The commanding officer of the third battalion, the artillery regiment and the field ambulance unit, were regulars. Also from the Canadian Active Force were the two staff officers. In every case each one of these officers had served with distinction during the war in the same capacity for which they had now been selected.

Initially, the organization, predicated upon the Canadian Army Active Force, which would supply instructors, the Canadian Army Special Force would be made up of a Royal Canadian Regiment, a Princess Patricia's Canadian Light Infantry Battalion, a Royal 22nd Regiment ("Van Dooz"), and the artillery unit, designated the 2nd Regiment, Royal Canadian Horse Artillery. The question now arose as to where the brigade should be trained. The Canadian winter weather ruled out the home ground as a suitable venue. Japan was considered — it would be close to the scene of action — but General Douglas MacArthur questioned the political wisdom of having a force that was not one of the occupying powers on Japanese soil. He suggested, and offered instead, Okinawa — then in US possession — as a feasible alternative. However, Brigadier J. F. Fleury, in charge of the newly established Canadian Military Mission, Far East in Tokyo, after a visit to the Okinawa, in a detailed report to General Foulkes, stressed that its facilities made it totally unsuitable and unacceptable as a collective training area. It was finally decided that Fort Lewis, Washington which was available, would make an ideal training ground in every respect, particularly with its accessibility to the embarkation port of Seattle. This marked the first time that a Canadian formation was to be trained in peacetime in the United States. And it was there that the Canadian Army Special Force took on the designation 25th Canadian Infantry Brigade. Its original name was seldom used again.

Meanwhile, the war in Korea had changed dramatically. On September 15, 1950, in a daring amphibious operation, MacArthur launched an assault on Inch'on, the port of Seoul, capital of South Korea, designed to sever the North Koreans' lines of communication. On the 26, Seoul itself fell. Now the American 8th Army broke out of the Pusan perimeter at the toe of the peninsula, where it had been holding out, to link up with the forces in the capital. The North Korean advance of four months earlier had been turned into a rout with the US and South Korean (ROK) armies chasing the enemy back towards the 38th parallel. By the end of the first week of October they had driven them across the parallel. By the middle of the month, Pyongyang, the

North Korean capital, had fallen and the US and ROK troops were fast advancing on the Yalu River dividing China from North Korea. MacArthur considered the war won. After a meeting with him, Brigadier Fleury wired General Foulkes:

> General MacArthur indicated Canadian Brigade would be of no repeat no significance from view small current operation. He suggests Canada might prefer to send immediately token force to show flag.

On the last week of October Foulkes was advised that the US joint chiefs of staff had recommended to the State Department that the Canadian contribution would be reduced to one battalion. And the way that the war was inevitability winding down it seemed likely that battalion would end up as an occupation force. However, the USJCS hinted that the remainder of the 25th Brigade would probably train in Fort Lewis that winter. It was agreed by both Canada and the US that as long as any uncertainty existed about the Korean situation, a trained force remained essential and there should be no let-up in training plans.

The 25th Brigade proceeded by rail to Fort Lewis on November 11. But the PPCLI, commanded by Lieutenant Colonel James Stone, the battalion picked to serve in Korea, spent less than four days there before embarking aboard the US Naval Ship *Private Jo P Marquez* from Seattle on the 25.

The departure left the remainder of John Rockingham's brigade very much up in the air and not without a tinge of envy. In recruiting the Special Force, great emphasis had been placed on overseas service, an opportunity for adventure, if you will. The result was an enlistment of a group that might be called soldiers of fortune. Now, it appeared that only a fraction would see overseas service and then merely in an occupation capacity.

This might well have created a morale problem had anyone other than Rockingham been in charge. No matter what the situation, he inspired confidence and, if anything, the training intensified, and morale was maintained at a high level. It was as if Rockingham had an insight into the future. And that future was right around the corner.

On October 31, Brigadier Fleury reported to the chief of staff committee in Ottawa that intelligence in Tokyo was puzzled by statements made by Chinese prisoners that they had been crossing the Manchurian border moving south towards Korea since October 19. The first ones were captured on October 25. This stunned everyone concerned. That this came as a surprise in view of Mao-tse-tung's threats that his People's Army would not stand idly by if Communist territory was violated, now seems incredible.

Moving at night and undetected from the air, by mid-November the Chinese had advanced five divisions, 180,000 strong across the Yalu River — the Korean border. Now the war took a new, entirely different turn. In the face of this situation, however, MacArthur had remained undeterred and, in fact, on November 24 launched a fresh offensive employing both the US Eighth Army and 10 Corps. They reached a point between Pyongyang and the Yalu before the Chinese waded into them in force and turned the offensive into a rout.

It was in this much changed atmosphere that Brigadier Fleury greeted the PPCLI on arrival in Yokohama. No more occupation, the troops were now slated for the real thing. The question was how fast they could be thrown into the fray to help stop the advance in the north. At 7:00 p.m. on December 18, the regiment disembarked at Pusan. After a period of training, an advance party of the PPCLI, now part of the 27th Commonwealth Brigade, reached the front near the town of Changhowon on February 12. The Canadians were about to see their first action in Korea. Nine days later the announcement was made that the rest of the 25th Brigade would follow.

On February 21, the minister of National Defence stated:

> Yesterday inquiry was received from the unified command of the United Nations forces in Korea as to whether training of the balance...was complete, and if so, could it be sent to form part of the United Nations Forces in Korea?
>
> This training is almost complete, and the government agreed today that the other elements in the Brigade group should shortly proceed to Korea and join the second battalion of the Princes Patricia's Canadian Light Infantry there.

At Fort Lewis, training proceeded apace, not without a few headaches. On December 1, after the Chinese intervention in Korea, Rockingham was informed that the 400 trucks and half-tracks that had been purchased from the US Army were to be returned for overseas shipment. This turned out to be only temporary. Then there were shortages, mostly nuisances, like the lack of stationery and ink. Other problems included, machine tools in the workshop that would only operate on direct current; and none of the American mortars which had been promised were ever delivered, though the Royal 22nd made do with six issued them in Valcartier.

Rockingham overcame the restrictions on the use of live ammunition for the heavier weapons by moving the anti-tank squadron, the artillery regiment, and the infantry anti-tank platoons to the firing range at Yakim, 80 miles east of the camp. The range was ideal for training purposes, with miles of rolling hills and valleys resembling conditions in Korea. He also considered it necessary for the infantry to train with tanks, and ordered the anti-tank squadrons to conduct tank-infantry training using its self-propelled M10 guns for this purpose.

By mid-February Rockingham had devised an ingenious live-firing exercise with which to round off the training. It was brilliant in its inception and accounted for the brigade's later success in the field while keeping casualties to a minimum. The first phase was a practice attack by an infantry company in advance supported by an allotment of weapons from a support company and a battery of field artillery. It required two platoon attacks accompanied by a company attack. The second was a battalion attack followed by consolidation on the objective. Each battalion was supported by the full weight of the guns of the 2nd RCHA, a troop from the armoured squadron, a troop of field engineers and a detachment from the signal squadron. The final stage was an attack in three phases by the entire brigade. In all cases live ammunition was used by both "them" and "us," and the exercises were monitored by observation towers along the route.

"Ignes Bellum" was followed by another of Rockingham's brainwaves. Operation Scramble was an exercise in rapid movement covering each of the operations of war. However, weather conditions prevented its being completed. The Fort Lewis training programme ended with a sand table exercise — "Finale" — on March 30 and 31. It was a lesson in the art of withdrawal.

When the ships *Marine Adder* and *General Patrick* docked at Pusan on May 4, 1951, the 25th Brigade had sailed into a type of war completely different from what it had originally been recruited to fight. On March 15, Seoul had been recaptured from the Chinese, and the UN forces were closing in towards the 38th parallel. Crossing it now became an issue. There were two schools of thought. Try again for a complete victory or accept a stalemate and attempt a negotiated peace. MacArthur favoured the first choice on the basis that "war's only object is victory." But he had no support from members of the United Nations, or from US President Harry Truman who reasoned that the alternative to stalemate was a "general war with Communist China" with the risk of a Third World War. MacArthur publicly criticized these views and was sacked for his pains. "We are trying to prevent a world war — not start one," Truman stated bluntly, and promptly replaced the "old soldier" with 8th Army commander, General Matthew Ridgeway.

Just prior to this turn of events, the PPCLI, as part of the 27th Commonwealth Brigade began moving into position to the high ground north-west of Hoengsong. Rockingham, who had flown to Korea on March 26, visited them three days later. But en route, his guide led him to the wrong ridge, one held by the British Argylls Regiment. As a result he was forced to descend the 600 foot-high ridge and climb another, equally high, before reaching the Patricias. It was midnight by the time he returned, a trudging journey through snow. It was there the battle of Kap'yong was fought between April 23 and 25 in which the PPCLI thwarted a Chinese attack aimed at capturing Seoul. By the 25 the regiment was surrounded and had to be supplied by airdrop until relieved. For its part in the battle the unit was awarded the US presidential citation.

One of Rockingham's first moves after his brigade had disembarked and set up in an empty prisoner-of-war camp nine miles from Pusan, was to convert his anti-tank squadron into an armoured one equipped with Sherman tanks. When he arrived in Korea earlier, Rockingham had learned that although the Chinese rarely used tanks, tank support for the infantry was essential. He also discovered that the enemy were experts at ambushing tanks all along the front and lines of communications. Rockingham also replaced the cumbersome 17-pounder anti-tank guns with American 75-mm recoilless rifles.

To acclimatize the troops with local conditions, Rockingham put Operation Charley Horse into effect which entailed climbing the mountainous hills surrounding the Pusan airport. On May 15 the brigade began moving north by wheeled vehicles.

A counter-attack by the US 10th Corps and the 1st ROK Corps on May 20 on the western section of the line completely upset the Canadian timetable. Instead of a period of settling in, the brigade found itself taking part in a fresh advance towards the 38th parallel. This operation must be viewed in the perspective with the now prevailing United Nations policy of creating a stalemate. The overall aim was simply to relieve pressure on the central and eastern sections of the line under attack, and prevent the Communists from launching a fresh offensive — nothing more.

On May 24, the 25th Brigade was placed under the command of the 25th Division and moved from Haech'on to an assembly area north-east of Uijongbu, near Sunae-ri from where it kicked off its first operation, code-named Initiate. Starting off at 9:30 a.m. on May 25, there was no opposition until mid-afternoon when the Royal Canadian Regiment were fired upon on Hill 70. The Van Dooz also met enemy fire north of Hill

329. By dusk both battalions had occupied defensive positions north of Changgo-ri. On May 27, the brigade had established positions covering Line "Kansas" after a further advance was made without contact. Next day the brigade had reached a point overlooking the 38th parallel in the area of Samdalbat. They had advanced nearly 30 miles through the mountainous countryside.

On May 29, with a Philippine battalion on the left and the Royal 22nd on the right, the brigade began an advance, Operation Followup, north of the 38th parallel. During this advance some Chinese foward positions were inadvertently bypassed and some Chinese taken prisoner.

On May 30, the RCR replaced the Van Dooz who now launched a drive in heavy pouring rain designed to overcome the formidable mountain barrier of Kakhul-bong. At first all went according to plan until around mid-day when the Canadians ran into determined Chinese resistance for the first time and with good reason. Kakhul-bong represented the Chinese main supply centre for materials from Manchuria, as well as being the hub of the enemy's lateral communications across this sector of the Korean peninsula. From the top looking south almost to the 38th parallel, any movement on the main road could be easily spotted. From this vantage point the Chinese were able to see every move the Royal Canadian Regiment made and gear their defences accordingly. The enemy defended it for all he was worth keeping up a steady rain of fire from mortars, small arms and machine-guns.

Reviewing the situation from Brigade Headquarters, Rockingham saw that although the brigade's advance had created a deep salient in the Chinese lines, his units on the left were without protection. On the right the closest troops were 8,000 yards behind, while the forward line of the left flanking unit was 7,000 yards back. One of the companies was in danger of being surrounded. Rockingham, as usual, wasted little time coming to a decision. He gave orders to withdraw. It was a slow and painful retreat. The regiment lost a lot of its equipment, six NCOs and men were killed in the fighting and two officers and 23 men were wounded.

On June 1, the 25th Brigade less the Royal 22nd, the Royal Regiment and the Royal Canadian Horse, was relieved by the 65th US Infantry Regiment. Four days earlier the PPCLI rejoined the brigade it had left six months earlier to act as an "occupation force." By June 3, the brigade became part of the 1st Commonwealth Division positioned south of the Imjin-Hantan rivers junction. On June 18, the Canadians, under the command of the US 1st Cavalry Division, were given the task of relieving the 28th ROK Regiment and the 65th Infantry Regiment of the 3rd US Division at the Ch'orwon end of the "Wyoming" position, a front stretching 7,500 yards south-west of the outskirts of the town which was included in their sector. Their assignment was to make deep patrols into no man's land and probe their defences, keep them off guard.

Within the brigade's sector the PPCLI was on the left and the RCR on the right with the Royal 22nd in reserve in rear of the RCR. The Princess Pats' position lay on the southern edge of a narrow valley, dominated by high ground on the far side. The RCR were on high ground overlooking Ch'orwon and the Ch'orwon plain stretching away to the north. The brigade faced north-west, but its boundaries extended north and south and within them, ahead of the forward defences, extended an area of hills interspersed with narrow valleys with quite level floors.

On June 21, the RCR made the first deep patrol into no man's land beginning at 6:30. a.m. consisting of tanks, infantry and a tactical air control party. During the afternoon the troops encountered sporadic resistance by small bodies of Chinese, but by 4:00 o'clock they had penetrated eight miles into enemy territory reaching the town of Hahoesun. Then when an observation plane reported an enemy concentration on a hill nearby, the patrol withdrew arriving back at the starting point around 7:00 p.m.

This was typical of patrols carried out by the 25th Brigade until mid-July — all of them difficult and increasingly dangerous. Rockingham himself took part in some of them. But insignificant though they may seem individually, collectively all these actions formed an important, integral part of the overall effort to bring the antagonist to the peace table. In this they succeeded. By June it had become obvious that a military solution to the Korean problem could never be achieved. On July 5, the Communists agreed to meet the United Nations negotiators at Kaeson, on the 38th parallel, three days later, to discuss terms of a ceasefire. Meanwhile, however, the war continued.

During the month of August the 25th Brigade became involved in a series of operations along the Imjin River. Then, in September it took part in Operation Minden that began with crossing the Imjin and establishing a bridgehead on the north side from which, alongside the 29th Brigade, it advanced north. This was followed by Operation Commando in October, a further penetration. These had been well-coordinated exercises in which all objectives had been achieved and did much to solidify the cohesion of the Commonwealth Division as a whole. But by this time the peace talks had reached their own stalemate, the negotiators wrangling over how to supervise an armistice and repatriate prisoners of war.

In November, reacting to Commando, the Chinese began a series of attacks in the area of the valley of Sami-ch'on and its eastern tributary. The RCR and the Princess Patricias bore the brunt. These actions that fell were typical of what had become a "limited" war with each side maintaining the pressure to strengthen its hand at the bargaining table. On one point, however, agreement had been reached. It was announced on November 27 that the forward line then existing would be the demarcation line in the event of an armistice. Fifteen days earlier restrictions on further UN offensive operations were laid down — infantry operations were limited to reconnaisance patrols and artillery to defensive and counter-battery responses. Rockingham's headquarters noted that "apparently the object is to show the enemy that we...will honour a cease-fire if one is agreed." However, these restrictions did not stay in effect for long. The talks bogged down again and the "limited" war resumed at its previous localized pace.

By April 1952. Rockingham had been in Korea for two years and few senior officers understood the Canadian military requirements as well. Training, reinforcement replacements, morale, equipment, rotation factors, all were operational considerations he knew from first-hand experience at the staff administration level. On April 10, Brigadier M.P. Bogert arrived in Korea to replace him. Rockingham who, once the 25th Infantry Brigade had been firmly established, had transferred to the Canadian Army Active Force, was now appointed to the position of director-general of Military Training and returned to Canada. For his service in Korea he was appointed companion of the Most Honourable Order of the Bath and awarded the US Legion of Merit (Degree of Commander).

In 1953, Rockingham attended the Imperial Defence College in England and that same year was appointed commander of the Third Canadian Infantry Brigade. On September 2, 1954 he took command of the First Canadian Infantry Division. A force of 14,000 troops, it was the Canadian Army's first peacetime division. Rockingham called it a "historic day for Canada and the most memorable day of my life." In 1955 he received an honorary Doctor of Laws (LLB) degree from the University of New Brunswick which he had attended briefly in the 1920s. In 1957 he became general officer commanding, Quebec Command. From 1961 to 1966 he served as GOC of Western Command with headquarters in Edmonton, Alberta, before retiring from the army with the rank of major general.

He then moved to Victoria where, from 1966 to 1972, he was employed by the Mannix Group and also served as councillor to the

Canada West Foundation. In 1969, he became governor of the BC Branch of the Royal Life Saving Society and in 1978 was appointed honorary colonel of the Canadian Scottish Regiment (Princess Mary's).

Rockingham retired to Qualicum BC. On July 24, 1987 he died in Vancouver Hospital at age 75. Memorial Services were held at Christ Church Cathedral in Victoria a few days later.

Wilfred Austin Curtis
1893–1977

10

AIR CHIEF EXTRAORDINAIRE
Wilf Curtis

The Fokker's Spandaus were spitting out deadly lead on a collision course with the Sopwith Camel whose pilot answered the enemy fire with his own Vickers machine-guns. Such eerie encounters, aerial versions of "chicken," were commonplace in the skies over the Western Front in 1917. It was a question of who was going to break first. In this instance it certainly wasn't going to be the Canadian pilot. Though his knees were knocking with fear, he counted on his German adversary being just as scared and made up his mind to hang in there regardless of the risk. It was just that same rugged determination than made Wilf Curtis, a stocky five-foot-nine bundle of energy, the ablest, most outstanding chief of the Air Staff Canada ever produced. During his six-year tenure from 1947 to 1953, the Royal Canadian Air Force grew from 13,000 to 50,000 men and women, with 41 squadrons, and 3,000 aircraft with a billion-dollar-annual budget. It absorbed half of Canada's defence allotment to become one of the most effective and efficient fighter forces anywhere.

Curtis came to the command with an abundance of unique qualities. He was the only RCAF officer to have served as an officer in all three services, the army, navy and air force. He was also the only reserve officer to assume the mantle of CAS — from 1932 until the start of the Second World War he had served with the air force auxiliary as a flight commander. An outstanding pilot, during the Great War he became a fighter ace with 13 victories, for which he was twice decorated. Highly successful in business between the two wars, his administrative skills

227

comfortably translated to his duties as an air force staff officer during World War II.

But when, on September 1, 1947, the Ministry of Defence announced the appointment of "Air Marshal W. A. Curtis as the new chief of the Air Staff of the Royal Canadian Air Force," the news was greeted with both consternation and resentment throughout the higher ranks, as well as in some not-so-high levels, of the service.

Curtis's achievements and abilities were widely known and respected, After all, he had currently served as vice-chief of the Air Staff under Air Marshal Robert Leckie (who recommended him as his successor). But, compared to the other senior officers in the air force, men who had made the RCAF a lifetime career, he was a mere junior with only eight years of "time in" — practically still a civilian. However, this was not the sort of situation that the affable, unflappable Curtis with the ready smile, would ever let bother him. He knew how to handle it. Characteristically he faced it and, with his considerable powers of persuasion, turned it around. Let's get on with things! The mood quickly changed and the dissension vanished as rapidly as it arose. This was hardly surprising, because, from a tender age Curtis had learned how to cope with crisis, win the confidence of others and succeed no matter what the problem.

Of United Empire Loyalist stock, Wilfred Austin Curtis came into the world on August 21, 1893 in a white two-storeyed house on the main street of Havelock, Ontario, a prosperous lumbering town 25 miles east of Peterborough, where his grandfather, Colin McKenzie Curtis, owned several of the town's largest mills.

Wilf was only 18 months old when disaster struck the Curtis family. One morning, while waiting for the tar to heat on a stove preparatory to finishing a roof patching job Colin had taken on, the bituminous liquid boiled and spilled over setting fire to the mills which burned to the ground. Wilf's parents moved to Toronto where his father took a job as a road construction boss with the city's works department, laying the municipality's brick roads.

When Wilf reached school age he attended Dovercourt Public School and then completed two years of a business course at the Central Technical School, making him eligible for a job with the Royal Bank of Canada. He joined it in 1909 at age 17 as a ledger keeper at the Bloor Street and Dovercourt Road branch. Later he worked as a teller and accountant at the bank's Ontario branches in Oshawa, Ingersol and Leamington.

When the Great War started in 1914, Curtis applied for pilot training with the Royal Naval Air Service. By 1915, having received no response from the navy, he enlisted in the 34th Infantry Battalion earning the rank of sergeant. He later transferred to the 21st Regiment in Windsor, Ontario, where he was commissioned as a lieutenant and posted to London, Ontario for an officers' training course. He had nearly completed his training when he was told to report to Admiral Sir Charles Kingsmill, director of the Royal Canadian Navy in Toronto. Kingsmill approved his application for pilot training at the Glen H. Curtiss Flying School at Long Branch, outside Toronto's western outskirts. This was a civilian organization which supplied flying training for the RNAS at the rate of $1.00 a minute's flying time. James McCurdy who, in 1919 made the first powered flight in Canada in the *Silver Dart*, managed the enterprise and, years later he and Curtis would become close friends.   23 FEB / 1909 /

Flimsy Curtiss Jennys were used for instructing and were flown only when the wind blew directly from the south across Lake Ontario. Crosswind take-offs were suicidal. McCurdy would warn his students, "Don't turn your back on our field or you'll smash our aircraft." By August 11, 1916, Curtis had completed his solo tests. Four hundred minutes in the air, just under seven hours flying time, had qualified him for his civilian flying licence. He received number 3391 issued by the *Federation Aeronautique Internationale* in Paris. His training had cost him $400, of which a grateful RNAS refunded $365, and admitted him into the flying service as a probationary flight sub-lieutenant.

The next step in the training programme was a six-week indoctrination course at London's Crystal Palace in England to teach the flying cadets how to become sailors. This rigorous instruction consisted of drilling daily from six o'clock in the morning until six that evening on the parade square under the harsh supervision of a tough Royal Marine sergeant major disciplinarian. From there the class was posted to the newly opened flying field at Cranwell in Lincolnshire, the site of the future Royal Air Force College, for advanced flying training.

As had been the case at Long Branch, the pupils received their instruction on Curtiss Jenny biplanes. On arrival at Cranwell, Curtis immediately became the butt of a joke. The senior cadets would tell the incoming class that Curtis was actually the son of the famous American aviator, Glen Curtiss, and had been flying since he was 13 years old. His first solo flight at Cranwell hardly warranted such distinction. He had been told to circle the field ten times. On the eighth circuit he saw a sinister black cloud looming towards the aerodrome. He turned tail to make a somewhat hasty wobbly landing. However, Tom Howe, his instructor assured him he'd made the right move.

Some days later, again on a solo flight, he was flying along at an altitude of 600 feet when he suddenly decided to shut off the engine and glide. But, up until then nobody had told him that without enough air speed the airplane would stall. And that is exactly what happened. The Jenny flicked over and crashed into the ground, a total write-off. Curtis was lucky it hadn't caught fire. He was also fortunate that his leather flying helmet had prevented a head injury, but he was badly banged up nonetheless. Enough to keep him in hospital at Chatham for two months before he was released and sent home.

Six weeks later he was back at Cranwell for further flight instruction, then, on June 6, 1917 he was posted to Dover for a two-week gunnery course. There, in a Sopwith Pup, he executed a loop for the first time at the safe altitude of 7,000 feet. It was a hairy experience all the same. Dust showered from the cockpit floor and the seat came loose. But, undeterred, Curtis tried seven more loops. He was determined to master every manoeuvre he could.

Having completed his gunnery training, on June 25, Curtis joined No. 6 (N) Squadron stationed near the Bray Dunes in Flanders, equipped at the time with the nimble little Nieuport scouts. It was with Naval Six that Curtis, who by then had 20 flying hours in his logbook, chalked up a couple of firsts. Early in July he was flying the tail position in formation, when without warning, the leader executed a quick steep turn to starboard. Curtis's Nieuport went into his very first spin from which it took him 2,000 feet to recover.

Some days later he spotted an enemy plane for the first time. He was on a lone patrol when three German Albatros fighters suddenly appeared ahead, one of them trailing some distance behind the other two. Curtis swung around for what he hoped would be a quick, easy kill. No such luck! The other two enemy pilots manoeuvred in behind him, forcing him to beat a hasty retreat for home.

Late in August 1917, Naval Six was disbanded due to a shortage of RNAS pilots and Curtis was posted to No. 10 Squadron stationed at Droglandt in Belgium. Attached to the Royal Flying Corps, Naval Ten was in the process of exchanging its Sopwith Triplanes for the newer Sopwith Camels when Curtis joined it. It was with No. 10 that he scored his first victory. That was on September 6. His flight was on patrol south-east of Dixmude when it encountered six Albatros scouts. Closing in on the nearest one, Curtis took careful aim and fired 250 rounds seeing "many tracers" striking the enemy plane's fuselage. The machine fell into a flat spin and fell 3,000 feet out of control.

His list of victims mounted steadily and by the end of October, Curtis had seven enemy aircraft to his credit including a double score on October 21. On November 4 he repeated the performance by racking up another pair of victories, but next day his flying career nearly came to an end. By this time he had been made a flight commander and promoted to the rank of flight lieutenant and was leading a flight of five Camels behind the enemy lines. At 8,000 feet the patrol spotted a formation of eight enemy fighters above them. Although outnumbered, Curtis climbed his flight towards the Germans then as they drew within range, both formations opened fire. Suddenly one of the enemy outside wingmen did a roll, "which," Curtis said later, "should have warned me that they were above average pilots." Curtis's own machine was struck by enemy fire and he found himself upside down, then the Camel went into a power-dive. His seat belt had come loose and he had to hang on for dear life to keep from falling out of the cockpit.

The Camel continued to dive from 12,000 feet down to 3,000 all the while pursued by enemy fighters, sniping at it, shredding the wings and fuselage with their fire. At 3,000 feet, Curtis dove his plane into a cloud and cut the engine to regain control of the machine. Curtis noticed that the main spar had been badly damaged and he hesitated about restarting the motor for fear the wings might give way from the acceleration. But he didn't have much choice. He was well behind enemy lines. It was either restart the engine or glide down and be taken prisoner. As he gingerly began to put power back on, his luck held. The Camel stayed in one piece and he made it back to Droglandt. Curtis was certain that the German pilots had marked him down as a "victory."

Then there was that head-on dogfight with the Fokker, an experience he would never forget. In the end the German pilot finally gave in and, as he turned, Curtis delivered the fatal blast that tore into the enemy machine sending it spinning to earth in flames.

As his score steadily grew, on November 20, he was awarded the Distinguished Service Cross for "conspicuous gallantry and devotion duty." The citation to the award added that he had: "on many occasions destroyed and driven down out of control enemy machines."

Curtis scored his final victory, his 13th, on January 23, 1918, on patrol at 7,000 feet over Staden. The Naval Ten pilots saw two enemy two-seaters and an Albatros scout silhouetted on top of a layer of cloud beneath them. The Camels dived down on the Germans who tried to escape into the cloud. Then, five more Albatros fighters suddenly appeared. Curtis attacked one of the two-seaters, firing 75 rounds from a range of 40 feet. The enemy aircraft broke in two and tumbled into the clouds.

Unfortunately, in that engagement, Curtis was injured, and a week later, was given sick leave to England and was awarded a Bar to his

DFC for "continuous skill and courage as a fighting pilot." The citation also noted that he had "destroyed several enemy machines and driven down others absolutely out of control."

In March, Curtis was invalided back to Canada. By November, fully recovered, he bought a train ticket to New York to board a ship and sail back to England where he hoped to get a posting to France to rejoin the fighting, when news arrived. The Germans had surrendered. The war was over.

In 1919 when Curtis received his discharge, he considered returning to banking but quickly rejected the notion. The excitement of aerial combat had aroused the adventure in him and he decided to strike out on his own. He remained in New York City where his first venture ended in failure. He put his savings into an ingenious gadget, a tilting, locking steering wheel auto accessory to retail at $35.00. But no one was interested and he soon abandoned the enterprise. He next took a job as a sales representative with a New York distributor of, ironically, German household goods and toys.

It was at this juncture that Curtis met Pearl Burford, daughter of a Toronto building contractor; she had come to New York from the Royal Conservatory of Music for advanced musical studies. Pearl and Wilf Curtis were married on October 15, 1924 and subsquently had three children, two sons and a daughter. By this time Curtis had returned to Toronto to form the insurance partnership of Moore and Curtis, later to become W. A. Curtis and Co., one of the city's most successful insurance brokerages.

But, despite the pressure of business, Curtis lost none of his military leanings or interest in flying. He joined the militia and as a captain in the Toronto Scottish Regiment attended weekly drills and summer camp exercises. At the same time he also directed his energies — and his money — to keeping the Toronto Flying Club flying. Three times he served as president of the organization that flew its trainers from De Lesseps Field on Trethewey Drive.

On October 5, 1932, when the RCAF formed No. 10 City of Toronto Auxiliary Squadron at Camp Borden, Ontario, Curtis became one of its first members and a flight commander, as a non-permanent air force officer with the rank of flight lieutenant. In 1935, with the rank of squadron leader, he took over as commanding officer. His energy, not to mention his enthusiasm, seemed boundless. One of his associates advised him, "Stick to business. Never mind the airplanes. You'll ruin yourself." But Curtis shrugged off the remark and, if anything, intensified and widened his interest in "the airplanes."

In 1933 at a Toronto convention of the Royal Canadian Legion, he tabled a recommendation that the government be petitioned to make the RCAF an autonomous service with its own chief of staff. Hitherto it had operated as virtually a branch of the army under the command of the chief of the General Staff. As a result of Legion pressure and agitation from other influential sources, by 1938 the air force had its own chief of the Air Staff and, down the line fittingly, the one who had made the original recommendation would hold that position.

By this time 60 per cent of Curtis's waking hours were spent administering to the needs of the Toronto Flying Club, whose financial woes never seemed to get sorted out, as well as working with the auxiliary air force squadron. Even his summer holidays were taken up flying with the RCAF out of Camp Borden and Trenton. Fortunately, his brother, Roy, was able to shoulder most of the insurance business load.

In 1938 with the expansion of the RCAF, two more auxiliary squadrons in Ontario were formed, one at London and the other at Hamilton, and the Toronto squadron was renumbered No. 110. As one of the most experienced auxiliary air force officers, Curtis was chosen to command the wing and given the rank of wing commander as a non-permanent officer. The following summer, as war clouds darkened the horizon, Curtis was given the additional responsibility of supervising the preparation of RCAF accommodation on the grounds of the Canadian National Exhibition in Toronto, preparatory to opening No. 1 Manning Depot, a processing centre for recruits. Time was of the essence. War seemed bound to break out no later than the fall and all indications pointed to a heavy enlistment, unemployment and the tradition set by Canadians in the air in 1914-18, being among the chief reasons.

By mid-August Curtis, close to exhaustion, retired to his cottage in Muskoka for a much needed rest from his business, the flying club and his air force duties. It was fated to be short-lived. On August 27, 1939, he received an urgent phone call from Air Commodore Harold "Gus" Edwards, the RCAF air member for Personnel, advising him that his services were required immediately. Next morning he reported to headquarters in Ottawa where Wing Commander Wilf Curtis was sworn in as a regular air force officer. Just in time. War broke out within the week.

There was lots of work for him to do. From Ottawa he directed preparations for sending Canadian squadrons overseas. His old auxiliary squadron, No. 110, mobilized and equipped with Lysanders for aerial reconnaisance, was one of the first to reach England.

Curtis was then sent to Toronto to recruit staff to operate the Manning Depot. That accomplished, his next assignment was selecting sites in Ontario for flying fields to implement the British Commonwealth Air Training Plan, a sizeable undertaking. But within months, under Curtis's direction, teams had combed the countryside and contracted land for fields at Mount Hope, Dunnville, Welland, Fingal, Goderich, Hagersville and Aylmer. It is worth mentioning that by the following spring aircraft were operating from the bombing and gunnery school at Fingal, testimony to the speed and thoroughness with which Curtis and his staff had tackled the task.

Curtis returned to RCAF headquarters in Ottawa, where he took over the post of director of postings and records and was promoted to the rank of group captain. Early in 1941 he was appointed station commander of No. 2 Service Flying Training School at Uplands, six miles south of the capital. Then in August he was back at headquarters as director of manning.

Curtis held that assignment until November 22, 1941 when he was posted overseas with the rank of air commodore as deputy to Air Marshal Harold Edwards, air officer commanding the RCAF overseas. His role in the United Kingdom was destined to be a formidable one. Before leaving Canada his orders from Charles "Chubby" Power, the minister of air for National Defence were far from explicit. "Put the RCAF on the map" he told him. But the implication was clear enough.

In November 1939, Prime Minister William Lyon Mackenzie King laid the groundwork for "Canadianization" when he spelled out his dictum that "Canadian personnel from the training plan [BCATP] will, on request from the Canadian government, be organized in Royal Canadian Air Force units and formations in the field." Regardless, from the start the British believed that Canadian formations overseas were really an integral part of the British Imperial forces. On the other hand, the Canadian government was determined to keep control of its overseas forces and preserve their Canadian identity. It was these diametrically opposed points of view that lay at the root of the AOC and his deputy at RCAF overseas headquarters at Lincoln's Inn Fields in the heart of London.

The manifestation of this situation was the influx of trained Canadian aircrews arriving in Great Britain without sufficient numbers of RCAF squadrons to absorb them with the result that they were being assigned to Royal Air Force units. By the time the number of RCAF squadrons had expanded to the point that they could comfortably accommodate these personnel, the RAF resolutely refused to surrender them. By 1943 the friction between the two services had reached a high point. On January 20 Edwards blew his stack. In haste and in anger he tactlessly bulletined Chubby Power, with a copy to the Air Ministry, in which he stated that, "I have requested that instructions be issued that no RCAF aircrew are to be posted to the United Kingdom except to Canadian units until the RCAF squadrons have one hundred per cent RCAF aircrew," and requested that his HQ take over postings and records of all RCAF personnel. He further added that "Canada should never have participated in the JATP [Joint Air Training Plan] but should have built up an air force of our own."

At 9:00 that morning when Edwards showed the signal to Curtis, his deputy was flabbergasted. "You didn't send that?" he asked. "Oh yes I did," Edwards replied, "four hours ago." When Curtis asked why Edwards hadn't shown him the signal earlier so that they could have talked it over the latter was intransigent. "If I did that," he said, "you would have talked me out of it and I didn't want that to happen." In the end the issue of Canadianization was gradually solved, not without a lot of wrangling on all sides. But in no small measure the oil that was poured onto troubled waters was the result of Curtis's restraining influence and common sense approach.

When the war in Europe ended in May 1945, Curtis returned to Canada as air member for Air Staff (later amended to air member for Air Plans) at RCAF headquarters in the Lisgar building in Ottawa with the rank of air vice-marshal. Among his responsibilities was the air force's participation in the war in the Pacific against Japan which, of course, never materialized.

With the advent of peace, under normal circumstances, Curtis would probably have retired from the air force and gone back into the insurance business. But by this time he was vice-chief of Air Staff under Robert Leckie who strongly urged the Ministry of National Defence to appoint him as his successor. On October 1, 1947, Curtis became chief of the Air Staff with the rank of air marshal. Added to his Great War decorations were the commander of the Order of the British Empire, the Efficiency Decoration, the USA Legion of Merit, the French Legion of Honour and Croix de Guerre with Palm.

By this time the RCAF had been reduced to a mere skeleton of what, at the end of World War II, had stood as the fourth largest air force in the world. Manpower was down from 250,000 to 13,000. Curtis described the situation:

> At the end of the war...we did not demobilize according to plan whereby we would lose so many instrument makers, and so

forth...We were in a pretty bad way for a while. We were short some 4,000 men from the approved establishment — which meant we had to set up a complete organization...to train men in all sorts of trades, including aircrew.

Our next task was to start some sort of worthwhile flying activity. During the war we did no photograph work in the north. The Department of Mines and Resources had been working on photographs taken before the war. We therefore set up a photo organization with first one, then two, and then three squadrons to photograph the north country. In 1948 we did some 911,000 odd square miles of photography, and that is a lot of territory to cover when one realizes that the bulk of it was in the north where most of the bases are 500 miles away from the areas where the flying was being carried out. It was really quite an achievement.

The war in Korea and the Cold War in Europe radically changed the government's attitude towards military spending. The North Atlantic Treaty Organization and the United Nations commitment in Asia forced an about face for Canada to meet its obligations. Under Curtis's able and energetic guidance and leadership, the role of the RCAF in both instances was nothing short of spectacular.

During the Korean War, the RCAF's contribution consisted of ferrying troops, mail and freight by North Stars from McChord Field at Tacoma, Washington to Tokyo and Misawa in Japan with refuelling stops at Alaska and the Aleutians en route. In all, it was a round trip of 24 hours flying time. During the nearly four years that the war lasted, Canadians flew seven million pounds of freight and 13,000 passengers and chalked up 34,000 flying hours without the loss of a single life or bit of cargo.

It was Curtis who convinced the government that Canada should make a major contribution to NATO. On April 4, 1949, the country became signatory to NATO committing the RCAF to four wings of three squadrons flying the latest and best fighter of the day, the North American F86 Sabre, built under licensing agreement by Canadair, Montreal. Curtis explained the reason for the choice, "We decided that our wisest course would be to try to standardize on equipment that we could get...*here*." Throughout the 1950s Canada stood as the principal air defence force on the continent.

At home the RCAF needed a special type of aircraft particularly suited to Canadian needs, one of all-weather, long-range fighter design suitable for flying in the north. The CF-100 developed from Curtis's credo that "if you must have an air force, you must have an aircraft industry to support it." By encouraging Avro Canada at Malton outside of Toronto to develop the aircraft, the RCAF not only created employment for engineers and the setting up of an engineering staff, but also helped the industry to support the air force. The resulting versatility of the CF-100 was one of its features with which Curtis was particularly pleased. He claimed that the aircraft was a credit to the Canadian aviation industry.

In November 1948, the first edition of the *Roundel*, the RCAF's postwar monthly journal, rolled off the presses with Curtis's introduction to Volume 1, Number 1. His words provide an interesting insight into the man:

> In Service as in civil life, these are days of increasing specialization. While specialization is absolutely essential to the operation of so complex an organization as an Air Force, the danger always exists that the specialist's view of the woods may become somewhat obscured by the trees. Against this danger there is only one safeguard: extensive reading and discussion. Only thus can we retain that wider perspective which gives full meaning to our individual tasks.
>
> Few of us have the time or even opportunity to ferret through the mass of available literature in the hope of here and there coming upon something that may contribute to our complete mental orientation. How many of us, indeed, can do much more than merely keep abreast of developments in our own variously limited spheres?
>
> The *Roundel* is an attempt to overcome the restrictions imposed upon our reading by lack of leisure. Drawing from all possible sources it will contribute as much material as the Editorial Committee considers to be of particular interest and value to all ranks and trades of the RCAF.
>
> No single issue, it is realized, can be composed entirely of articles which will make an instant appeal to every member of the service. I cannot too strongly recommend that every member of the Service read the *Roundel* from cover to cover. To peruse only those portions which relate directly to one or two particular trades would defeat the whole purpose of the magazine.

On a visit to No. 2 Fighter Wing at Grostenquin in France, in November 1952, Curtis was suddenly afflicted by severe stomach pains. He was flown to England and rushed to the RAF hospital at Uxbridge where his appendix was removed. However, during the operation a stoppage in the main bowel was discovered and he was transferred to Westminster Hospital in London where he underwent further surgery. The doctor prescribed two months' convalescence. During that time he received a visitor, a tall man wearing the RAF uniform of an air commodore. It was his old instructor from Cranwell days, Tom Howe.

When Howe learned of Curtis's operations he became worried that they might have been caused by the "gliding" crash he'd been lucky enough to survive 36 years earlier. Curtis assured him the current ailments were unrelated to the accident which, despite two months in hospital, left him without a scar. Curtis, whose weight had dropped from 175 to 151 pounds, confided to Howe that he was planning to retire. On January 31, 1953, he left the RCAF and he and his wife returned to live in Toronto.

In retirement Curtis remained active and maintained his connections with the air force and the aircraft industry. He was elected president, then grand chairman of the RCAF Association. He became vice-chairman of A.V. Roe (Canada) Ltd., and subsequently of the parent company, Hawker Siddley (Canada) Ltd. In such a capacity he was understandably upset and chagrined when the Conservative government under Prime Minister John Diefenbaker cancelled the Arrow on "Black Friday," February 20, 1959.

In 1956, Curtis was approached by a group of influential Toronto citizens to head up an organizing committee to inaugurate a second university for the community. One spokesman said, "We were looking for a man who was prominent in public life and who was an administrator." By 1959 the Ontario Legislature passed a bill without a single dissenting vote to incorporate York University. Before the campus was built, various buildings were used as temporary quarters. In 1961 Curtis became the university's first chancellor.

Air Marshal Wilf Curtis, air chief extraordinaire, died of a stroke on Sunday August 7, 1977 at Sunnybrook Veteran's Hospital in Toronto. The funeral was held in St. Clements Church. He was 86 years old.

Jacques Albert Dextraze
1919–1993

11

JADEX
Jacques Dextraze

On a bright spring day in 1976, Private Kathy Horlock, a cheerful brunette newly enlisted in the Air Force, was standing rigidly at attention as part of a 1,000-man honour guard. The occasion was an official inspection of the Canadian Forces Base at Cold Lake, Alberta by the chief of the Defence Staff. A steady procession of staff cars slowly wended their way along the route. To Kathy they all looked the same — long and black and somewhat forbidding to one who had been in the service for less than six months. Suddenly one of them stopped right in front of her. Down came the driver's window ("just like in the movies," Kathy recalled). A gloved hand beckoned her over. She marched forward, then came to attention and saluted, which she should have done before the car stopped.

Seated in the back seat was the base commander and, next to him a slim, wiry, dark-eyed figure with a stern gaze, none other than the CDS himself, General Jacques Dextraze. He looked Kathy straight in the eye, scowled but said nothing. The base commander leaned forward, pointed to the pennant on the left front fender of the limousine and barked, "Don't you recognize that flag?" It had four stars on it — the CDS' pennant. "Yes — Sir," Kathy gulped. "Well next time make sure you salute it!" With that he told the driver to proceed and the cavalcade continued on. It was an unnerving experience, one Kathy would never forget. It was also a characteristic image most people had of "Jadex" who was known as a strict disciplinarian, demanding and unforgiving. This belied a friendly personality laced with a keen sense of humour.

For most people it was hard to assimilate the immaculately uniformed officer, whose dark eyebrows and moustache accentuated his intense, harsh expression, with the youngster whose father called a "rough guy," one who went hunting when he was only eight, liked to read cowboy stories and war books, and broke windows and crockery. "That boy is either going to be a big zero or else an A-1 man," Fred Dextraze said. "There's no in-between with him."

This was no exaggeration. His son would join the army at the very lowest rank of a private and, before his military career ended, rise to be a four-star general, the highest rank in the service. From peeling potatoes to directing Canada's armed forces, Jadex is the only one ever to earn such a distinction. His business career was equally meteoric. Starting out as an office boy, he eventually became chairman of the board of one of Canada's two national railways.

Jacques Albert Dextraze was born in Montreal, Quebec on August 15, 1919, the son of a paper box manufacturer, Albert "Fred" Dextraze, and his wife, the former Amanda Bond. When he reached 11 years old, in 1930, his father packed him off to boarding school at College Saint-Joseph in Berthiervile, Quebec. When he finished school at age 17, he started out as an office boy with the Dominion Rubber Company Ltd., in Montreal.

When World War II started in September 1939 Dextraze tried to join the army but was turned down at first because of flat feet. However, he managed to talk his way into Les Fusiliers Mont-Royal Reserve with the rank of private. In 1940 he was placed on the Active Service list. He quickly and easily adapted to army life and seemed to thrive on the discipline. He was soon promoted to corporal, then sergeant and applied for officers' training, coming second in his class. He was commissioned in 1942 before being sent overseas. During his embarkation leave, on September 2 of that year, he married Françoise Pare.

On August 19, while Dextrase had been attending the officers' school, Les Fusiliers in Great Britain had been cut to ribbons at Dieppe when the battalion landed on the wrong beach. Dextraze became one of 30 replacements picked out of 65 eligible officers. Later, the regimental commanding officer, Lieutenant Colonel Guy Gavreau, described him at the time. "It was the way he stood that impressed me. That and his neatness. You could drop [him] into mud up to his neck and he'd still look immaculate." Gavreau also found him to be totally dependable, more so than any of his other officers. He only needed to be given an order once, but as he later admitted, "it was best if you gave the order pleasantly."

Dextraze's first assignment was that of battalion intelligence officer. Later, he was promoted to captain and by 1944, before D-Day he had been appointed a company commander with the rank of major. It was during the Battle of Falaise in July that Dextraze won his first decoration, the Distinguished Service Order.

At St. André-sur-Orne, the Germans, holding out in a church, controlled a front 8,000 yards wide. In an attempt to secure it the Black Watch Regiment had been caught in a vicious crossfire in which nearly 100 men were killed and many more wounded. Dextraze decided to take the church head-on. Charging at the head of his company, he and his troops captured it at bayonet point then turned it into their own fortress against counter-attacks. This action not only earned Dextraze the DSO but also the sobriquet "Mad Jimmy."

On December 25, Dextraze was appointed commanding officer of Les Fusiliers with the rank of lieutenant colonel. Towards the end of the war, as the Canadians thrust into Holland, Dextraze won a bar to his DSO at Groningen in what was one of the most astounding episodes of the conflict, not to mention one of the more daring. All by himself, he drove his carrier two miles behind enemy lines to a convent which served as the German headquarters in the area. He climbed the stairs, hands in his pockets, and casually confronted the German general in charge who thought he had come to surrender. Instead, Dextraze calmly lit a cigarette, deliberately not offering the enemy officer one, and told him that he was surrounded. He then delivered the ultimatum that he would give the general 15 minutes in which to surrender his forces. To emphasize his point, he offered to show him his troop dispositions as evidence and they drove off in the carrier. The sight of FMRs everywhere was enough to convince the German general that to continue fighting would be suicidal. He promptly surrendered and proffered his hand to Dextraze. There was still a war on and this was improper military procedure so Dextraze correctly refused to honour the gesture, though he later confessed, "I felt sorry for the guy."

After the war in Europe ended, in June 1945, Dextraze was given command of the Hastings and Prince Edward Regiment, part of the Canadian Army Pacific Force formed to take part in the war against Japan. When that country capitulated in August, Dextraze took his discharge from the army and went to work for the Singer Sewing Machine Company as a logger in Thoro, Quebec, a company lumber town between Ottawa and Montreal.

By 1948, after taking a course in forestry at Duchesnay, in Quebec, the company recognized his talents at handling men and delegating authority and appointed him woodlands manager. By this time the Dextrazes had three sons, Jacques, Robert and John. Then, on June 26, 1950, the news broke like a thunderclap around the world that the North Korean Army had crossed the 38th parallel. The United Nations immediately moved to resist the invasion. A little more than a month later Canada announced that a special force would be created for the country to play its part.

The Department of National Defence was anxious to re-enlist as many World War II veterans as possible, and particularly experienced officers with distinguished combat records. The call went out to Dextraze to take command of a new battalion of the Royal 22nd Regiment, the famous "Van Doos." At first he resisted. It meant giving up a $10,000 a year job, a substantial salary at the time, with the promise of a promotion to general manager and being separated from his family. But in the end his sense of duty prevailed and he accepted the appointment. When his regiment was posted to Fort Lewis in Washington in November for training along with other units of the newly formed 25th Canadian Infantry Brigade, Francoise and the children moved to an apartment in Montreal.

At Fort Lewis, Dextraze worked with a single sense of purpose — to prepare his men for battle so that casualties would be kept to a minimum, and to instill in them a sense of pride. It began with discipline; he was a stickler for dress, obedience and behaviour and no one set a better example. He drove himself as hard as he drove his men, sometimes even harder. He believed that casualties could be prevented if his men were trained properly to keep their minds and bodies alert. Once, in Europe, while driving his carrier, his vehicle was hit by a German bazooka. But his keen reflexes allowed him to leap from the carrier before the shot landed.

Dextraze placed a heavy premium on physical fitness. Every morning at 5:15, all officers would report to the commander on the parade square for 45 minutes of physical training followed by a 30-minute run led by the CO himself. After showering, shaving and breakfast at eight o'clock, Dextraze would take over the battalion parade. Most of the tactical training during the day took place on the double. At 4:00 p.m. from Monday to Friday, Dextraze would lead the entire regiment through an hour of fitness training.

This emphasis on PT — Physical Training — was not surprising. Dextrase, a lithe, wiry figure of a man, was the epitome of fitness. Athletic and strong, he was known throughout the brigade as a champion boxer. During his military career he would promote the sport throughout the army so successfully that he was subsequently inducted into Canada's Boxing Hall of Fame.

On Tuesday and Thursday evenings Dextraze conducted officers' training. Saturdays were reserved for administration chores. Paperwork crossing Dextraze's desk was always initialled JDX, earning him the nickname "Jadex." Those who served under him called themselves "Jadex Men."

By the time the Van Doos were ready to set sail for Korea from Seattle, the regiment was a well-coordinated unit, its personnel confident and proud of themselves. Along with the rest of the brigade, the regiment reached the port of Pusan in South Korea in early May 1951, and after a short period of familiarization and orientation training, moved into the front line at the end of the month. When it was learned that the American and ROK troops were sustaining casualties from trenchfoot, Dextraze ordered all platoon commanders to inspect their men's feet once a day, everyday. Socks were to be changed and if possible feet were to be washed. Any officer disregarding this instruction faced the penalty of being sent home to Canada and possible dismissal from the army. The same rule applied to the issue of Atebrine tablets to prevent malaria. Platoon commanders were to see that each man took one tablet a day. One officer neglected this procedure and was sent home by Dextraze and given his discharge.

The regiment first went into action in Korea on May 25 as part of Operation Initiate, along the valley of the P'och'on River with the objective of clearing hills adjacent to it on the right. It made contact with a small force of Chinese and by nightfall had reached a defensive position north of designated Hill 329. Next day it advanced towards the 38th parallel west of Samdalbat but its only encounter was with some deserters and stragglers. By May 29, the advance had covered over 40 miles and was well beyond the parallel. Dextraze was highly pleased with the exercise. His regiment had performed well.

In July, truce talks began and patrols were limited in scope though no less dangerous. However, on one occasion during an advance around the Imjin River, the Chinese made wireless contact requesting a parlay, though nothing came of it. Then on September 12, the Van Doos, whose position centred on Hill 172, were given the task of clearing three hills across the Imjin Valley. These were carried out with thorough precision and coordination. The attack began at 1:30 in the afternoon with an air strike. Then one company, with another in support under cover of artillery fire, according to the regimental diarist, "literally fired the troops down the slope from Hill 172, across the valley, and on the middle objective." Dextraze himself provided the tank support. In his own words, "We were watching Therrien's (the platoon commander) progress up the flank of the hill through our binoculars. I would talk to Therrien, [finding out] where the fire was coming from." This information was passed on to the individual tank commanders who then opened fire. Some of the Chinese bunkers engaged in this way were no more than 40 or 50 yards ahead and this supporting fire contributed greatly to the attacking company's success. However, the captured objective proved to be untenable and Dextraze ordered the company to return to Hill 172.

Between mid-October and the last week of November, the Chinese tried to regain as much territory as possible before November 27, since the front as it existed on that day would become the truce talks' demarcation line in the event of an armistice within the next 30 days. The Van Doos, along with other battalions from the Commonwealth Brigade, were ordered to defend a front four miles long in the Kowang-Hi region north-east of Sami-cho'on.

On November 22 the Royal 22nd took up a position on the right flank of the Sami-cho'on River where Dextraze expected his regiment to perform in typical "Van Doos manner — no withdrawal, no platoons overrun, no panic." By 6:30 that morning the three rifle companies were in readiness in their given positions. But some of these positions were "hot dog stand" or "sandbag castle" types — built-up instead of dug-in, making them highly vulnerable to Chinese artillery and rocket fire. Enemy shelling began early that afternoon. Things were made all the more uncomfortable with rain turning to snow by nightfall. Next day the sun melted the snow turning the area into a quagmire. Towards noon the Chinese shelling increased and by 4:20 it had intensified to the point where it was obvious an attack would follow. Ten minutes later, the Chinese began advancing down one of the surrounding hills in pairs; they were sitting ducks for the French Canadians. But sheer weight of numbers began to tell and by evening the Van Doos were subjected to one assault after the other, the Chinese shouting and blowing bugles.

On the following day the attacks continued without letup, the enemy sometimes in groups of 500. One assault at 5:45 that afternoon was typical. The first of three waves was armed with burp guns, the second wave carried heavy matting for getting over the barbed wire, and the third carried bayonets attached to sticks. As soon as one man was knocked out by defensive fire, another took his place. Platoon leader Lieutenant R. MacDuff said, "They came over the wire like buffalo over a bridge and there was no stopping them." Dextraze described the next attack which followed 15 minutes later:

> At the time this particular attack took place which led to the loss of the platoon position. MacDuff was...at the rear of the platoon with his section leaders which enabled the Chinese to overrun the most forward section. MacDuff, when he realized the fighting was getting close...went to his forward section...to rally them...but it proved impossible to do so....

What saved the situation was the mortar and artillery fire support. At midnight, a Royal 22nd scout platoon under Corporal Leo Major was sent out, by which time the enemy had begun to withdraw. But there was still some resistance as the field communication with the task force leader and the battalion commander indicates:

COLONEL DEXTRAZE: Are you "Buick"? [code name for completion
of task]

CORPORAL MAJOR: Tout est fait.

DEXTRAZE: Good show, Joe. [code name]

MAJOR: Tout est fait, slow but sure.

Dextraze: Good show, Joe...

MAJOR: We are being attacked by infantry...

DEXTRAZE: Come back with your men.

MAJOR: I am not pulling out, just changing position...Engage with
mortars and machine-guns.

DEXTRAZE: I shall have some artillery brought down in a few minutes...Do you need anything else?

This was typical of Dextraze who drilled into his officers the need for proper fire support. With this support and Major's able directing of his fire it enabled the platoon to repulse four separate enemy counter-attacks. That night the regiment had gone through 3,500 rounds of 81-millimetre mortar ammunition and one complete set of mortar barrels had been burnt out. During the four days the battle lasted, the Van Doos lost 16 men, 36 wounded and two taken prisoner. It also marked the last large-scale attack against the battalion in the fall of 1951.

Prior to the Battle of Kowang-Hi, Dextraze became the focus of attention in the Canadian press on two different occasions, one directly, the other by association. The first of these occurred on September 23, when a story appeared in the Ottawa French-language newspaper *Le Droit* that Dextraze would "soon be returning to Canada," as a result of differences of opinion with the 25th Canadian Infantry Brigade commander, Brigadier John Rockingham. The latter vehemently denied the rumour, replying that there has "never been any difference of opinion between us."

The second incident was more serious. Early in November the independent member of Parliament for Chicoutimi, Quebec, P. E. Gagnon alleged in the House of Commons that French Canadian troops in Korea were being singled out to serve in the most exposed positions and were being given the most unpleasant fatigue duties. Defence Minister Brooke Claxton immediately replied that, "there is not a single word of truth" in the charges. Dextraze denounced them as a "damned lie." "We've fought our fair share," he added, "no more, no less than any other. The statement has no foundation." Rockingham suggested that Gagnon visit the fighting zone to see for himself that there was no discrimination against French Canadians.

But Gagnon answered that until an investigation was made he would not withdraw his charges. To this Rockingham countered, "Why doesn't he come out here and investigate personally? I'll give him a jeep and turn him loose and he can go anywhere he wants." That appeared to end the matter. No more was heard from Monsieur Gagnon.

On December 15, 1951, Dextraze's tour in Korea came to a close, but not his military career — far from it. He returned to Canada to attend the Staff College in Kingston, Ontario. On April 12 of the following year, for his services as commander of the Royal 22nd Regiment, he was awarded the Order of the British Empire.

Between 1953 and 1957 Dextraze served in various staff capacities in Ottawa before taking command of the Infantry School at Camp Borden. In 1960 he was promoted to the rank of full colonel and given command of Camp Valcartier, Quebec. In 1962 he rose to the rank of brigadier and was appointed commander, Eastern Quebec Area (part of Quebec command) until 1963 when he became chief of Staff Headquarters, United Nations in the Congo (now Zaire). For his services in rescuing missionaries there, he was made a commander of the Order of the Most Excellent Order of the British Empire (Military) with Oak Leaf cluster, to become the only Canadian to receive this order for bravery. The citation, which speaks for itself, is published here (with the exception of the *Canada Gazette*) for the first time:

During the missionary rescue operations carried out by the ONUC helicopter force in Kwilu province in the Republic of the Congo on 22 and 23 February 1946, Brigadier Dextraze played an important part both in direction and in actual participation. As the original planner of the operation, he initiated rescue drills which proved completely successful. He imbued all members of the force with his own brand of fiery enthusiasm and was generally responsible for the efficiency and success of the rescue operations. On several occasions, Brigadier Dextraze either flew the control aircraft personally or accompanied the rescue helicopters in order to gain first hand knowledge of the situation. During the rescue operation at Kishua Nseke on 29 January 1964, he controlled the ground operations from the Otter aircraft and carried out such close low level reconnaissance and protection missions that the rescue helicopters were able to effect the rescue quickly and with the minimum danger. On this occasion despite the hazards imposed by the presence of armed Jeunesse, he displayed superb leadership and control. During the Gungu and Totshi rescues on 30 January 1964 he commanded the operation personally from the lead helicopter and was directly responsible for the saving of four missionaries. On Sunday 23 February 1964, Brigadier Dextraze while visiting the troops in the rescue area received information that the mission at Kafumba was in immediate danger. He carried out a close air reconnaissance of the area and saw the mission being attacked by a heavily armed Jeunesse group and that the missionaries had placed several SOS signs on the ground. Realizing that the ANC troops were somewhere in the vicinity, he set out to locate them. He dropped messages to the ANC troops requesting them to follow his line of flight to Kafumba mission and then proceeded to the mission area where he dropped further messages to the besieged missionaries, telling them to head through the jungle towards the oncoming ANC force. Having satisfied himself that the remaining missionaries were safely in ANC hands, he returned to the rescue area. As a result of brigadier Dextraze's quick thinking and his superb handling of the situation, the ANC arrived at the mission in time to drive off the Jeunesse and thus save over thirty missionaries and students who would otherwise have been killed by the Jeunesse. Throughout the same day Brigadier Dextraze remained in control of the successive helicopter rescue missions which rescued in all five wounded missionaries, seventeen teachers and retrieved the bodies of the two Belgian UNESCO teachers who had been killed. Whatever success was achieved by the ONUC rescue forces in the Kwilu operations must be attributed to the outstanding qualities in planning, leadership and command of Brigadier Dextraze. This work is therefore worthy of high recognition.

On his return to Canada on October 5, Dextraze took command of the 2nd Canadian Infantry Brigade Group at Petawawa, Ontario until 1966 when he took over as chief of Staff Operations and Training, Mobile Command headquarters in Montreal. In 1967 he was promoted to major general and became deputy commander of Mobile Command. In 1970 he was made deputy chief of Personnel at National Defence headquarters in Ottawa and the following year was elevated to the rank of lieutenant general. Between 1971 and 1972 Dextraze served as chief of Personnel before becoming chief of the Defence Staff with the rank of full general.

What concerned Dextraze most when he took over his duties as CDS, was the credibility the armed forces had lost with the government, chiefly through the unification debates during the 1960s. "We hadn't painted a picture of intellectual honesty," he admitted. Dextraze worked hard to correct this impression by presenting himself as a "reasonable person" to the politicians, Prime Minister Pierre Elliott Trudeau in particular. During his five years in office, though he only met privately with Trudeau five times, Dextraze developed what he called "a sound and honest relationship" with the prime minister. He worked hard to reinforce this "special position," as he termed it, by being truthful and forthright in expressing the needs of the Canadian Forces as he perceived them, while at the same time being sensitive to Trudeau's own attitude and needs as well as the political situation.

High on Dextraze's list of priorities was a new battle tank for the Canadian Forces which needed such modern weaponry to save the integrity of the country's commitment to NATO. This ran contrary to the 1970 White Paper on defence which opposed rearmament of any kind. Prime Minister Trudeau agreed with the document as did the senior Cabinet ministers and his personal staff. Moreover, at this time, Trudeau was decidedly hostile to the NATO strategy of deterrence and, in fact, wanted out. But the situation was too tricky and sensitive to abandon the treaty altogether. There were other relationship considerations with the participating nations, particularly West Germany, which could affect trade.

It was fortunate that Dextraze had established that "sound and honest relationship" with the prime minister so that he was able to circumvent Defence Minister Jim Richardson, who, since he was not a military man, was powerless to influence the Cabinet. He pointed out that to maintain a credible presence in Europe, new, modern tanks for the Canadian Forces were essential. Next, he explained, in staff college terms, laying out the tactical advantages in terms of the mechanized battlefield. He deliberately avoided any political overtones.

When he received the "green light," as Trudeau called it, to go ahead, he was able to proceed directly and immediately because he had already taken steps to arrange to tag onto the German Leopard tank production line for Canada's needs. This marked an impressive victory for Dextraze in the face of considerable political and bureaucratic opposition.

On the home front the defence of Canada by Canadians occupied a good deal of Dextraze's energies and thinking. He harboured a serious concern that the FLQ crisis and separatist thinking in Quebec might eventually erupt into an "Irish situation." He believed that Ottawa was highly vulnerable to terrorist attacks and that the Canadian Forces were not well enough equipped to cope with the threat either intellectually or professionally over the long term. But he was confident that problem could be corrected, given time and proper training.

By focusing attention on the Canadian Forces in matters of direct interest to the politicians, Dextraze gradually softened Trudeau's opinion and distrust of the military professionals. Unlike some of his predecessors, he brought a strong believability to his office. He was a decorated war hero, a francophone, who won the respect of everyone who served under, or worked with him. And he was in no way a "headquarters officer" stereotype. He was persuasive and intelligent and an able administrator and negotiator. In short he was ideal for the job of CDS and it gradually began to show. Once he felt that he had earned a measure of confidence with the politicos, he decided to "stop the bloody erosion of the forces," and gain back some of the stability and capacity in Europe, as well as press for major equipment to support defence missions at home and elsewhere.

Dextraze had become frustrated with the Cabinet's refusal to "make up their minds about what we want as a country and how we want to defend it." By 1973 he himself had developed some very set ideas about what the actual defence of Canada meant and what could be done about it. Chaired by Dextraze, the Defence Structure Review process started "half way," as he put it, with the politicians breathing down his neck in search of a quick and easy fix to solve their foreign policy and trade problems in Europe. "We decided what we thought we needed and it was highly influenced by the dollars and cents we had in the bank at the time," Dextraze said.

In leading this review Dextraze had to stumble almost every inch of the way over obstacles that appeared in his path, but with the sober realization that this was all part of the game between the military and the political. However, he succeeded in overcoming most of these barriers with the result that the decline in military personnel was reversed and the Canadian Forces began a slow recovery.

The review provided for the purchase of the tanks for NATO and a decision to buy a fleet of long-range aircraft, ostensibly on the pretext they would be used for surveillance when, in actual fact, their mission was to hunt submarines.

Dextraze also won his argument for an AVGP (armoured vehicle general purpose), which could move about the country quickly. It was publicly advertised as a tank trainer. Actually it answered Dextraze's concern for having a weapon available as a deterrent to any conflict that occurred within Canada for whatever reason. "People would think twice before they got violent or more violent when you introduced them to Cougars or Grizzlies and we intended to have the means to make them think twice." Many among the military as well as the deputy minister of defence, Sylvain Cloutier, opposed this decision, but Dextraze was able to bull it through.

He was, however, on more than one occasion, willing to compromise. He was convinced that Ottawa needed a resident military force to deter internally and externally mounted terrorist actions. He proposed that the crack Canadian Airborne Division, or at least part of it, be moved from its home base in Edmonton to the capital city. But the government felt that this might cause some public alarm generally and give the FLQ and others too much publicity, precisely what they wanted. Dextraze settled for the regiment being moved to Petawawa within easy distance of Ottawa, should terrorism break out.

The Defence Structure Review was an important document, though it never succeeded in changing the government's understanding of national defence. It was not designed to give the country a new strategic military direction nor was it structured simply to pry more money out of the treasury. Its purpose was to provide a guide to material requirements and the defence spending needed to acquire them. Hitherto, Richardson had no way of explaining to his Cabinet colleagues what was needed for national defence and how much of a budget was required to meet that need. But in 1977, when Dextraze retired as chief of the Defence Staff, problems still existed because of Trudeau's determination to discipline Canada's military establishment and bring defence policy under national strategy.

In civilian life, Dextraze made his home in Ottawa. He became chairman of the board of Canadian National Railways, a position he held until May 1982. He also served as a director of the Canadian Safety Council, the Atlantic Council of Canada, and the Consortium of Atlantic-Pacific Affairs. He was grand patron of the Korean Veterans Association, and honorary president of the Canadian Infantry Association as well as the Canadian Amateur Boxing Association. In addition, he was made honorary patron of the Big Brothers Association of Ottawa and District, as well as Dominion honorary vice-president of the Royal Canadian Legion, and vice-patron of the Royal Canadian Military Institute. In addition to his other decorations and honours, he also became a Knight of the Most Venerable Order of the Hospital of St. John of Jerusalem, and Knight of the Military and Hospitaller Order of Saint Lazarus of Jerusalem. Dextraze continued to maintain his interest in the Canadian Forces. As an example, in 1989, he came out publicly against women in combat roles.

On May 9, 1993 General Jacques Dextraze CC, CBE, CMM, DSO and Bar, CD, LLD, died of cancer at age 73 in the National Defence Hospital. His funeral was held at Notre Dame Basilica in Ottawa and he was buried in Cote des Neiges Cemetery in Montreal with full military honours.

No monument has been built to commemorate and honour this great Canadian military leader, a shameful disgrace both nationally and provincially. This is not merely an oversight. It's worse than that. It demonstrates a disregard and disrespect on the part of the Canadian government, not to mention the public, for those who risked their lives in the service of our country to preserve our freedom and all that we hold sacred. Let us hope that one day this will be corrected.

AFTERWORD

What was it that these great Canadian military leaders of ours had in common? The most obvious gift was just that, the ability to lead. They inspired confidence in those who served under them. All were highly talented strategists and tacticians. Each, in his own way, was individually innovative.

By capturing Michilimackinac Island, Brock won over the Indians as allies, a key factor in the War of 1812 against the Americans. Tecumseh's use of the threat of terror was instrumental in forcing the capitulation of Detroit. Salaberry's style of backwoods fighting defeated an overwhelming force of Americans and saved Montreal. Currie brought science to the battlefield. Hose rescued the navy from obliteration by resurrecting the reserve on a national basis to give Canadians from coast to coast visible proof that a navy even existed. McEwen's emphasis on training, practice and preparation produced one of the finest bomber groups among the Allied air forces. Simonds developed such novel battle techniques as artificial moonlight to direct night armoured assaults. Thanks to Mainguy's intuitive efforts, the troubled postwar navy received a much needed refit. Hodson refined wing fighter tactics to the nth degree. Rockingham exhibited his talent for flexibility by taking a freshly recruited brigade and adapting it to the unique combat conditions demanded in the hills and valleys of Korea. Curtis's drive and determination fashioned a peacetime RCAF into one of the finest, most efficient defence forces in the world. Dextraze displayed his powers of persuasion and political savvy in bending the government's will to the need for strengthening and reorienting our armed forces.

Every one of these leaders, one way or another, proved to be capable administrators. And of course all of them, without exception, were extremely brave, as the decorations they earned for courage, above and beyond the call of duty, testify. We can take justifiable pride in their achievements. May the meaning and memory of their greatness never fade.

BIBLIOGRAPHY

Bishop, Arthur. **Canada's Glory: Battles that Forged a Nation,** Toronto: McGraw-Hill Ryerson, 1996.

Bishop, Arthur. **Courage at Sea.** Toronto: McGraw-Hill Ryerson, 1995.

Bishop, Arthur. **Courage in the Air.** Toronto: McGraw-Hill Ryerson, 1992.

Bishop, Arthur. **Courage on the Battlefield.** Toronto: McGraw-Hill Ryerson, 1993.

Berton, Pierre. "The Crisis and The Colonel." *Maclean's Magazine,* February 15, 1951.

Berton, Pierre, and Scott R. Cameron. **The Death of Isaac Brock.** McClelland & Stewart, Toronto, 1991.

Brown, George and Michel Lavigne. **Canadian Wing Commanders of Fighter Command in World War II.** Battleline Books, Langley, BC, 1984.

Canadian Defence Quarterly Vol IV, No 1, October, 1926.

Cooke, David C. **Tecumseh Destiny's Warrior** New York: Julian Mesner.

Cosgrove, Edmund. **Canada's Fighting Pilots**. Toronto: Clarke, Irwin, 1965.

Dancocks, Daniel G. **Sir Arthur Currie: A Biography.** Toronto: Methuen, 1985.

Dunmore, Spencer and William Carter. **Reap the Whirlwind: The Untold Story of 6 Group, Canada's Bomber Force of World War II.** Toronto: McClelland & Stewart, 1991.

Edgar, Lady. **General Brock.** Toronto: Morang & Co., 1926.

Encyclopedia Canadian. Toronto: Grolier of Canada, 1968.

German, Tony. **The Sea Is at Our Gates: the History of the Canadian Navy**. Toronto: McClelland & Stewart, 1990.

The Globe and Mail. August 7, 1967.

Graham, Dominick. **The Price of Command: A Biography of General Guy Simonds.** Toronto: Stoddart, 1993.

Gurd, Norman S. **The Story of Tecumseh.** Toronto: William Briggs, 1912.

Lamb, W. Kaye. **The Hero of Upper Canada.** Toronto: Rous & Mann Press, 1962.

MacFarlane, John M. **Canada's Admirals and Commodores.** Vancouver: Maritime Museum of British Columbia.

The Toronto Daily Star. May 9, 1940; August 7, 1967.

Wohler, Patrick J. **Charles de Salaberry: Soldier of the Empire, Defender of Quebec.** Toronto: Dundurn Press, 1984.

Wood, Herbert Fairlie. **Strange Battlefield: The Operations in Korea and Their Effects on the Defence Policy of Canada.** Ottawa: Department of National Defence, 1966.

Zaslow, Morris. **The Defended Border.** Toronto: Macmillan Canada, 1964.

INDEX

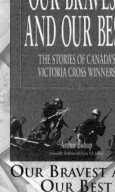
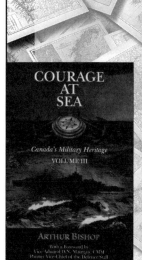
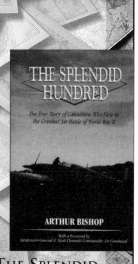